Gassendi's Ethics

GASSENDI'S
ETHICS

Freedom in a Mechanistic Universe

Lisa T. Sarasohn

Cornell University Press

ITHACA AND LONDON

First published 1996 by Cornell University Press.

Printed in the United States of America

⊗ The paper in this book meets the minimum requirements of the American National Standard for Information Sciences—Permanence of Paper for Printed Library Materials, ANSI Z39.48-1984.

Library of Congress Cataloging-in-Publication Data

Sarasohn, Lisa T., 1950–
Gassendi's ethics : freedom in a mechanistic universe /
p.   cm.
Includes bibliographical references and index.
ISBN 0-8014-2947-1 (cloth : alk. paper)
1. Gassendi, Pierre, 1592–1655—Views on ethics.   2. Ethics.   3. Gassendi, Pierre, 1592–1655. Syntagma philosophicum.   I. Gassendi, Pierre, 1592–1655. Syntagma philosophicum.   II. Title.
B1887.S27   1996
170'.92—dc20   96-18279

To David

Contents

Preface

I t took the French priest and philosopher Pierre Gassendi more than twenty-five years to complete his project of rehabilitating Epicurus and transforming the philosophy of the ancient atomist into his own system. I have been working on this project almost as long. Shortly after the invasion of Cambodia and shortly before the disintegration of the Nixon administration, my adviser and mentor, Amos Funkenstein, suggested innocently enough that I work on the revival of Epicureanism in the seventeenth century. After a sobering look at Gassendi's *Syntagma Philosophicum*, I began what became a very long journey. Delving into Gassendi's Latin is something like running the rapids on the Rogue River: batches of smooth passage interspersed with tortuous turnings. Hundreds of pages later, I finally have the opportunity to ask others along on the ride.

This work is a traditional study in the history of ideas. I am convinced that with an author as little known as Gassendi, any analysis must begin with a close study of the text. This is particularly true of his ethical teachings, which have not yet been translated into any modern language and present an impenetrable barrier to the casual reader. Although to some extent I let the text speak for itself, I have contextualized the material and not allowed the terms "freedom" and "pleasure" to exist as free-floating units mysteriously progressing through time and place. I have used Gassendi's definitions, which are certainly not modern but rather grounded in the theological and humanistic soil of the seventeenth century.

My own method was dictated by Gassendi's approach to the history of philosophy. His invariable procedure in constructing an argument was to present the views of those who had written on the subject before him. This practice results in many long lists of quotations from his almost inexhaustible knowledge of the thought of antiquity, the Middle Ages, and, more rarely, his own time. Gassendi's aim was not to demonstrate his humanistic prowess but rather to allow his readers the freedom to judge the worth of any doctrine themselves. Tolerance for the ideas of others was an ethical value to the French philosopher, who disavowed dogmatism and embraced the free exchange of ideas.

I present Gassendi's moral philosophy as it was meant to be read: as a dialogue with his predecessors and contemporaries. The early seventeenth century teemed with great philosophy. Hobbes and Descartes were reshaping the philosophic universe at the same time Galileo was restructuring the natural world. Gassendi realized the implications of the new philosophy; he was a working experimental scientist himself. He understood that in a world of matter and motion, a place needed to be found for humanity.

Gassendi could accept neither Hobbes's materialism nor Descartes's realism, because he believed both destroyed the possibility of human freedom. In a Hobbesian universe man was integrated into matter; in a Cartesian world man and nature were sundered. Gassendi tried to entwine nature and humanity in a much more complex interrelationship, which preserved a special place for man without entirely divorcing him from the other parts of God's creation. An argument along these lines is perhaps more interesting than the rationalist/empiricist split often used to characterize the difference between Gassendi and Descartes.

Some of Gassendi's attitudes toward Hobbes and Descartes were conditioned by his own probabilistic epistemology. He was not looking for new velleities, because he believed they were not possible to achieve. The best an individual could do was to try to understand the appearance of things and make provisional decisions on this basis. Gassendi is one of the links between the humanism and skepticism of the late sixteenth century and the hypothetical and probabilistic approach to knowledge of the late seventeenth century. Although the argument about the nature of the early Scientific Revolution continues, Gassendi's natural and ethical philosophy clearly shows that at least this founder of the mechanical philosophy was part of an emerging probabilistic tradition.

Following the route of traditions, however, is perilous. In this book I make several suggestions about possible lines of influence on Gassendi and about the thinkers he influenced. I do so even though direct lines of filiation are often difficult or impossible to discover. There were not many early modern thinkers who casually admitted that they lifted an idea from someone else; it was not part of their style. Nevertheless, close readings of the texts show similarities in vocabulary and metaphor that are very suggestive. Ideas do not develop in a vacuum, and the content of any person's ideas is affected by his intellectual context, which shapes the way arguments are framed and determines what issues are considered significant.

A study of context and tradition shows that Gassendi was profoundly affected by theological presuppositions and arguments. This insight leads to a broader interpretation of Gassendi himself, for he is considered an enigma by modern historians, who assume a never-ending battle between science and religion stretching back at least to the seventeenth century. Gassendi's so-called materialism and heterodoxy fade as a truer picture of the savant emerges. I suggest that the nature of early modern thought cannot be understood until theology is seen as a fruitful and dynamic partner in the articulation of a new world-view. In this viewpoint, my work coincides with that of Margaret Osler, who also emphasizes the theological dimensions of Gassendi's and others' philosophies.

All translations in the following pages are my own unless otherwise indicated. In translating Gassendi, I have tried to be as literal as possible without completely sacrificing style and intelligibility. I treat most of the other primary sources the same way. Where needed, I have modernized the English texts in order to facilitate ease of understanding. In all cases, I have tried to use the original editions, although sometimes I was forced to use modern renditions. Some of my happiest times during the whole process were spent in the basement of the William Andrews Clark Library making my way through the volumes of Gassendi's *Opera Omnia*. The weight of the tomes reflected the impact of his thought.

In this work, I have tried to avoid gendered language, but it has not always been possible. It is anachronistic to make seventeenth-century philosophers speak in the language of indefinite articles. When Gassendi said "man" he usually meant man; like his contemporaries, he did not view women as truly rational beings.

Over the years, I have received various kinds of support for my work on Gassendi. A graduate fellowship at the Clark Library at UCLA began my evolution as a Gassendist. In 1982–83, a Mellon Fellowship in the Humanities at the University of Pennsylvania contributed greatly to the maturation of my thought. I spent a wonderful summer at the glorious Folger Shakespeare Library in 1987. The librarians at each of these institutions were more than helpful in providing material and space for my research. In addition, I have received grants from the College of Liberal Arts and the Center for the Humanities at Oregon State University.

There are many people I wish to thank for their support and comments on my work. First of all, I owe a debt of gratitude to my teachers, Amos Funkenstein and Robert Westman. Margaret Osler has been my constant companion and foil in my studies of Gassendi. Her careful reading of my text, and her invaluable suggestions, turned an inchoate mass into something resembling an argument. Gianni Paganini, the other person in the world interested in Gassendi's ethics, has been generous in sharing his work and ideas with me. Barbara Shapiro was a thoughtful and helpful reader who made me consider the context of Gassendi's thought. There are many others whose suggestions and criticisms have enriched this work: Richard S. Westfall, Paul Farber, Peter Steinberger, Mordechai Feingold, Maristella Lorch, Mario Biagioli, Thomas Franzell, and the anonymous reader for Cornell University Press. My editor at Cornell, Roger Haydon, never ceased to believe in the worth of this project. My thanks also to Lisa Turner for her careful copy editing.

Parts of this text grew out of earlier article-length studies. Some material in Chapter 1 appeared in "Epicureanism and the Creation of a Privatist Ethics in Early Seventeenth-Century France," in *Atoms, Pneuma, and Tranquillity: Epicurean and Stoic Themes in European Thought,* ed. Margaret J. Osler (Cambridge: Cambridge University Press, 1991), 175–95. Parts of Chapter 6 first appeared in "Motion and Morality: Pierre Gassendi, Thomas Hobbes, and the Mechanical World-View," *Journal of the History of Ideas* 46 (1985): 363–79. The first is adapted by permission of Cambridge University Press and the second by permission of The Johns Hopkins University Press. An early article, "The Ethical and Political Philosophy of Pierre Gassendi," *Journal of the History of Philosophy* 20 (1982): 239–60, The Journal of the History of Philosophy, Inc. inspired parts of Chapters 2 and 6. It is adapted by permission.

I also thank my two sons, Alex and Peter, who somehow reconciled themselves to the reality of a mother cloistered with a computer they wanted to use. Most of all, I thank my husband, David, whose encouragement and belief in me is the main reason I was able to finish this book. He also had the great good will to read and edit my work, even though he is an American historian and a journalist with perhaps a less than active interest in early modern intellectual history. This book is dedicated to him, my friend and ally.

LISA SARASOHN

Corvallis, Oregon

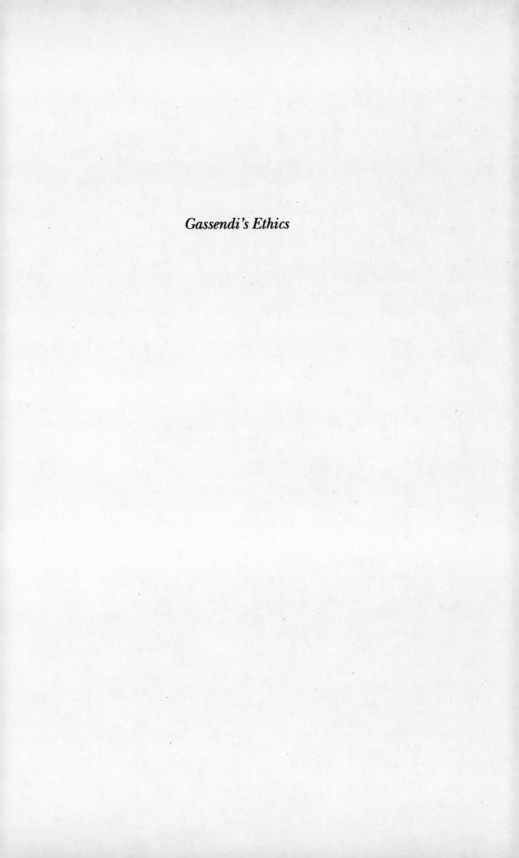

Gassendi's Ethics

CHAPTER ONE

Introduction:
Life and Context

A Life in Pursuit of Freedom

Pierre Gassendi (1592–1655), a French priest and philosopher, was absorbed by the idea of freedom. It animated his ethical philosophy, in which human nature is defined by its capacity to choose freely. Freedom underlay his philosophy of nature, in which God freely creates the natural order. Freedom was the cornerstone of his epistemology and his logic, in which probable knowledge of the natural and moral universe frees men to choose the most likely natural explanation of phenomena and the best possible course of action. The theme of freedom gives coherence and unity to his ethical, scientific, and epistemological doctrines.

Gassendi integrated ideas of human freedom into a neo-Epicurean ethic where pleasure is the highest good, while at the same time maintaining a consistent belief in Christian providence. Gassendi was one of the first philosophers to examine the implications of the new philosophy of nature for human beings. While adopting the mechanistic world-view, that the universe was composed of nothing but matter in motion, he rejected the idea of natural necessity—implicit in some of the new scientific viewpoints—to pursue his vision of human free choice in a universe contingent on the will of God.[1] The basic premise of Gassendi's moral

---

[1] On Gassendi's role in the establishment of the mechanical philosophy, see E. J. Dijksterhuis, *The Mechanization of the World Picture*, trans. C. Dikshoorn (Oxford, 1961), 425–30; Richard S. Westfall, "The Foundations of Newton's Philosophy of Nature," *British Journal for the History of Science* 1 (1962): 171–82; Olivier René Bloch, *La philosophie de Gassendi: Nominalisme, matérialisme, et métaphysique* (The Hague, 1971); Margaret J. Osler, *Divine Will*

philosophy, as I show here, is that morality is impossible unless human decisions are freely made. The teleological assumption of this ethical theory is that such decisions are motivated by the calculation of what will bring the greatest amount of pleasure or happiness to an individual. For Gassendi, a moral life consists in the rational and free pursuit of pleasure. Pleasure, correctly understood, is tranquillity of the soul and absence of pain in the body.

Gassendi's evaluation of human liberty grew out of sources as diverse as the new understanding of motion and the traditional understanding of the relation of the faculties of will and intellect. His work demonstrates that humanism and science were not mutually exclusive fields of intellectual endeavor, but were intimately related.[2] One of the most interesting aspects of his ethical thought and his natural philosophy is the degree to which he was able to integrate probabilistic traditions of thought into a coherent whole. His philosophic work is a system in the most basic sense: all of the parts are aspects of a unified vision. While Gassendi's ethics, physics, and logic all reflected the philosophy of the ancient atomist and hedonist Epicurus, Gassendi combined these elements with Christian theology and the mechanical philosophy. A true savant and humanist, Gassendi used what he wanted in an effort to present the most persuasive account of humanity and the world.

If a modern student has heard of Gassendi at all, it is because he wrote the "Fifth Objections" to Descartes's *Meditations* (1641) and rehabilitated the philosophy of Epicurus. As the seventeenth century's standard-bearer of empiricism, Gassendi was engaged in an aggressive action against Cartesian rationalism, making some good hits along the way. Recently, however, Gassendi studies have undergone a kind of renaissance: he has been credited by Margaret Osler as a founder of the mechanical philosophy, by Lynn Joy as an heir to humanist historiography, and by Thomas Lennon as the proponent of an empirical philosophy that flourished in the second half of the seventeenth century and deeply affected John Locke.[3]

Because of these efforts, Gassendi is well on his way to taking a more

---

and the Mechanical Philosophy: Gassendi and Descartes on Contingency and Necessity in the Created World (Cambridge, 1994), 8–9, 180–200.

[2] On the relationship of humanism and science, see Barbara Shapiro, "Early Modern Intellectual Life: Humanism, Religion, and Science in Seventeenth-Century England," *History of Science* 29 (1991): 45–71.

[3] Osler, *Divine Will and the Mechanical Philosophy*; Lynn Sumida Joy, *Gassendi the Atomist: Advocate of History in an Age of Science* (Cambridge, 1987); and Thomas M. Lennon, *The Battle of the Gods and Giants: The Legacies of Descartes and Gassendi, 1655–1715* (Princeton, 1993).

prominent place in the history of science and philosophy. My task in this book is to show that Gassendi was equally important in the history of ethical theory. Gassendi's notions of freedom and pleasure formed part of the mainstream liberal tradition in the late seventeenth and eighteenth centuries. Ironically, a Catholic priest became one of the progenitors of a moral tradition antithetical to the absolutist, religious world in which he lived and wrote.

Gassendi was an odd candidate to be a disciple of ethical libertarianism. His own career was circumscribed by the demands of seventeenth-century social and intellectual life. He came from a humble background; his parents were prosperous peasants in the village of Champtercier near Digne in southern France. After his intellectual abilities were recognized at an early age, he won rapid social advancement.[4] Like many other promising scholars, he found his best career opportunity in the priesthood. At the age of nineteen, in 1613, he was appointed principal of the College of Digne. In 1616, he was elected theological canon of the cathedral church at Digne and ordained as a priest. In 1635 Gassendi completed his ecclesiastical rise by becoming dean of the Digne cathedral.

Gassendi had done extremely well for himself. In early modern times, the canonical office was a stepping-stone to yet higher clerical preferment.[5] The office, however, at least at Digne, required the residency of the officeholder. Absence for longer than a month deprived the canon of his income.[6] Although Gassendi enjoyed his clerical duties, he also wanted the time and leisure necessary for his scholarly pursuits.[7] For a while Gassendi was able to devote himself to philosophy during a professorship at the nearby University of Aix. His university career ended, however, when the Jesuits took over the university in 1623. Lynn Joy has pointed out that the termination of Gassendi's teaching career at Aix precipitated his dependence on private patrons or other members of the intellectual community to support his scholarly activities.[8]

Gassendi prized his personal freedom. He wanted to be as free as the

[4] Gaston Sortais, *La philosophie moderne depuis Bacon jusqu'à Leibniz*, 2 vols. (Paris, 1920–22), 2:1–10.
[5] Roland Mousnier, *The Institutions of France under the Absolute Monarchy, 1598–1789*, trans. Brian Pearce (Chicago, 1979), 1:328.
[6] Pierre Gassendi, "Notitia ecclesia Diniensis," in *Opera Omnia*, 6 vols. (Lyon, 1658; reprint, Stuttgart-Bad Cannstatt, 1964), 5:693–94. In future citations *Opera Omnia* will be referred to as *Opera*.
[7] Pierre Gassendi, *Pierre Gassendi: Lettres familières à François Luillier*, ed. Bernard Rochot (Paris, 1944), 53, 77–78, 94.
[8] Joy, *Gassendi the Atomist*, 29.

conditions of his life permitted, both as a philosopher and as a man. He shared this aim with Epicurus, who had urged the wise man to withdraw from public participation. Epicurus stated that the best chance for happiness a human could have would be detachment from the world of affairs. Detachment would make the individual self-sufficient, which is a condition necessary to human freedom.[9]

Such an antisocial ethic had not been well received by the public-spirited philosophers of antiquity, but Gassendi defended it: "Epicurus ought not to be charged with shame, because he established a kind of life more innocent and more peaceful; and there was a society of men, who, having laid aside ambition, pursued tranquillity. This assuredly always may be permitted without shame, and especially it may be permitted in our own time."[10] The growing absolutism of Richelieu and Mazarin and the terror of the Thirty Years' War encouraged this attitude not only in Gassendi, but in many other savants as well.[11]

Thus, Gassendi argued that the private life is "a calm and useful condition" which results in "the quiet of the soul and the freedom to study." In short, Gassendi endorsed the Epicurean maxim that it is better "to live apart," enjoying a contemplative and happy life.[12] This kind of philosophic attitude created a tension between Gassendi's aspirations and his realities, which perhaps colored his moral doctrines, and makes his biography of interest to students of his ethics.[13]

Unlike Epicurus, able to live apart in his Garden, Gassendi and other intellectuals were caught up in the matrix of private and public relationships that constituted the patronage system of early modern France. The patron-client relationship bound together people of unequal social status in a mutual and reciprocal association where various material and immaterial goods and gifts were exchanged and some degree of trust and loyalty created.[14] Patronage impinged on freedom in two ways: The

[9] Epicurus, *Epicurus: The Extant Remains*, trans. Cyril Bailey (Oxford, 1926), 115, 98–99, 119.

[10] Gassendi, "Ethics," in *Syntagma Philosophicum* in *Opera*, 2:762, 764. In future citations, *Syntagma Philosophicum* will be referred to as *SP*. All translations made directly from the *Opera* are my own.

[11] Nannerl O. Keohane, *Philosophy and the State in France: The Renaissance to the Enlightenment* (Princeton, 1980), 119–82.

[12] Gassendi to Valois, April 11, 1641, in "Letters," *Opera*, 6:105, and "Ethics," *SP*, *Opera*, 2:717–19.

[13] I pursue this argument in more detail in "Epicureanism and the Creation of a Privatist Ethic in Early Seventeenth-Century France," in *Atoms, Pneuma, and Tranquillity: Epicurean and Stoic Themes in European Thought*, ed. Margaret J. Osler (Cambridge, 1991), 175–96.

[14] Sharon Kettering, *Patrons, Brokers, and Clients in Seventeenth-Century France* (New York, 1986), 3, 20. Other important studies of patronage in early modern Europe include the

various social obligations limited the time that could be used in study and constantly exposed a heterodox thinker to supervision by political and religious authority. Unlike Epicurus, Gassendi could not avoid these dangers to his liberty, and the Frenchman's philosophy reflected these exigencies—although often he was much more concerned about loss of time than loss of freedom of thought. The question Gassendi had to answer was how could a wise man be free, and obtain pleasure whether operating within the world or living apart from it?

To a certain extent Gassendi was very lucky in his patronage relationships. He was the kind of person whom people liked: affable, humble, loyal, and kind.[15] In 1618, while a student at the University of Aix, Gassendi had met his earliest patron, Nicolas-Claude Fabri de Peiresc, with whom Gassendi managed to be a close friend as well as a client. For a while, at least, Gassendi avoided the more onerous aspects of seventeenth-century patronage. In his biography of Peiresc, Gassendi described their relationship,

> I account it a great ha;ppiness, that he prized me so dearly, and that it was his pleasure to have me so frequently with him, and to make me privy to all his private thoughts and inclinations and besides other matters, to utter his last words, and breathe out his very soul itself, into my bosom. . . . For, seeing that as oft I think, speak, or hear of that man, I feel my mind filled with a most intimate and sweet passion of joy and pleasure.[16]

Peiresc, a member of the Nobility of the Robe, served as councillor to the Parlement of Aix, but his chief importance was as a patron of arts and letters. A noted humanist and naturalist himself, he "perhaps more than any other person of his period lays a firm foundation for the Re-

---

following: Peter Burke, *Venice and Amsterdam: A Study of Seventeenth-Century Elites* (London, 1974), and *The Italian Renaissance: Culture and Society in Italy* (Cambridge, 1986); Francis William Kent, *Household and Lineage in Early Modern Florence* (Princeton, 1977); Richard C. Trexler, *Public Life in Renaissance Florence* (New York, 1980); William Beik, *Absolutism and Society in Seventeenth-Century France* (Cambridge, 1985); and Kristen B. Neuschel, *Word of Honor: Interpreting Noble Culture in Sixteenth-Century France* (Ithaca, 1989).

[15] On Gassendi's many close friendships and relationships, see the eighteenth-century biography by Joseph Bougerel, *Vie de Pierre Gassendi: Prévôt de l'Église de Digne et Professeur de Mathématique au Collège Royal* (Paris, 1737; reprint Geneva, 1970).

[16] Pierre Gassendus, *The Mirrour of True Nobility and Gentility: Being the Life of the Renowned Nicolas Claudius Fabricius Lord of Peiresck*, trans. W. Rand (London, 1657), iii–iv. I have modernized the spelling of this faithful translation of Gassendi's work. The Latin original can be found in Gassendi's *Opera, Viri Illustris Nicolai Claudii Fabricii de Peiresc, Senatoris Aqvisextiensis Vita*, 5:239–362. It will henceforth be referred to as *Life*.

public of Letters, as it will be found to exist during the next hundred years."[17]

All of the notable intellectuals of the early seventeenth century visited Peiresc in Aix or else corresponded with him. According to Gassendi, "he proved a large sanctuary always open to learned men, for to him all had recourse that had business at Court . . . and no man ever went away, whose patronage he did not cheerfully undertake."[18] Peiresc encouraged Gassendi in his study of Epicurus, a project that began about 1629 and continued until the philosopher's death in 1655.

Peiresc introduced Gassendi into the intellectual community of Paris, where Gassendi met François Luillier, another patron of letters, councillor to the Parlement of Metz and a Master of Accounts. Gassendi lived and traveled with Luillier between 1629 and 1632, and then again from 1641 to 1648. Gassendi described Luillier as his "comrade, friend, and patron."[19] Like his relationship with Peiresc, this was an association of equals, regardless of differences in social class. Unlike Peiresc, who was universally respected, Luillier had a much more dubious reputation: he was not only a freethinker, but also a moral libertine.

Gassendi's friendship with Luillier, among others, has led the modern historian of libertinage, René Pintard, to characterize him as a secret libertine, at least in terms of the radical heterodoxy of his thought.[20] But the friendship likely had to do more with patronage than moral outlook. Gassendi wrote a friend, "You ask me how only with Luillier I can live most freely? Since he loves me sincerely, so he is not the opponent of that most honest condition [of freedom]."[21]

---

[17] Harcourt Brown, *Scientific Organizations in Seventeenth-Century France (1620–1680)* (Baltimore, 1934), 5. Robert Westman, discussing Peiresc's role in helping publish a Latin translation of Galileo's *Dialogue*, remarks, "Peiresc was one of a new breed of men in late 16th and early 17th century France who had been trained either for the law or the clergy and who found in the promotion of natural knowledge a way of expressing their rise to higher social rank as *conseillers* to the *parlements* or members of the diplomatic corps or abbots of wealthy religious houses" (Robert S. Westman, "The Reception of Galileo's *Dialogue*, A Partial World Census of Extant Copies," in *Novita celesti e crisi del sapere*, ed. P. Galluzzi [Florence, 1984], 336).

[18] *Life*, 171–72. Gassendi's objectivity about Peiresc might be questioned. His work is definitely a panegyric, but much of it seems to concord with Peiresc's personality and actions. In a less guarded moment, Gassendi wrote to his friend Luillier, "Peiresc becomes jealous if any other person than he mediates between his friends or if he does not have the principal part. . . . In this he is only being himself" (*Lettres familières*, 19–20).

[19] Gassendi to Jacob Golius, July 8, 1633, "Letters," *Opera*, 6:33.

[20] René Pintard, *Le libertinage érudit dans la première moitié du XVIIe siècle* (Paris, 1943), 127–28.

[21] Gassendi to Gabriel Naudé, July 15, 1633, "Letters," *Opera*, 6:57.

This "freedom" is contrasted by Gassendi with the lack of freedom he would experience if he accepted another man, of higher rank, as his patron: "there is another who solicits me exceedingly, so that I may vow to him brotherhood, and indivisible and perpetual society. . . . I will never escape him if I go with him to Paris, for he desires me for his own, and I am impotent to deny anything in his presence. Therefore I will save myself from this misfortune."[22] In other words, with Luillier, as with Peiresc, Gassendi was able to maintain his personal liberty, while another, more typical, patronage relationship would result in servitude and "perpetual society." The community of freethinkers and savants with whom Gassendi associated in Paris also gave him the scope and freedom he needed to develop his philosophical ideas.

Luillier and Gassendi attended the meetings of freethinkers and others at the Cabinet of the brothers Dupuy, who were also great patrons and facilitators of learning. Here Gassendi found a new kind of community of thinkers, who could discuss and debate the new ideas in science, philology, and history.[23] The kind of institutionally defined public space, described by Steven Shapin and Simon Schaffer in their account of the Royal Society, or by Roger Hahn in his history of the Royal Academy of Science, did not yet exist in this period. Instead private and informal associations like the Dupuys' provided the forum for cooperative scientific and intellectual activities.[24]

Within the confines of the Cabinet, all opinions were welcomed and all ideas were tolerated: "Each man, therefore, proposed his opinion in complete independence."[25] The friendships Gassendi formed with three other intellectuals, Gabriel Naudé, Elie Diodati, and François de

[22] Ibid. Gassendi had returned to Digne in 1631 to perform his clerical duties. He remained there until 1641. According to Sortais, Gassendi's Parisian friends urged him to return to Paris during this period. The "great man" referred to here, according to Sortais, is probably Henri-Louis Habert, lord of Montmer, who offered the philosopher a place in his household and a pension of three thousand livres (Sortais, *Philosophie moderne*, 9). This was a great deal of money at the time, when an income of six thousand livres was enough to support a "gentleman" (Robert Mandrou, *Introduction to Modern France, 1500–1655*, trans. R. E. Hallmark [New York, 1975], 43).

[23] Pintard, *Libertinage érudit*, 87. Keohane, in her study of early modern French intellectual and political life, argues that the libertines "took seriously the Epicurean counsel to avoid the business of the world. They conformed to its demands as far as necessary, and found their true pleasure in the company of friends" (146).

[24] Roger Hahn, *The Anatomy of a Scientific Institution: The Paris Academy of Sciences, 1666–1803* (Berkeley, 1971), 4–12; Steven Shapin and Simon Schaffer, *Leviathan and the Air-Pump: Hobbes, Boyle, and the Experimental Life* (Princeton, 1985), 78.

[25] Pintard, *Libertinage érudit*, 30.

la Mothe le Vayer, produced an even more intimate group, which the members called the Tetrade. Pintard believes that this association, also, like the one with Luillier, was a cover for all sorts of freethinking.[26]

Olivier René Bloch, a more recent interpreter of Gassendi's thought, echoes this theme when he argues that Gassendi was a ideological materialist, who disguised the heterodoxy of his thought under a hypocritical theological conformity.[27] Bloch's analysis, in turn, exaggerates Pintard's argument, who softened his critique of Gassendi in later works by suggesting he was not an intellectual heretic, but rather a prudent and cautious individual conforming to the political necessities of his time.[28]

The idea that intellectuals were in a conspiracy of silence to prevent others from perceiving their radicalism is echoed by Robert Mandrou in his analysis of seventeenth-century intellectual patronage. He suggests that patronage, while protecting the savant from the repressive institutions of the French Church and State, also exposed the thinker to continual dangers. He argues that intellectuals were led, so to speak, to put themselves under the direct and personal protection of those whose task it would be, if the intellectuals revealed themselves completely, to destroy them. These thinkers labored under a double duplicity, increasing the degree of oppression that they felt and experienced.[29] This argument is particularly compelling if one recognizes that many patrons were members of the ecclesiastical hierarchy and the high nobility. In theory, every patron was a potential persecutor.

Some scholars have argued that Gassendi did not complete his early critique of Aristotle and delayed the publication of his work on Epicurus out of fear of ecclesiastical persecution.[30] Indeed, he wrote to a friend in 1630 about his work on Aristotle,

---

[26] Ibid., 128. Naudé was a doctor, but more important, librarian first to Francesco Cardinal Barberini and then to Mazarin. La Mothe le Vayer was tutor to the duke of Orleans and Louis XIV and a prolific author. For more on these *libertins érudits,* see J. S. Spink, *French Free-Thought from Gassendi to Voltaire* (London, 1960), 17–22; Richard H. Popkin, *The History of Scepticism from Erasmus to Descartes* (New York, 1964), 89–112; and Robert Mandrou, *From Humanism to Science, 1480–1700,* trans. Brian Pearce (Atlantic Highlands, N.J., 1979), 183–98. Naudé and La Mothe le Vayer had very active public careers. Whether they shared Gassendi's attitude toward patronage remains to be investigated. Diodati was a Swiss diplomat who was instrumental in the dissemination of the works of Galileo. See Pintard, *Libertinage érudit,* 129–31.

[27] Bloch, *Philosophie de Gassendi,* 485–87.

[28] See Joy, *Gassendi the Atomist,* 17, for an excellent historiographical account of the difference between Bloch's and Pintard's interpretations of Gassendi.

[29] Mandrou, *From Humanism to Science,* 218.

[30] Henri Berr, *Du scepticisme de Gassendi,* trans. B. Rochot (Paris, 1960), 45–51, argues that Gassendi ceased his attack on Aristotle because of the persecutions of two anti-Aristotelians in 1624, while Bernard Rochot, *Les travaux de Gassendi sur Épicure et sur*

Liberty in these things for me is somewhat greater than the condition of the current time bears. . . . Therefore I will do another kind of thing, and I will await a better fortune, which unless it smiles on me, I will blind myself to the Muses. I have another commentary on an ancient philosopher, but I will certainly hold it for myself and my friends.[31]

In the 1630s, Gassendi also had very much in mind the example of Galileo, a scholar who wandered too far into the public battlefield and too far away from the intellectual world, and sank into the morass of ecclesiastical politics. In Galileo's case, a miscalculation of patronage priorities led to his downfall.[32]

Nevertheless, if Gassendi lived in constant fear of the Church authorities, it is odd that he would have chosen to write on a figure as controversial as Epicurus. Indeed Gassendi may have been inspired to pursue his Epicurean studies by the example of Galileo in the first place. While Gassendi was interested in Epicurean morality as early as 1624, he did not begin his major project of vindicating Epicurus and rehabilitating his philosophy until 1629, possibly because of his contact with Isaac Beeckman, a Dutch atomist. Other historians have suggested that Gassendi's interest in Epicurus was inspired primarily by his rejection of Aristotle, or because of Gassendi's own theological concerns.[33]

There was, however, another work implicitly endorsing atomism that Gassendi certainly knew about. Galileo's *Assayer*, published in 1623, contained a materialistic and atomistic natural philosophy. Pietro Redondi argues, "*The Assayer* immediately summoned up before contemporary eyes two names: Democritus and Ockham."[34] In 1625, Gassendi wrote a letter to Galileo, with whom he had not corresponded before, praising the Italian extravagantly, and particularly "a little book recently published by you (Galileo)," which Diodati, Galileo's European factor, had given him.[35] The "little book" is probably *The Assayer*, and in it Gassendi would have found his Epicurean leanings confirmed by Galileo.

---

l'atomisme, 1619–1658 (Paris, 1944), 17, argues that Gassendi was never in danger from the established authorities because of his work on Epicurus.

[31] Gassendi to William Schickard, August 25, 1630, "Letters," *Opera*, 6:36.

[32] Mario Biagioli, *Galileo Courtier: The Practice of Science in the Culture of Absolutism* (Chicago, 1993), and Richard S. Westfall, "Science and Patronage: Galileo and the Telescope," *Isis* 76 (1985): 11–30.

[33] See Barry Brundell, *Pierre Gassendi: From Aristotelianism to a New Natural Philosophy* (Dordrecht, 1987), x; and Margaret J. Osler, "Providence and Divine Will and the Theological Background to Gassendi's Views on Scientific Knowledge," *Journal of the History of Ideas* 44 (1983): 549–60.

[34] Pietro Redondi, *Galileo Heretic*, trans. Raymond Rosenthal (Princeton, 1987), 59.

[35] Gassendi to Galileo, July 18, 1625, "Letters," *Opera*, 6:4.

In his controversial study, Pietro Redondi argues that the possible heretical implications of atomism for the Catholic doctrine of the Eucharist might have gotten Galileo into trouble in 1624, and that he was defended against the charge of heresy by Father Giovanni di Guevara, a scholastic philosopher who was father general of the Order of Regular Minor Clerks.[36] Guevara traveled to France in 1627 in the suite of Cardinal Francesco Barberini, a patron of Peiresc, who entertained him in Marseilles.[37] According to Redondi, "these two friends (Barberini and Guevara) and defenders of Galileo had many philosophical discussions" on their journey, which no doubt would have included Peiresc while they visited him.[38] Gassendi was Peiresc's constant companion during these years, so perhaps this encounter provided yet another impetus for the French scholar to devote himself to Epicurean atomism.

Clearly Gassendi must have been aware of some of the perils Galileo had experienced in the 1620s, but they did not dissuade him from undertaking his own potentially dangerous philosophical studies. He knew that when Galileo's real problems with the Church began in 1633, Peiresc tried to use his influence as a client of Barberini to get the cardinal to intercede for Galileo.[39]

Gassendi was certainly cautious, but there were many reasons besides fear of the Church why he did not put his work out into the public arena. He was sincere in his respect for the Church and its injunctions—a sentiment repeated many times in both his private correspondence and published works—and truly happy to disseminate his ideas only within the circle of his friends. For most of the 1630s, these friends included an overlapping and intricately related community of patrons, natural philosophers, and humanists, who all shared an interest in the new philosophy, and whose interests usually ran together.[40]

Ultimately, Gassendi's actions suggest that Robert Mandrou's characterization of the dangers inherent in a patronage relationship for a heterodox thinker does not really fit Gassendi's situation. Gassendi's fear of the "perpetual servitude" involved in a patronage relationship was not so much fear of persecution, should his protectors discover his true

---

[36] Redondi, *Galileo Heretic*, 165–75.
[37] Gassendus, *Life*, 201.
[38] Redondi, *Galileo Heretic*, 169.
[39] See my article, "French Reaction to the Condemnation of Galileo," *Catholic Historical Review* 74 (1988): 34–54.
[40] On the development of the scientific community within the context of patronage, see David S. Lux, *Patronage and Royal Science in Seventeenth-Century France: The Académie de Physique in Caen* (Ithaca, 1989), and Lisa T. Sarasohn, "Nicolas-Claude Fabri de Peiresc and the Patronage of the New Science in the Seventeenth Century," *Isis* 84 (1993): 70–90.

opinions, as the fear that the duties of a client would cheat him of the time, repose, and freedom he needed for his studies. Likewise, Bloch's accusation of theological duplicity and hypocrisy overlooks the fact that in the seventeenth century, sincere religiosity could coexist with unconventional ideas, which themselves could be expressed with caution and conformity to societal norms.

Such a pattern can be seen in the work and life of Marin Mersenne (1588–1648), the Minimin monk who was yet another promoter of knowledge in the early seventeenth century, who has never been accused of dubious morality. During the 1630s, a number of mathematicians and natural philosophers, including Gassendi, began to meet regularly at his cell. Like Peiresc, Mersenne knew everyone in Europe involved in the mechanical philosophy, and through his vast correspondence encouraged productivity, communication, and controversy among these scholars.[41] Gassendi and Mersenne became close friends and it was Mersenne, also a good friend of Descartes, who initiated the dispute between these two founders of the mechanical philosophy.

Throughout his life, Gassendi shared his work with Mersenne, who transmitted Gassendi's ideas to other intellectuals in France and all over Europe. Gassendi and Mersenne developed similar epistemologies and they devoted themselves to the new ideas in natural philosophy. Both devout members of the clergy, they saw no inconsistencies between free inquiry and piety.

The more Gassendi's renown grew in the 1640s and 1650s, the more he suffered from the constraints of the patronage system—constraints not on his philosophical liberty, but on his time and personal independence. As Orest Ranum has pointed out, the great sought clients whose glory would increase their own.[42] Such was Gassendi's fate.

Gassendi found himself in a very precarious position in 1637, after Peiresc died. He shortly thereafter attracted the attention of the governor of Provence, Louis-Emmanuel de Valois, count of Alais, a close connection of the royal family. In 1638, Gassendi was "invited to wait upon" Valois and thus he entered the nobleman's service until the latter's death in 1653. The nature of this new patronage relationship is indi-

---

[41] For Mersenne's life and works, see Robert Lenoble, *Mersenne ou la naissance du mécanisme* (Paris, 1943); Peter Dear, *Mersenne and the Learning of the Schools* (Ithaca, 1988); and Marin Mersenne, *Correspondance du P. Marin Mersenne, religieux minime,* ed. C. de Waard, B. Rochot, R. Pintard, A. Beaulieu, 17 vols. to date (Paris, 1933–88). Mersenne's *Correspondance* will be cited as *CM.*

[42] Orest Ranum, *Artisans of Glory: Writers and Historical Thought in Seventeenth-Century France* (Chapel Hill, 1980), 31–32.

cated in Gassendi's first letter to Valois, written in 1639, when he wrote, "you bind me willingly, and I become yours by right."[43]

Gassendi's ties with Valois exposed him to many of the inconveniences of patronage that he had longed to avoid. From the very beginning of their relationship, Valois sought to gain offices and rewards for Gassendi, and the savant could only accede to his wishes. Between 1639 and 1641, Valois attempted to have Gassendi elected an Agent General of the French clergy, a national post that normally led to the episcopate. To this end, Valois enlisted the aid of Count Leon le Bouthillier Chavigny, the secretary of state, and finally the king himself. Gassendi thanked him for these efforts in the following way: "Hence it is not marvelous if I feel myself weighed down by so much benevolence, but also oppressed (which is hard for a soul acknowledging gratitude), and I foresee no time sufficient to give you the thanks I owe you."[44]

This kind of rhetoric is familiar in the context of seventeenth century patronage, but differs sharply from the words Gassendi used to describe his state of mind after the appointment was blocked, "not for all the gold of Croesus would I wish to have been inflicted with these burdens. The voice of the Assembly [of the Clergy] has released me like the rose from the thorns."[45]

This theme continued in later letters: "Nothing could be more sweet, than not to have displeased you, because I took the initiative of claiming the tranquil life for myself. . . . I esteem especially the quiet of the soul and the freedom for study."[46] Clearly, Gassendi regarded his service to Valois as servitude, and the rewards of patronage as a prison that would destroy tranquillity and freedom. Although Gassendi remained a client of Valois for many years, and attended him sporadically, he tried to keep his distance. He lived with Luillier, and limited his service to Valois to advising him and instructing him in Epicurean philosophy in letters.[47] Interestingly enough, Valois, while an agent of the state, was not incensed but rather intrigued by these somewhat unorthodox ideas.

Nevertheless, Gassendi was not able to avoid more public involvement. In 1645, Cardinal Alphonse de Richelieu, the cardinal-minister's brother and archbishop of Lyon, who had known Gassendi from his time as archbishop of Aix in 1626–1628, helped procure a professorship of mathematics at the Collège Royal for his client. This new patron

---

43 Gassendi to Louis de Valois, July 30, 1639, "Letters," *Opera*, 6:95.
44 Gassendi to Louis de Valois, September 19, 1639, ibid., 6:97.
45 Gassendi to Louis de Valois, March 1, 1641, ibid., 6:104.
46 Gassendi to Louis de Valois, March 20, 1641, ibid., 6:105.
47 Gassendi to Louis de Valois, ibid., 6:117–60.

carefully reassured Gassendi that he would not actually have to teach at the Collège, but could continue to pursue his scholarly activities without distraction.[48] In 1653, Gassendi came under the protection of Henri-Louis Habert, seignor of Montmor, with whom the philosopher lived until his death in 1655. Montmor was the patron of a scientific group that would, in the next decade, evolve into the Royal Academy of Sciences.

Between 1641 and 1655, Gassendi wrote the "Ethics" of the *Syntagma Philosophicum*, and rewrote the "Physics."[49] Concepts of freedom and tranquillity are basic to the "Ethics," and thus it reflects the moral imperatives of Gassendi's own life. But the "Ethics" is more than a theoretical rendition of biographical factors. Gassendi's moral philosophy drew on many prior traditions, and is also a rejoinder to other philosophic theories of his own time. Moreover, Gassendi's ethical ideas are part of a unified vision of the universe and humanity's place within it, which is novel and important in its own right.

The Intellectual Context

Gassendi's life encompassed an age of great philosophic speculation. The Aristotelianism which had dominated philosophy, and indeed all learning, was disintegrating. It no longer offered the answers demanded in an age that had rediscovered the entire classical heritage, and at at time when new ideas proliferated as quickly as the printing press could propagate them. The crisis of authority which had characterized the sixteenth century—the result of intellectual ferment, religious upheaval, and the new discoveries of science—continued into the seventeenth century.

As a young man, Gassendi had spent a brief time as a university professor, expounding on Aristotle and then confounding him.[50] Scholastic Aristotelianism still ruled in the universities of Europe; students were required to learn it and professors to teach it.[51] This academic demand led Gassendi to produce his first philosophic challenge to authority, the *Exercitationes paradoxicae adversus Aristoteleos* (1624).

In the late 1620s, Gassendi abandoned his direct attack on Aristotle, perhaps because two anti-Aristotelians, Jean Bitaud and Étienne de

---

[48] Joy, *Gassendi the Atomist,* 195–96. Joy mentions that this office was worth 600 livres.
[49] On the dating of the "Ethics" of the *Syntagma Philosophicum,* see the Appendix.
[50] Gassendi's anti-Aristotelianism is the theme of Brundell, *From Aristotelianism.*
[51] L. W. B. Brockliss, *French Higher Education in the Seventeenth and Eighteenth Centuries: A Cultural History* (Oxford, 1987), 186–95.

Claves, had been condemned by the Sorbonne.[52] By 1628 or 1629, Gassendi had embarked on his studies of Epicurus, which would occupy him in one form or another for the rest of his life, culminating in his own neo-Epicurean philosophic treatise, the *Syntagma Philosophicum* (1658) published three years after his death in 1655.

Gassendi was a polymath and a humanist. While he abandoned the authority of Aristotle, he still felt he needed the warrant of ancient philosophy to validate his own. As Lynn Joy has recently pointed out, a humanistic historiographic style is basic not only to the form of his exposition, but also to its content.[53] Gassendi believed that philosophically correct understanding had to be based on an evaluation of all preceding and contrasting philosophic schools, even if he personally favored Epicureanism. As a result, all of his works include complex and verbose explorations of philosophy from antiquity until the seventeenth century.

Epicurus's own defense of freedom and pleasure had developed against the background of the Hellenistic Age, when the moral norms constructed during the Greek classical era were under assault. New ethical doctrines, including Epicureanism, Stoicism, and skepticism, which were more congenial to the emerging individualism and cosmopolitanism of the period, were being articulated. Aristotelian *eudaemonia*, the idea that the goal of human life is happiness, was still the substratum of ethical thought, but new schools of philosophy interpreted happiness differently than Aristotle had.[54] Aristotle had argued that happiness is the rational operation of the soul, where reason established a virtuous mean between the extremes of passion. In doing so, man fulfills his potential as man—he is a rational creature.[55]

Quite differently, Epicureanism and Stoicism taught that happiness consisted of a kind of tranquillity (Epicurean *ataraxia*) or imperturbility (Stoic *apatheia*) of the soul for the wise man. Epicurus thought this came from the pursuit of pleasure and the avoidance of pain. The Stoics argued that a virtuous life following reason in conformity to natural law was the source of internal calm.[56]

Epicurus believed that a man could be tranquil only if he understood the way the universe worked, that all physical events were based on

52 Spink, *French Free-Thought*, 89–90.
53 Joy, *Gassendi the Atomist*, 165.
54 Phillip Mitsis, *Epicurus' Ethical Theory: The Pleasures of Invulnerability* (Ithaca, 1988), 1–58.
55 J. McDowell, "The Role of *Eudaemonia* in Aristotle's Ethics," in *Essays on Aristotle's Ethics*, ed. A. O. Rorty (Berkeley, 1980), 359–76.
56 Philip P. Hallie, "Stoicism," in *The Encyclopedia of Philosophy*, ed. Paul Edwards, 8 vols. (New York, 1967), 8:19–22.

atomic indeterminism, and that all human action resulted from a corresponding freedom in the human soul.[57] Such knowledge would free one from fear of death and fear of the arbitrary nature of the gods. The Stoics found no comfort in such an anarchic universe, and instead postulated a cosmos governed by natural law and fate, a universe where the divine was immanent. There was a limited role for human freedom in the Stoic schema; it was largely understood as obedience to God's law as expressed in the universe.[58] Thus, these two ancient philosophies set up the parameters of the debate on freedom, pleasure, and virtue, but only for a world devoid of a Christian God.

Gassendi adopted and Christianized Epicurean atomism, and used it to create a natural philosophy that would support the new mechanistic world-view. Epicurus had articulated a physical system where, in order to undermine the terrifying prospect of death and the interference of the gods, all cosmology was reduced to the action of eternal solid atoms moving through a void universe, itself devoid of proactive divine beings. According to Epicurus, atoms compose the material substratum of all material substances, including human beings, whose atomic structure simply decomposes after death.

Gassendi believed that the atoms and the void—matter in motion—could be integrated into a divinely conceived mechanistic universe. The great bulk of the *Syntagma Philosophicum* was an explication of an atomistic natural philosophy connected, as Margaret Osler recently argued, to the providential workings of a voluntaristic deity.[59] Even in the midst of these physical preoccupations, however, Gassendi included intimations that his physics were meant to be read as a part of a system which included ethics.[60]

Gassendi insisted that the world is absolutely contingent on God's will, which is "most free." God created the world when it pleased him to do so; God is "so free, that no necessity is stronger, so wise, that no accident of fortune can sport with him, and so good, that he is never hampered by envy." This omnipotent, voluntaristic God created the world for the pleasure of human beings, not because he had to, but because he

[57] On Epicureanism, a good modern account is John M. Rist, *Epicurus: An Introduction* (Cambridge, 1969).

[58] On ancient Stoicism, see A. A. Long, *Hellenistic Philosophy: Stoics, Epicureans, Sceptics,* 2d ed. (Berkeley, 1986).

[59] Osler, *Divine Will and the Mechanical Philosophy,* 1–12.

[60] See for example, Gassendi's discussion of fate and fortune in the "Physics" where he explicitly refers the discussion of chance and freedom to the ethical section of his philosophy (Pierre Gassendi, "Physics," in *SP, Opera,* 1:337).

wanted to. He endowed them with self-consciousness, rationality, and freedom so that they could appreciate and use all of the things of the natural world for their own benefit.[61]

In other words, a most free God created humans in his own image, who are therefore also most free, and allowed to pursue their own pleasure and utility by God's special providence. Instead of being curbed by providence or fate, human liberty is enhanced by it. The natural necessity of Gassendi's universe is limited by God's freedom on one side and human freedom on the other. Physics, therefore, is enfolded within theology and ethics, and can only be understood these terms.

When Gassendi commented on theology and ethics, he also had to consider traditional Church theological teaching, although theology was so diverse that many of his own doctrines could be accommodated to it without necessitating a desertion of his basic tenets. In a Christian cosmos, providence usurped the role of fate or fortune, and human freedom was conditioned by God's foreknowledge and omnipotence. Ethics itself became an adjunct of theology. The question of freedom and determinism became more difficult, because theologians had to decide whether man was free in two different ways: Could man freely make decisions in this world, and could he freely earn his own place in the scheme of salvation and damnation?

Saint Augustine, in the fifth century A.D., formulated the fundamental Christian teachings on ethical matters. In ethics, as in so many areas, Augustine can be interpreted in different ways, but his major thesis concerning free will was that after the Fall, the human capacity to will freely was perverted and destroyed. Without grace, man can only will freely to do evil. Only grace enables the will to possess the freedom to choose the good and to do good works. Without grace, no act can be virtuous in itself. Thus, humans, corrupted by the Fall, are fallible and helpless without God. Their ultimate fate, to be saved or damned, is also dependent on God's decree. One who is saved will be enfolded in the eternal fruition of the beatific vision—for all Christian theologians, pleasure is assimilated to divine bliss.[62]

Augustine's doctrine of grace and will was the product of a controversy with a contemporary philosopher and theologian, Pelagius. Pelagius denied that man's ability to will the good freely was destroyed by

---

[61] Ibid., 1:337, 318, 329–30.
[62] On Augustine's doctrines and his impact on later times , see Étienne Gilson, *The Christian Philosophy of St. Augustine*, trans. L. E. M. Lynch (London, 1961); Jan Miel, *Pascal and Theology* (Baltimore, 1969), 41–42; and J. B. Schneewind, ed., *Moral Philosophy from Montaigne to Kant: An Anthology*, 2 vols. (Cambridge, 1990), 1:4–7.

the Fall, and that grace was the only way to overcome human depravity and fallibility. Pelagius vindicated the unimpaired abilities of human reason and will. Human beings, through their free will, can do good works and even achieve salvation without God's intervening grace.[63] Thus, by the end of antiquity there existed diametrically opposite views on freedom and determinism in both the classical and Christian traditions.

The debate about freedom and determinism, with concomitant doctrines concerning virtue and pleasure, had a long and vigorous history in the middle ages.[64] The Augustinian view was carried on by Saint Bernard of Clairvaux and Saint Bonaventura among others, but the most famous scholastic, Saint Thomas Aquinas, was more sympathetic to the possibility of human freedom, even within a divinely ordained universe.[65]

Aquinas's theory is complex, and will be explored in detail in Chapter 4, but in sum he argued that human beings retained their power of free choice after the fall and can know eternal law and the self-evident laws of morality through their reason. Aquinas developed a psychological theory of the faculties of will and intellect to explain how human beings can act as free moral agents. His intellectualist account stressed the importance of the reason in free choice, but also allowed the will to operate autonomously in appetitive decisions. To a certain limited extent, Aquinas even allowed human beings to participate in their own salvation and achieve happiness in the vision of God.[66] His views dominated later scholastic thought on these issues.

Gassendi knew these traditions well, as the numerous references to Augustine and Aquinas in the *Syntagma* demonstrate. Perhaps in early modern time these ethical debates became even more pressing; certainly, as people died for their beliefs, the stakes were higher. The Reformation had focused theology once again on the role of grace in human life and the question of predestination. To differing degrees, Luther and Calvin agreed with the Augustinian teaching that human reason was corrupted by the fall, and that good works were impossible without the

---

[63] John A. Mourant, "Pelagius and Pelagianism," in *Encyclopedia of Philosophy*, 6:78–79.
[64] On the history of these themes in the middle ages, see Étienne Gilson, *Reason and Revelation in the Middle Ages* (New York, 1938); David Knowles, *The Evolution of Medieval Thought* (New York, 1962); and Gordon Leff, *Medieval Thought: St. Augustine to Ockham* (Baltimore, 1968, 1958).
[65] Vernon J. Bourke, "St. Thomas Aquinas," in *Encyclopedia of Philosophy*, 8:105–14.
[66] A good selection of Aquinas's ethical writings, with commentary can be found in Thomas Aquinas, *St. Thomas Aquinas on Politics and Ethics*, ed. and trans. P. E. Sigmund (New York, 1988).

intervention of divine grace. While human beings can make rational decisions in matters pertaining to this world, declared the Reformation theologians, they are incompetent to choose in spiritual matters without the aid of grace and the law revealed in Scripture. Man's ultimate destiny is not preconditioned on free human actions, but it is predestined.[67]

Legions of Catholic theologians rose to the defense of a more libertarian theology. The most significant were Jesuits, who came close to arguing that salvation is possible through acts without reliance on divine grace. Among the most ardent defenders of human liberty was the Spanish Jesuit Luis de Molina (1535–1600). He developed the doctrine of the middle knowledge of God, where God knows what anyone would do in a future contingent situation, but does not thereby determine the agent to do that action. This doctrine preserves human freedom, as does his doctrine of the liberty of indifference, in which humans can either act or not act, do one thing or its opposite. Molina's doctrine of human liberty is articulated within the framework of a psychology of the faculties, which makes the will almost totally autonomous and free.[68]

Molinism was central to Gassendi's theory of freedom, and it will be discussed in greater detail in Chapter 4. The French philosopher must have been aware that these doctrines were attacked not only by Protestants, but also by Catholic Dominicans and Jansenists, who held more firmly to the Augustinian line. Jansenism, in particular, animated religious debate in France at precisely the time Gassendi developed his ethical theories.[69] In terms of the history of theology, Gassendi took his place most definitively in the tradition of Christian libertarianism versus the deterministic doctrines of Augustine and his followers.

Gassendi was also familiar with a more secular ethical tradition associated with the Italian and Northern Renaissance. The problems facing the humanists were the same ones that confronted Gassendi in the seventeenth century: how to accommodate classical and Christian systems of morality—and how to provide an ethical system which identified the summum bonum and showed how to integrate this good it into the practice of one's life.[70] More specifically, earlier thinkers had also ana-

---

[67] On the theological beliefs of the reformers, see Steven E. Ozment, *The Age of Reform, 1250–1550: An Intellectual and Religious History of Late Medieval and Reformation Europe* (New Haven, 1980).

[68] A good short account of Molinism can be found in Miel, *Pascal and Theology*, 50–52.

[69] Ibid., 53–74.

[70] Jill Kraye, "Moral Philosophy," in *The Cambridge History of Renaissance Philosophy*, ed. Charles B. Schmitt and Quentin Skinner (Cambridge, 1988), 325; and Brian P. Copenhaver and Charles B. Schmitt, *Renaissance Philosophy* (Oxford, 1992), 196–97.

lyzed the role of freedom and pleasure in human life. They used skepticism and rhetoric to reinforce their positions in moral philosophy, as Gassendi would do. When Gassendi developed his own moral system focusing on freedom and pleasure, he continued an unbroken tradition originating in the early Renaissance.

In 1624, in two different places, Gassendi enumerated some of the modern philosophers he most admired: the Florentine, Pico della Mirandola (whether he meant Giovanni (1463–94) or Gianfrancesco (1469–1533) is difficult to determine), the Northern humanist, Desiderius Erasmus (1466/9–1536), the Spanish humanist, Juan Luis Vives (1492–1540), and the French thinkers, Peter Ramus (1515–72), Michel de Montaigne (1533–95), and Pierre Charron (1541–1603), and the Flemish scholar, Justus Lipsius (1547–1606).[71] While Gassendi did not often cite either these thinkers or the earlier Renaissance ethical writers in his mature philosophical writing, it is clear that he operated within the context of Italian and French humanist thought.

Gassendi's adoration of freedom had good Renaissance antecedents. From the time of Petrarch, humanists had grappled with the problem of human liberty and its relationship to traditional Christian teachings.[72] Francesco Petrarch (1304–74) believed men should be able to live freely among friends without being subject to any kind of coercion.[73] Following him, the Florentine chancellor, Coluccio Salutati (1331–1406) had argued that human beings possess free will, and that an ethical life could only be one of active participation in the events of the day.

[71] The two sources for these names are Pierre Gassendi, "Preface" to *Exercitationes paradoxicae adversus Aristoteleos* (originally published Grenoble, 1624), in *Opera*, 3:99, and Gassendi to Henri du Faur de Pibrac, June 10, 1624, in "Letters," *Opera*, 6:2. Craig Brush believes Gassendi was referring to Giovanni Pico della Mirandola's nephew, Gianfrancesco Pico della Mirandola, who had written a skeptical attack on various pagan authors in the early sixteenth century (Pierre Gassendi, *The Selected Works of Pierre Gassendi*, ed. and trans. Craig B. Brush [New York, 1972], 18). Charles B. Schmitt, in *Gianfrancesco Pico della Mirandola (1469–1533) and His Critique of Aristotle* (The Hague, 1967), 175–78, also makes a powerful argument for the influence of the younger Pico on Gassendi's epistemology. Clearly Gassendi learned much from Gianfrancesco Pico, but his ethical thought also has resonances to the earlier work of Giovanni. Giovanni Pico's "Oration on the Dignity of Man" was well known in Gassendi's time, and I will assume that Gassendi was familiar with it. In the letter to Pibrac, Gassendi also mentioned that he admired the following authors among the ancients: Seneca, Cicero, Lucretius, Horace, and Juvenal. Seneca, Cicero, and Lucretius are the main sources for information about ancient Epicureanism, Stoicism, and skepticism.
[72] A good short account of the history of early modern ethics can be found in the introduction to Schneewind, *Moral Philosophy*, 1:1–30.
[73] Nancy S. Struever, *Theory as Practice: Ethical Inquiry in the Renaissance* (Chicago, 1992), 4–37.

But Salutati, like Petrarch before him and Gassendi after him, seemed sometimes to prefer a contemplative life of political withdrawal.[74] The debate about the relative worth of the *vita activa* and *vita contemplativa* was a basic problem for anyone discussing ethics in the Renaissance and the sixteenth and seventeenth centuries. Ethics was the study of how one should act, not just what one should think.

The discussion of freedom and the proper way for a person to conduct his life continued throughout the fifteenth century. This period saw the recovery of ancient Greek writings, which enriched and stimulated philosophical discussions. One of the most famous scholars of the age was Giovanni Pico della Mirandola, who was a Neoplatonist, but used all philosophical traditions in his writings. In his *Oration on the Dignity of Man*, Pico went so far as to argue that a human being "with freedom of choice and with honor" could make himself either bestial or divine: he was "the maker and molder" of his own destiny.[75]

Pico was part of the Neoplatonic school created by Marsilio Ficino (1433–90) in the late fifteenth century. Both Pico and Ficino believed that human reason allows man to transcend any form of determinism, whether providential, fatal, or natural. As Charles Trinkaus argues, Pico in modern times, "but also in the Renaissance, has come to symbolize a Renaissance liberation of the human spirit from an earth-born determinism."[76]

For Pico, prelapsarian man, at least, had the power to operate outside of the hierarchy of being established by God, and raise himself even to the Godhead through his own efforts. The proclamation of the dignity of man was at the center of Renaissance humanism, and the notion that human beings must be free to operate autonomously in the human sphere was fundamental to this concept. Pico, and his most optimistic peers, assumed that since God had become manlike, men could become Godlike, and create and rule over their own mental universes.[77] Gassendi also thought a person controlled his perception and understand-

---

[74] On Salutati, see Charles Trinkaus, *In Our Image and Likeness: Humanity and Divinity in Italian Humanist Thought*, 2 vols. (Chicago, 1970), 1:69–89.

[75] Giovanni Pico della Mirandola, *Oration on the Dignity of Man*, trans. Elizabeth L. Forbes, in *The Renaissance Philosophy of Man*, ed. Ernst Cassirer, Paul O. Kristeller, and John Randall, Jr. (Chicago, 1948), 224–25.

[76] Trinkaus, *In Our Image*, 2:525.

[77] Kraye, "Moral Philosophy," 309–10, and Trinkaus, *In Our Image*, xiv. The concept of the dignity of man has also been discussed by Ernst Cassirer, *The Individual and the Cosmos in Renaissance Philosophy*, trans. Mario Domandi (New York, 1963), and in the many works of Paul Osker Kristeller. See, for example, Paul Oskar Kristeller, *Renaissance Thought and Its Sources* (New York, 1979).

ing of the world, and in fact, created his own moral life—if not as a deity, then as a freely acting part of the divine plan.

In arguing for human freedom, Pico was appalled by anything that challenged liberty. He disliked astrology, against which he wrote the *Disputationes adversus astrologiam divinatricem.*[78] Many Renaissance humanists viewed astrology with disdain, because they thought it made human beings subject to natural necessity.[79] It was an early paradigm of a world ruled by intrinsic laws of nature.

It is not surprising, therefore, to find that Gassendi also inveighed against astrology, which he too perceived as a threat to human autonomy. Chapter 5 will show that Gassendi viewed the denunciation of astrology as a fundamental ethical stance. Such an attack was also associated with skepticism about the possibility of essential knowledge. Gianfrancesco Pico had, in the sixteenth century, used the weapons of skepticism to undermine astrology.[80] Gassendi probably utilized the anti-astrological arguments of both the uncle and the nephew in his own defense of human freedom against the claims of the astrologers.

Scholars of the fifteenth century were also interested in the nature and role of pleasure as well as freedom.[81] Ficino argued that pleasure could be viewed as a good if it was controlled by reason and the will. He identified Epicurean pleasure with divine love, thus beginning the process of rehabilitating Epicurus, which continued to a certain extent in the work of Lorenzo Valla (1407–57).[82] Valla was the first modern European to deal extensively with Epicurean philosophy, although he wrote his dialogue, *De voluptate* or *De vero bono* (1431), probably without knowing Lucretius's *De Rerum Natura*, which was rediscovered by Poggio Bracciolini in 1417, but not printed until many years later.[83] Thus, Valla depended on the accounts of Epicureanism found in Cicero and Sen-

---

[78] Giovanni Pico della Mirandola, *Disputationes adversus astrologiam divinatricem*, ed. E. Garin, 2 vols. (Florence, 1946–52). On Pico and astrology, see Trinkaus, *In Our Image*, 97.
[79] Eugenio Garin, *Astrology in the Renaissance: The Zodiac of Life*, trans. Carolyn Jackson and June Allen, revised trans. Clare Robertson (London, 1983), 8.
[80] On Gianfrancesco Pico and astrology, see Brian P. Copenhaver, "Astrology and Magic," in *Cambridge History of Renaissance Philosophy*, 288–90.
[81] On discussions of pleasure during the Renaissance, see Kraye, "Moral Philosophy," 376–86, and Copenhaver and Schmitt, *Renaissance Philosophy*, 198–200.
[82] Copenhaver and Schmitt, *Renaissance Philosophy*, 199.
[83] Maristella de Panizza Lorch, *A Defense of Life: Lorenzo Valla's Theory of Pleasure* (Munich, 1985). I am following Trinkaus's analysis of Valla's treatise here (103–170). On other Epicurean themes in the Renaissance, see Howard Jones, *The Epicurean Tradition* (London, 1989); Kraye, "Moral Philosophy," 374–86 and Chapter 2 of my unpublished dissertation, "The Influence of Epicurean Philosophy on Seventeenth-Century Ethical and Political Thought: The Moral Philosophy of Pierre Gassendi" (UCLA, 1979).

eca, and his exposition is far from the detailed and sophisticated analysis Gassendi would later develop.

Valla used Epicureanism as a ploy to discredit any natural system of ethics. Starting from Augustinian premises, Valla did not believe that the human will or reason, unaided by grace, could achieve anything. What he did argue was that Epicurus was correct in postulating that pleasure is the highest good, and the Stoics were nothing short of absurd in maintaining that human beings would want virtue for its own sake. In his account, Valla transmuted the meanings of both Epicureanism and Stoicism for his own purposes. His aim was to show that pleasure is indeed the highest good, but only within the Christian system of grace and redemption, where the highest pleasure is the beatific vision of God. Thus, divine love should be the aim, the summum bonum for which human beings should strive.[84]

Gassendi also viewed God as the ultimate end of the wise man who correctly understands the nature of pleasure, but whether Gassendi was directly influenced by Valla is difficult to determine. Gassendi's view of the virtues, as Lynn Joy points out, was different from Valla's. For Valla, virtue is an act of will, which does not depend on prudence.[85] For Gassendi, all actions depend on reason and prudence, and the pursuits of the pleasures of this world serve a moral and social purpose.

Valla was also interested in the question of human liberty. In the dialogue, *De libero arbitrio,* Valla wrestled with the question of how God's foreknowledge and will can coexist with human freedom, a question which he ultimately decided was beyond human comprehension.[86] In the last part of the "Ethics," Gassendi came to the same conclusion, while still favoring the Molinist solution to the problem.

While Valla's Epicureanism is quite different from Gassendi's, the one aspect of Valla's thought that would have been most congenial to Gassendi was his epistemology.[87] Valla was an empiricist who believed that cognition begins with sense data, which are then synthesized by the mind. Since this kind of knowledge is fallible, it is necessary to follow a discursive process, arguing from one side and the other—*ad utramque*

---

[84] Trinkaus, *In Our Image,* 110–41.
[85] Lynn Sumida Joy, "Epicureanism in Renaissance Philosophy," *Journal of the History of Ideas* 53 (1992): 573–83; 575.
[86] Lorenzo Valla, "Dialogue on Free Will," trans. Charles E. Trinkaus, in *Renaissance Philosophy of Man,* 147–82.
[87] There is no evidence that Gassendi knew Valla's work, but he was a very famous scholar and it would have been most unusual for Gassendi not to have read him. Valla and Gassendi's Epicureanism are compared by Joy, in "Epicureanism in Renaissance Philosophy."

partem—to arrive at the most probable truth. Valla developed his ideas from Cicero's account of Academic skepticism in the *Academia*, as well as from his own knowledge of ancient rhetoric, which also aimed at persuasion of the most probable truth through arguing the pros and cons of a position.[88] Gassendi used a similar form of rhetorical argumentation, as the next chapter will show.

Rhetoric is the art of speaking and writing eloquently and well. In the Renaissance it routed Aristotelian logic from its monopoly of the methodology of reasoning. Renaissance humanists found its less dogmatic claims more in keeping with their relativistic and individuated points of view.[89] In the ancient world and the Renaissance, rhetoric was usually interpreted as an ethical enterprise, whose purpose was to persuade humans to choose and do the good.[90] Thus, Valla's epistemological and rhetorical doctrines were part of his ethical teachings.

The tradition of Academic skepticism and probabilistic rhetoric was maintained by Peter Ramus, who integrated it into his new dialectic which aimed at probable rather than demonstrative knowledge and employed techniques borrowed from traditional rhetoric. Ramus's new method was developed to undermine Aristotelian logic, and it was enormously popular in late sixteenth-century France. Ramus's anti-Aristotelianism undoubtedly appealed to Gassendi, but he could not have appreciated the divorce Ramus had posited between dialectic and morality.[91] What Gassendi did like was the idea that discourse should present two sides of a question and discourse should be used to argue the most probable solution. Ramus's influence was far-reaching in terms of the structure and the content of Gassendi's ethical philosophy as I will show in Chapter 2.

Gassendi admired the universal scholar, Desiderius Erasmus, who was also affected by the revival of Academic skepticism and rhetoric, perhaps through reading Valla. This knowledge of the skeptical and rhetorical tradition resulted in what Barbara Shapiro has called the "irenic, non-theological, moralistic, slightly probabilistic strains" of his discourse.[92] Living a century apart, Erasmus and Gassendi strongly resemble each

[88] On Valla and ethics, as well as the relationship of rhetoric and Academic skepticism, see Dear, *Mersenne and the Learning of the Schools*, 28–38.
[89] Donald Wilcox, *In Search of God and Self: Renaissance and Reformation Thought* (Boston, 1975), 74–88.
[90] Brian Vickers, "Rhetoric and Poetics," in *Cambridge History of Renaissance Philosophy*, 726–35.
[91] Copenhaver and Schmitt, *Renaissance Philosophy*, 237–38.
[92] Shapiro, "Early Modern Intellectual Life," 45–71; 61.

other. Both found in skepticism and rhetoric a way of moderating the escalating passions of their respective times—they presented an ethical stance that was an alternative to either religious fanaticism or dogmatic philosophic systems.

Erasmus, and his friend and fellow humanist, Thomas More, were seeking a philosophy which could combine tolerance, human pleasure, and Christianity.[93] Erasmus utilized the idea that a calculus of pleasure and pain leads men to realize that false pleasures of the flesh are ultimately destructive, and the only true pleasure is to live a virtuous life, which promises joy while living and eternal bliss in the hereafter.[94] In two of his colloquies, *De contemptu mundi* (1486) and *The Epicurean* (1533), Erasmus argued, "In plain truth, there are no people more Epicurean than Godly Christians" because they understand that leading a virtuous life will lead to the ultimate pleasure of the vision of God, a conclusion which is very much in keeping with Lorenzo Valla's argument in *De vero bono*.[95]

The other significant moral tradition which was revived in the generation immediately preceding Gassendi's own was neo-Stoicism. Its best known protagonists were the Flemish philosopher, Justus Lipsius, and the French thinker, Guillaume du Vair (1556–1621).[96] A virtual community of neo-Stoics flourished in France in the early seventeenth century. As an advocate of Epicureanism, Gassendi criticized Stoicism in the *Syntagma*, but the neo-Stoics maintained some doctrines that Gassendi would have found agreeable. They emphasized the importance of divine providence and prudence or right reason—that is, a practical wisdom directed to living a virtuous life, as did Gassendi. Lipsius was interested in questions concerning probable and certain knowledge and the relationship of knowledge to ethical actions. He associated the destiny of the Stoics with divine providence, but he allowed for the possibility of liberty and contingency in the natural world.[97] The neo-Stoics in general

---

[93] On Thomas More's Epicureanism, see Edward Surtz, *The Praise of Pleasure: Philosophy, Education, and Communism in More's Utopia* (Cambridge, 1957); and Edward Surtz, *The Praise of Wisdom: A Commentary on the Religious and Moral Problems and Backgrounds of St. Thomas More's Utopia* (Chicago, 1957).

[94] Desiderius Erasmus, *The Colloquies*, ed. and trans. C. R. Thompson (Chicago, 1965), 538.

[95] Ibid., 546.

[96] Anthony Levi, *French Moralists: The Theory of the Passions, 1585 to 1649* (Oxford, 1964), 57–58. On the neo-Stoics, see Jason Lewis Saunders, *Justus Lipsius: The Philosophy of Renaissance Stoicism* (New York, 1955); Margaret J. Osler, ed., *Atoms, Pneuma, and Tranquillity*; and Mark Morford, *Stoics and Neostoics: Rubens and the Circle of Lipsius* (Princeton, 1991).

[97] Copenhaver and Schmitt, *Renaissance Philosophy*, 264.

emphasized the importance of the intellect in judgment and they made this faculty appetitive, thereby making the faculty of will superfluous.[98] The accommodation of liberty and providence and the emphasis on the intellect were both important themes in Gassendi's ethical thought, as Chapter 3 will show.

Neo-Stoics, like their ancient progenitors, viewed the passions with suspicion if not outright disdain, but Gassendi adopted an ethic based on the desire for pleasure and the avoidance of pain. Fundamentally, this meant that Gassendi's ethics was utilitarian and egoistic, and he faced the problem of making such an non-Christian view of morality acceptable to Christian sensibilities. The pioneering work of his humanist predecessors set the stage for his most ambitious foray into moral philosophy.

It is clear that the ethical thought of the fifteenth and sixteenth century was undergoing a transformation which admitted the possibility of integrating a previously heterodox philosophic tradition into moral systems based on Aristotle and Christianity. When Gassendi undertook to create a Christian Epicurean ethics based on pleasure and freedom intertwined with a skeptical epistemology and rhetorical reasoning, he was part of an emerging moral reformulation of western thought which sought rules for living not in prescriptive moral maxims but in a consciousness of human character and motivation.

While Gassendi was well acquainted with the ideas and concerns of many of the thinkers I have mentioned, it was his immediate French predecessors who shaped the intellectual milieu in which he lived. Montaigne towered over the other thinkers of his age, and he anticipated Gassendi in combining Epicurean, Stoic, and especially skeptical themes into his writings. Montaigne was truly in the Pyrrhonic tradition; for him, all human knowledge was presumption. He reversed Pico's image of man as the highest of all creatures. Montaigne asked, "Is it possible to imagine anything so ridiculous as that wretched and puny creature, who is not even master of himself, exposed to offenses from all things, and who yet proclaims himself master and emperor of the universe, concerning which it is not within his power to know the slightest part, let alone govern it?"[99]

While not as negative as Montaigne, Gassendi also believed that man

---

[98] Levi, *French Moralists*, 27.
[99] Michel de Montaigne, "Essays: In Defense of Raymond Sebond," in *Classics of Western Thought*, Vol. 2: *Middle Ages, Renaissance, and Reformation*, ed. Karl F. Thompson, 3d ed. (San Diego, 1980), 392.

was "from the condition of his nature liable to innumerable evils and miseries."[100] The only way out of this predicament for both philosophers was rational introspection, in which the autonomous self tries to determine what is truly natural and necessary for personal happiness. If we cannot know and control the world, we can attempt to know and control ourselves. Both Montaigne and Gassendi advocated withdrawal from the affairs of this world—if possible—and the pleasurable experience of a retired life full of amiable conversation with friends.[101] When Montaigne advocated this style of life, he found a follower in Gassendi.

Montaigne was at the forefront of a skeptical upheaval about the possibility of knowledge itself. Gassendi was influenced by this tradition in his early life and skeptical motifs remain prominent in his entire work. Much of the attack on Aristotle, by Gassendi and others, found inspiration in the revived skepticism of Pyrrho of Elis (c. 360–c.230 B.C.), whose denunciation of the possibility of knowledge created what Richard Popkin has called the "crise pyrrhonienne" of the sixteenth and seventeenth centuries.[102] This crisis, fundamental to the basic crisis of authority, found its supporters in those bruised by the religious fanaticism and brutality of the age of religious wars.[103]

Popkin makes the argument that Gassendi and his friend Marin Mersenne developed a form of "mitigated skepticism" based on Pyrrhonic teachings.[104] Pyrrhonic skepticism rejected the possibility of knowing anything which was nonevident, because all knowledge based on inference from indicative signs is suspect: our fallible senses cannot reveal infallible truth. The aim of Pyrrhonic skepticism is complete suspension of belief, an imperturbility of mind (*ataraxia*), which allows the individual to live without anxiety and frustration. Pyrrhonic skepticism opposed the teaching of Academic skepticism, another ancient sceptical tradition associated with Carneades (c. 213–128 B.C.). The Academics argued (dogmatically, in the opinion of the Pyrrhonists) that no knowledge was ever possible, and human beings should instead seek to find what is most probable and live accordingly.[105]

Recent studies have shown that Academic skepticism was a viable phi-

[100] Gassendi, "Ethics," in *SP, Opera*, 2:662.

[101] Keohane, *Philosophy and the State*, 98–105.

[102] Popkin, *History of Scepticism*, 1.

[103] On the crisis of the seventeenth century, see Theodore Rabb, *The Struggle for Stability in Early Modern Europe* (Oxford, 1975), and the historiographical account in the introduction to Geoffrey Parker and Lesley M. Smith, eds., *The General Crisis of the Seventeenth Century* (London, 1978).

[104] Popkin, *History of Scepticism*, 132–54.

[105] Richard H. Popkin, "Skepticism," in *Encyclopedia of Philosophy*, 7:449–61.

losophy and a fertile source of ideas in the Renaissance and early modern periods. Scholars have linked its success with the growing popularity of rhetoric over logic as an art of discourse.[106] Gassendi's mitigated skepticism allows for probable knowledge of appearances; the more likely context for this idea is not the Pyrrhonic aim of suspension of judgment, but the Academic skeptical method of finding the most probable truth and—in morals—the action most likely to increase pleasure and reduce pain.

Nevertheless, Gassendi found the Pyrrhonic skepticism of Pierre Charron (1541–1603) very congenial. As Popkin has shown, Charron's combination of skepticism and fideism profoundly affected Gassendi and Mersenne and the so-called *libertins érudits* of the early seventeenth century.[107] Charron used all of the traditional skeptical tropes found in Sextus Empiricus to challenge the claim that human beings could have genuine knowledge of things. In his earlier works, particularly the *Exercitationes*, Gassendi followed this line, although later he was more sympathetic to the idea that knowledge of appearances is possible. Still, like Charron, Gassendi viewed human beings as fundamentally fallible when it came to epistemological matters.

But both Charron and Gassendi agreed that in questions of morality, some conclusions can be reached. Both advocated conventionalism—people should accede to the traditions of their country and religion—but both also advocated human freedom. Charron proclaimed, "the principal and most legitimate charge we have . . . is our conduct. This is why we are here; we should maintain ourselves in tranquillity and liberty."[108] Liberty and the pleasure of tranquillity are the two anchors of Gassendi's ethics, and they play an equal role in the thought of his skeptical predecessor.

Charron also developed a faculties theory which was close to Gassendi's psychology. Charron argued that virtue is the product of reason taking control of the will and thus controlling the passions.[109] For Charron, reason is "sovereign" in ethical matters, even if it has less power in speculative matters.[110] It is reason that chooses what is necessary to pursue and what is necessary to flee in order to achieve virtue and wisdom

---

[106] See for example, Lisa Jardine, "Lorenzo Valla: Academic Skepticism and the New Humanist Dialectic," in *The Skeptical Tradition*, ed. Myles Burnyeat (Berkeley, 1983), 253–86. Dear, *Mersenne and the Learning of the Schools*, applies the same argument to Mersenne, 41.
[107] Popkin, *History of Scepticism*, 67–112.
[108] Quoted in Keohane, *Philosophy and the State*, 136.
[109] Ibid., 138.
[110] Levi, *French Moralists*, 2.

in both private and public life. The combination of freedom, reason, and choice became an important motif in Gassendi's thought, where he integrated these themes with the Epicurean idea that pleasure is the highest good. It is not surprising that Gassendi referred to the earlier thinker as "my dear Charron."[111]

Gassendi thus lived in a world that was askew. The old authorities of Church, State, and thought were being challenged and replaced. Gassendi escaped the kind of existential despair that captured some of his contemporaries and he avoided the new dogmatism of his contemporaries, Descartes and Hobbes.[112] Gassendi shared their espousal of the mechanical philosophy but he reacted to other of their ideas in his ethical philosophy. He rejected Descartes's theory of human freedom centered on the will and clear and distinct ideas. He repudiated Hobbesian materialism and natural necessity. The latter part of this book will show the extent to which Gassendi shaped his own thought in polemical discussions with his two great philosophic peers.

When Gassendi read ancient and modern debates about freedom and pleasure, and when he studied natural philosophy, he found the possibilities liberating and inspiring—even if they resulted in a more humble view of human ability. His own ethical philosophy was conditioned by a tolerance of philosophic disagreement and the hope of providing an ethic that would allow him and his friends the ability to live freely and pleasurably. In an early letter, he wrote, "A writer who is wise and candid removes all fables, however much they seem to be established by authority and utility."[113] Freethinking in the face of authority became, for Gassendi, the defining characteristic of a philosopher: "I love the liberty of philosophizing greatly. . . . It is shameful for those who take pride in being philosophers not to take risks; and who, if they are not supported by the word of authority, they fear, hesitate, waver and fall down."[114]

Both the structure and the content of Gassendi's philosophy are dialectical, and hence I present Gassendi's ethics as part of a polemical

---

[111] Gassendi, *Exercitationes, Opera,* 3:99.
[112] The example of Pascal is best known: "Such is our true condition, rendering us incapable of certain knowledge or of absolute ignorance. We sail over a vast expanse, ever uncertain, ever adrift, carried to and fro. To whatever point we think to fix and fasten ourselves it shifts and leaves us; and if we pursue it escapes our grasp, slips away, fleeing in eternal flight. Nothing stays for us." (Blaise Pascal, *Pascal's Pensées,* trans. H. F. Stewart [London, 1950], 25). Pascal eventually resolved his despair in devotion to religion.
[113] Gassendi to Albertus Myreus, August 1, 1629, "Letters," *Opera,* 6:24. This letter may reflect Gassendi's knowledge of the philosophy of Francis Bacon. Sortais argues for a Baconist influence on Gassendi in *Philosophie Moderne,* 2:34.
[114] Gassendi to Thomas Fienus, June 6, 1629, "Letters," *Opera,* 6:17.

process in which his engagement with other philosophers and philosophies prompted the articulation of his own ideas. In Chapter 2, however, I begin with a discussion of Gassendi's own view of moral and natural philosophy and the role skepticism and rhetoric played in both the content and structure of his philosophy. In Chapter 3, I describe Gassendi's moral philosophy in detail to see how he developed his own ideas about freedom and pleasure. The connection between Gassendi's moral and natural philosophy will also be explored: principles of motion are vital to both.

In Chapter 4, I show how Gassendi's ideas about freedom developed in the context of prior theological speculation about free will, a discussion which Gassendi continued with Descartes, his great philosophic opponent. Gassendi attacked Descartes' theory of error in order to validate his own insistence on uncertainty in judgment, which is crucial to his philosophy of freedom.

Chapter 5 describes Gassendi's attack on astrology, one of the several systems he felt undermined human liberty. Gassendi's relationship with Hobbes is the subject of Chapter 6. In it I argue that Gassendi saw Hobbes as a reborn Democritus—both the ancient and modern materialists envision a cosmos governed by natural necessity. Gassendi expanded his notions of freedom in partial response to the challenge of their ideas. Gassendi also was stimulated by Hobbes in his discussion of political philosophy, the subject of Chapter 7. As elsewhere in his eclectic system, Gassendi drew on past and present ideas about political life in articulating a political ethics, which was based on the idea of the freedom and well-being of the individual.

Gassendi developed an ethical theory which not only accommodated Epicureanism to Christianity, but presented a view of humanity and morality which was itself impressive and influential. The most important student of Gassendi's ideas was John Locke, who, as detailed in Chapter 8, made many of these ideas part of the liberal tradition of the Enlightenment. Gassendi's ideas were not only fundamental for the development of natural philosophy and logic, but also to the evolution of modern ethical theory. In the concluding chapter I will point the direction for further studies of Gassendi's influence on the late seventeenth century and the Enlightenment. The priest absorbed by freedom made a major contribution to its advance.

Probability in Ethics, Natural Philosophy, and Epistemology

The Parts of Philosophy

In the *Oration on the Dignity of Man*, Giovanni Pico della Mirandola confidently explained how to reach "knowledge of things divine." The path, he revealed, ran through the study of natural philosophy, moral philosophy, and dialectic, which, with theology, makes us "full of divine power" so "we shall no longer be ourselves but shall become He Himself who made us."[1]

Gassendi did not share Pico's mysticism—or his level of aspiration—but he also thought that the study of the philosophic disciplines would lead to a valuable goal. For Gassendi, the study of logic, ethics, and natural philosophy led not to the Godhead, but rather to the creation of a wise, free, and virtuous man, who conducts his life correctly in order to obtain the greatest happiness possible for human beings. For Gassendi, as for Pico, the study of all forms of philosophy was necessary for the wise man, who could develop his potential only with the aid of knowledge.

Until quite recently Gassendi's ethical writings have been ignored, disparaged, or misunderstood. The "Ethics," which comprises Part 3 of the *Syntagma Philosophicum*, has been treated as a minor adjunct to his serious philosophical work. Bloch has charged the "Ethics" with being full of "la platitude et l'inconsistance." Bernard Rochot calls them "très conformiste." Gaston Sortais argues that, "La doctrine morale de Gassendi n'est guère en somme que le système d'Épicure épuré et rectifié."

[1] Giovanni Pico della Mirandola, *Oration on the Dignity of Man*, 229–35.

René Pintard describes Gassendi's moral philosophy as "pagan and independent of religion."[2]

Some of the more recent critics have also downplayed the ethical theory; Howard Egan dismisses the "Ethics" as "a minor treatise of under two hundred pages," while Lynn Joy rarely mentions the "Ethics" at all in her study of Gassendi's atomism.[3] Thomas Lennon barely discusses Gassendi's ethics and suggests that, "Gassendi's main concern with respect to hedonism is to defend it against the traditional charge of its being 'pig philosophy.' "[4] Of recent commentators, Margaret Osler and Richard Kroll have acknowledged that Gassendi's ethical writings are an important part of his philosophical synthesis. According to Kroll, "The metaphors informing both Epicurus's and Gassendi's physical and cognitive speculations serve to iterate their ethical aims and, in doing so, to distinguish them from other philosophical systems."[5]

At the beginning of the *Syntagma*, Gassendi set himself several tasks. He wanted to define the parts of his philosophy, fit them into different categories of knowledge, and relate them to his basic epistemological premises—themselves tied to a rhetorical rather than logical process of reasoning.[6] Gassendi had a passion for dualities and definition. He counterpoised ethics and physics, art and science, action and contemplation. His entire work was devoted to sorting out the relationships between these seemingly antithetical areas, in order to avoid "complete obscurity."[7]

Gassendi characterized ethics, physics, and even logic in terms of an empiricism which denied that any knowledge based on the senses was certain and evident. He repudiated the claims of Aristotle and his followers about the possibility of demonstrative or certain knowledge. He denied the Cartesian position that one can make true judgments based on clear and evident ideas. The conclusions reached in either natural or

---

[2] Sortais, *Philosophie Moderne*, 148; Pintard, *Libertinage érudit*, 492; Bernard Rochot, "Gassendi: Le Philosophe," in *Pierre Gassendi: Sa vie et son oeuvre* (Paris, 1955), 99; Bloch, *Philosophie de Gassendi*, 376–78.

[3] Howard T. Egan, *Gassendi's View of Knowledge: A Study of the Epistemological Basis of his Logic* (Lanham, Md., 1984), 53. Joy, *Gassendi the Atomist* (Cambridge, 1987), 5. Egan's remark is curious since his study is of the "Logic" which comprises even fewer pages in the *Syntagma*.

[4] Lennon, *Gods and Giants*, 153.

[5] Richard W. F. Kroll, *The Material Word: Literate Culture in the Restoration and Early Eighteenth Century* (Baltimore, 1991), 97; Osler, *Divine Will and the Mechanical Philosophy*, 42.

[6] On the historical position of the "Logic," see Fred Michael, "La place de Gassendi dans l'histoire de la logique," in *Corpus: revue de philosophie*, ed. Sylvia Murr, 20–21 (1992): 9–36.

[7] Gassendi, "Logic," in *SP, Opera*, 1:123.

moral philosophy, Gassendi argued, are probable rather than certain, because they are based on fallible judgments about sense impressions. In the current scholarly debate about whether the early scientific revolution was characterized by a new dogmatism or by probabilism, Gassendi's work is clearly evidence for the latter view.[8]

Gassendi distinguished two kinds of truth; the first "truth of existence" characterizes what the thing really is as a sensate object and can never be wrong, but the second "truth of judgment" is the proposition we have drawn based on our sensate impressions, and in judgment there is always a possibility of error.[9] Therefore, the reasonings used in physics and ethics are analogous because both employ judgment, even while the goals of the two philosophic disciplines remain distinct: to acquire knowledge of the universe or to lead a virtuous and happy life. This similarity holds even if ethical decisions are primarily practical and not based on propositional forms of logical discourse. Ethical decisions are the result of reasoning, even if this reasoning does not follow logical rules. They are systematic and lead to a conclusion about what is more or less true as well as to what is more or less good.[10]

Gassendi also struggled with normative questions that had preoccupied thinkers from antiquity onward: what is the relative value of contemplation versus action; is it better to know or to do? Gassendi did indeed set up clear boundaries for his philosophy—and thus managed to avoid obscurity in philosophic discourse—in sketching the relationship between ethics and physics and in defining the characteristics of the moral life of the archetypical wise man.

The discursive strategy Gassendi adopted, which had skeptical and

---

[8] Barbara J. Shapiro, *Probability and Certainty in Seventeenth-Century England: A Study of the Relationships between Natural Science, Religion, History, Law, and Literature* (Princeton, 1983), 39, writes, "while the work of Bacon demonstrates that empiricism need not have resulted in probabilism, empiricism, as preached by Gassendi and practiced by the virtuosi of the Royal Society, clearly moved in that direction. Unless we are somehow to read Gassendi and the Royal Society virtuosi entirely out of the scientific movement, it is going to be impossible to break the link between the new science and the new, positive treatment of probabilism." The argument that the empirical scientist of the early seventeenth century still sought for absolute, demonstrative knowledge is given by Ian Hacking, *The Emergence of Probability: A Philosophical Study of Early Ideas about Probability, Induction, and Statistical Inference* (Cambridge, 1975), 26, and William A. Wallace, "The Certitude of Science in Late Medieval and Renaissance Thought," *History of Philosophy Quarterly* 3 (1986): 281–91.
[9] On Gassendi's logic, and the different categories of truth, see Osler, *Divine Will and the Mechanical Philosophy*, 107–9.
[10] Howard Jones, *Pierre Gassendi's Institutio Logica (1658)* (Assen, 1981), 160–63. This is a modern edition of the last part of Gassendi's "Logic" (Gassendi, "Logic," in *SP, Opera,* 1:91–124). All material used from this translation will be cited as Jones, *Institutio Logica.*

rhetorical antecedents, was intimately connected with his notion of freedom and tolerance. Gassendi would not acknowledge that any argument can compel assent. A free person always has the ability to weigh alternatives and decide for himself what is best or truest. Gassendi believed that traditional logic was tyrannical. Only other forms of discourse would allow the wise man to think—and act—as he chooses.[11]

Whether the wise man should live a contemplative or active life was a question of particular interest to the Italian humanists. They were reacting to the elevation of the contemplative life in medieval scholasticism, which viewed contemplation as an activity bringing man closer to God. The schoolmen admired Thomas Aquinas's dictum: "Man's ultimate happiness consists in the contemplation of truth for this operation is specific to man and is shared with no other animal."[12]

This view was attacked repeatedly during the Renaissance, when many humanists valued action over contemplation. Petrarch's internal debate on this subject is well known; ultimately—and rather unwillingly—he conceded that the active life is better than the contemplative: "It is better to will the good than to know the truth."[13] Many humanists came to value ethics over natural philosophy, because they viewed the latter as arid and useless when it came to the problem of how one should live.

In contrast to the humanists, Gassendi wanted to endorse a life of both action and contemplation, dedicated to finding and living the best life possible and enriched by the study and exercise of natural philosophy. Gassendi repudiated the passivity associated with the contemplative life and the study of the sciences, without rejecting contemplation itself. He had learned from Francis Bacon that natural philosophy should be not only contemplative, but active, and the natural philosopher should seek to imitate the workings of nature.[14] Ethics had been characterized

---

[11] See Brian Vickers, "Rhetoric and Poetics," 731, and Victoria Kahn, *Rhetoric, Prudence, and Skepticism in the Renaissance* (Ithaca, 1985), 66. In the context of an analysis of Salutati's view of rhetoric and free will, Kahn writes, "It is because we have free will and are morally responsible that persuasion is necessary, and it is for this reason that it will be necessary to present different, and even contrasting, arguments to an audience. . . . So the belief that we do indeed have free will justifies a rhetoric of contradiction as that which allows us to respond appropriately to any given situation."

[12] *St. Thomas Aquinas on Politics and Ethics*, 8. In this statement Aquinas was only echoing Aristotle; see *Nicomachean Ethics*, trans. Martin Ostwald (Indianapolis, 1962), Bk. 10, chap. 7, 288–89.

[13] Francisco Petrarca, "On His Own Ignorance," trans. Hans Nachod, in *Renaissance Philosophy of Man*, 105. The debate about the relative value of the active and contemplative life is discussed by Eugene F. Rice, *The Renaissance Idea of Wisdom* (Cambridge, Mass., 1958), 30–57.

[14] Gassendi, "Logic," in *SP, Opera*, 1:61–62.

since the time of the Greeks as an active discipline; it became Gassendi's task to reconcile the seemingly contradictory aspects of ethics and physics, without making the two indistinguishable.

The *Syntagma Philosophicum* is divided into three sections. Although the pages concerned with natural philosophy far outnumber the others—93 for the "Logic," 201 for the "Ethics," and 1,285 for the "Physics"—Gassendi began his work with a long preface analyzing and justifying the traditional divisions of philosophy and the mutual interdependence of its parts.[15] In this preface, Gassendi emphasized the equal importance of ethics and physics in the philosophical corpus and their dependence on logic, propaedeutic to both, which gives the rules of correct reasoning.

Gassendi's initial analysis of the parts of philosophy falls into the venerable tradition of the classification of knowledge. Aristotle had distinguished four parts of philosophy: metaphysics, natural philosophy, mathematics, and ethics, where the first three are theoretical and the last practical and the study of logic is preliminary to each.[16] Philosophy had been divided into logic, physics, and ethics by the Hellenistic philosophers. To a large extent, these divisions were still reflected in the philosophy courses of the French universities where Gassendi had studied.[17] In his own philosophy, Gassendi merged metaphysics, natural philosophy, and mathematics under the heading of natural philosophy, and retained the distinction between the theoretical sciences and ethics. His division parallels the system of classification used by the Hellenistic philosophers, and especially by the Stoics.

Many early modern philosophers wrote compendia incorporating all the parts of philosophy. Charles B. Schmitt has pinpointed this practice in textbook writers of the time, but it seems equally applicable to more serious thinkers. Schmitt also mentions that the many contemporary discoveries in natural philosophy increased the size of the sections covering these areas, relative to those dealing with logic and ethics.[18] To some extent, this tradition may explain the disproportion in Gas-

---

[15] Gassendi, "Concerning Philosophy in General,"in *SP, Opera,* 1:1–30.
[16] Lisa Jardine, *Francis Bacon: Discovery and the Art of Discourse* (Cambridge, 1974), 96–108, discusses the traditional classification of knowledge and Bacon's changes to this schema.
[17] Brockliss, *French Higher Education,* 185–89.
[18] Charles B. Schmitt, "The Rise of the Philosophic Textbook," in *Cambridge History of Renaissance Philosophy,* 802. On the Renaissance divisions of philosophy, see also William A. Wallace, "Traditional Natural Philosophy," in *Cambridge History of Renaissance Philosophy,* 209–12, and Brockliss, *French Higher Education,* 187–203, who traces the permutations and ambiguities inherent in disciplinary classification schemes in early modern France.

sendi's work. But the more likely reason is that Gassendi was fascinated by problems in natural philosophy, which in his system led directly to an exposition of theology, with an emphasis on the relationship between God and his creation.[19] A natural philosopher himself, Gassendi wanted to emphasize the importance and relevance of his studies for a new philosophy of nature, but he also recognized that a new physics of matter in motion had broad implications for moral philosophy—and therefore necessitated a reformulation of ethical thought.

Thus, at the very beginning of his work, Gassendi stated, "there are two parts of philosophy, one is concerned with truth, and the other with what is right. One may call the first physics, or nature, when one scrutinizes the truth of all things; the other is ethics or morality, when one acts sufficiently to introduce upright morals into man. Moreover, consummate wisdom, or virtue, which is the highest perfection of the soul, flows from both."[20] In the first case, one follows the truth to achieve wisdom, and in the second one acts correctly to achieve virtue. The first is speculative, and the second active, but both are needed to produce a wise and virtuous human being.

The relationship of the various parts of philosophy was a particularly pressing problem for Gassendi—not only because of its traditional place in philosophic discussions, but also because of the character of the ancient philosophy he was defending. Epicurus had made physics subservient to ethics, practically stripping the study of the universe of any function but an ethical one: Gassendi remarked, "Epicurus made moral philosophy so great, that he thought physics ought to be cared for only so far as it is useful in removing certain kinds of agitations, and it therefore contributes to morality."[21]

Gassendi repeatedly cited Epicurus's teaching that physics was an adjunct of ethics because it contributed to the ultimate end of ethics: pleasure, or the tranquillity of the soul and the absence of pain in the body. In particular, physics contributes to tranquillity by liberating us from our irrational concerns, and by providing a natural explanation for things which terrify us: If we know the natural causes of all events in the world

---

[19] Gassendi's theological ideas are contained in the "Physics," in *SP, Opera*, 1:283–337. Gassendi's concept of God and nature has been analyzed in Margaret J. Osler, "Providence, Divine Will, and the Theological Background to Gassendi's Views on Scientific Knowledge," *Journal of the History of Ideas* 44 (1983): 549–560, and *Divine Will and the Mechanical Philosophy.*
[20] Gassendi, "Concerning Philosophy in General," in *SP, Opera*, 1:1.
[21] Gassendi, "Ethics," in *SP, Opera*, 2:660.

we will be freed from both the fear of death and the fear of the gods.[22] This knowledge makes us self-sufficient, which in turn makes us free.

Nevertheless, Gassendi noted—with some obvious agitation of his own spirit—that Epicurus had still been so interested in physics that he "obtained the cognomen 'physicist' (*physica*) among the Athenians." Gassendi editorialized that "although physics also contributes to the calming of the passions, still the contemplation of nature is philosophy's special gift, and because of this it may be esteemed a special part of philosophy."[23]

It was important to Gassendi to be able to classify and rank the categories of knowledge to which physics and ethics belonged as either arts or sciences. Aristotle had connected physics with theoretical knowledge and ethics with practical knowledge (*Topics*, 6, 6).[24] Renaissance humanists continued this tradition and considered physics a science and ethics an art. Whether a field was an art or a science meant a difference in its worthiness, and in the level of certitude it could promise.[25]

Many other thinkers in the sixteenth and seventeenth and later centuries also ranked categories of knowledge, perhaps because the growth of skepticism in the sixteenth century forced them to analyze whether any kind of knowledge could generate certainty. They responded to the ambiguities and assaults on tradition of the time with a compulsive need to classify.[26] Taxonomies of knowledge can be found from Bacon to Diderot and d'Alembert and even on to the Vienna Circle in the twentieth century.[27]

What is interesting about Gassendi's discussion is that he distinguished the categories of art/ethics and science/physics, only to reintegrate them as he examined their methodological and epistemological underpinnings. While trying to preserve the autonomy of physics, Gassendi recognized the inextricable links between physics and ethics. Toward the end of the introduction to the *Syntagma*, Gassendi stated,

[22] Gassendi, "Physics," in *SP, Opera*, 1:128.
[23] Gassendi, "Concerning Philosophy in General," in *SP, Opera*, 1:28.
[24] G. B. Kerferd, "Aristotle," in *Encyclopedia of Philosophy*, 1:154–55.
[25] A broad account of the classification of the arts and sciences from antiquity until the eighteenth century is given in Paul Oskar Kristeller, *Renaissance Thought and the Arts* (Princeton, 1990), 163–227.
[26] See Zachary Sayre Schiffmann, *On the Threshold of Modernity: Relativism in the French Renaissance* (Baltimore, 1991) for a very interesting study on the reaction to relativity and skepticism during the sixteenth and seventeenth centuries.
[27] Robert Darnton, "Philosophers Trim the Tree of Knowledge: The Epistemological Strategy of the *Encyclopédie*," in *The Great Cat Massacre and Other Episodes in French Cultural History* (New York, 1985), 191–214.

"Since these [logic, physics, ethics] have been considered the three parts of philosophy, the order in which they ought to be treated or taught remains to be discussed. Notwithstanding that they are connected by a certain kind of chain, so that they answer for each other's mutual works [*ut operas sibi praestant mutuas*], they should be examined separately."[28] There is an explicit tension in the relationship Gassendi posited between ethics and physics: they are symbiotic and characterized by a similar methodology, but also separate because their goals are different.

Thus, in the "Logic," the first section of the *Syntagma,* Gassendi adopted the traditional characterization of ethics as an art: an active skill or craft which teaches "knowledge about things that can be done or made." And because "anyone who is teaching a craft (or art) should give rules on making and finishing a work," the philosopher should describe the means for acquiring virtue and the good life. Physics, however, is a science, "which provides knowledge of speculative and contemplative subjects," and "anyone teaching a science should guide the mind by speculation to the knowledge of things." To accomplish this end the physicist must investigate his surroundings "until he has accounted for the entire body of the universe and made its workings clear."[29] Although Gassendi classifies physics as a science, he does not mean that it can provide complete knowledge or *scientia.* The knowledge we acquire by the investigation of the physical universe is problematical at best: a knowledge of appearances, not essences.

Gassendi first turned to methodology to explicate the relationship of physics and ethics.[30] Gassendi endowed both categories with a methodological homogeneity:

> To turn secondly to the sciences, whose instruction is in matters of observation and research, we find the same procedure applies (as in the arts). For although in matters of this kind our role is not a creative one, nevertheless, since we regard them as the work of a creator, either nature or nature's designer, we philosophize about them in the same way we do

[28] Gassendi, "Concerning Philosophy in General," in *SP, Opera,* 1:29.
[29] Gassendi, "Logic," in *SP, Opera,* 1:123. Brockliss (*French Higher Education,* 1) states, "In early-modern France (as in the rest of Europe) it was customary to separate knowledge into two distinctive categories: the arts and the sciences. The first offered an understanding of how a phenomenon might be applied; the second how it might be explained."
[30] The importance of methodology in the early modern period has been emphasized by many historians. See, for example, the ground-breaking study by Neal W. Gilbert, *Renaissance Concepts of Method* (Cambridge, 1960), and Cesare Vasoli, "The Renaissance concept of philosophy," in *Cambridge History of Renaissance Philosophy.*

about our own creations. Our way of proceeding in the sciences, then, is the same as in the arts.[31]

So Gassendi recommended that the prudent man use his reason, foresight, and experience in making a judgment. Thus he would have full cognizance of the past, present, and future implications of an action, and therefore increase his chances of making a decision which would lead to happiness.[32] This procedure is analogous to the process for investigating nature: According to Gassendi, the more one knows about what one is observing, the more likely one is to approach its true nature, without ever actually achieving this goal. In order to know the properties of natural objects, the natural philosopher is urged to investigate, "how much is by divine law or from what natural principles it is established; or whether or from what natural causes it has been produced, or whether or on account of what ends it has been made, and with what properties it has been bestowed."[33]

Gassendi recommended using the same method for physics and ethics. The distinction between contemplative science and active ethics almost disappears when he depicted the actual activity of the scientist. Gassendi adopted Cicero's metaphor. A physicist is like a hunter of nature, who just as a hunter

> does not pursue a wild animal sluggishly like an onlooker, but hunts with keen senses and tracks it down zealously. . . ; likewise a physicist obtains the idea of the nature of things, or truth, not by considering it superficially and lazily, but by investigating it with many different kinds of experiments and observations. . . . Even though its nature keeps slipping away in many ways, he perseveres and seeks it in his search.[34]

Gassendi characterized this kind of science as "active physics," *physica actuosa*, and he emphasized the idea of experimentation in his descriptions of both physics and the physicist. He was, no doubt, influenced by Bacon in his choice of words and in his theory of experimentation. In

[31] Jones, *Institutio Logica*, 162–63.
[32] Gassendi, "Ethics," in *SP, Opera*, 2:745–46.
[33] Gassendi, "Physics," in *SP, Opera*, 1:126.
[34] Ibid. Paoli Rossi has pointed out this factor of Gassendi's thought and its relationship to the establishment of empirical science in the seventeenth century. He and others have commented on its similarity to Vico's principle of "verum-factum." Paoli Rossi, "Hermeticism, Rationality and the Scientific Revolution," in *Reason, Experiment, and Mysticism in the Scientific Revolution*, ed. M. L. Righini Bonelli and William R. Shea (New York, 1975), 252–54.

his discussion of Bacon in the "Logic," Gassendi noted Bacon's use of the term *scientia activa* and described Bacon's theory of experimentation, which is very close to Gassendi's own. They differ, however, because Bacon believed certain truths could be established through experimentation and reason, while Gassendi felt only probabilities could be ascertained.[35] Thus, for Gassendi, the contemplative science of physics is transformed into the active, empirical investigation of nature, and the theoretical physicist into the active investigator of the universe.

Likewise, ethics is an active rather than a contemplative pursuit. At the beginning of the "Ethics" Gassendi wrote, "the moral part of philosophy is not purely speculative, as if it were placed in the naked contemplation of morals; but it is in truth active, or it consists in this, that it forms morals, imbues righteousness and rules, and it is consequently a science, or if you prefer, an art of acting well and from virtue."[36]

The integration of the two previously distinct categories of art and science in relation to ethics is analogous to Gassendi's redefinition of physics as an active science. Both disciplines share similar characteristics and in some ways become indistinguishable. In part, this fusion may also reflect the ambivalent status of ethics in the traditional philosophy curriculum of the seventeenth century, where ethics was sometimes characterized as a science, because the knowledge of good and bad and the rules of right behavior were grounded on the law of nature and, as such, were considered self-evident.[37] Gassendi was obviously more attuned to the classical and humanist tradition which held that ethics was an art which taught the rules of living. His further mingling of the categories of art and science is directly related to the fact that he thought that ethics and natural philosophy have the same epistemological status.

Gassendi's epistemology is empiricist and rests ultimately on a doctrine of signs. Sense presents us with a perceptible sign, which when carefully examined by reason—both initially and after a conclusion is reached—results in knowledge possessing a high degree of probability.[38] But since reason, or the faculty of judgment, is always fallible, this knowledge cannot rise from conjecture to certitude. This epistemology is crucial for understanding Gassendi's theory of human freedom, which is examined in the next chapter.

Gassendi was also responding to the skeptical crisis of the sixteenth

[35] Gassendi, "Logic," in *SP, Opera*, 1:63–64.
[36] Gassendi, "Ethics," in *SP, Opera*, 2:659.
[37] Brockliss, *French Higher Education*, 225.
[38] Jones, in his introduction to *Institutio Logica*, xlv–xlvii, has a good analysis of Gassendi's theory of indicative signs. See also, Popkin, *History of Scepticism*, 145–46.

and early seventeenth centuries. About 1576, the humanist Henri Estienne had published a Latin edition of the work of Sextus Empiricus, the second-century follower of the radical skeptic Pyrrho of Elis.[39] Pyrrhonian skepticism proclaimed, and Gassendi in his youth had once believed, that nothing could be known, because all knowledge is based on our highly fallible senses. Under the influence of Sextus Empiricus, Gassendi declared in his first work, the *Exercitationes paradoxicae adversus Aristoteleos,* "Quod nulla sit scientia, et maxime Aristoelea," that is, "There is no knowledge, and especially Aristotelian knowledge."[40]

As he matured, Gassendi developed ideas first articulated in the *Exercitationes.* Gassendi retained the epistemology of skepticism, but resolved the challenge which arose from its negative conclusions about any possibility of knowledge. Richard Popkin has called this view "mitigated skepticism": it holds that while we cannot have absolute knowledge of the essences of things in nature in the Aristotelian sense, we can know, as Popkin interprets it, "convincing or probable truths about appearances."[41]

As Gassendi asserted, "it is permitted to survey the external faces of things and to unravel something about the works of nature . . . still we cannot penetrate into these things. . . . Clearly, I do not say this so that we may be deterred from the investigation and contemplation of these kinds of things, since however small what we perceive may be, it is therefore more precious than gold."[42] The study of nature becomes an activity where we can achieve some degree of knowledge, but we can never penetrate into its secrets which only God knows.

Like physics, the science or art of ethics rests on an empiricist epistemology. To Gassendi, every individual seeks pleasure and avoids pain—and the calculation of what will increase pleasure and decrease pain lies in the mental faculty of judgment or reason, which is also responsible for ascertaining the probable truth about the natural world. "The faculty of judging is reason itself and is called judgment," explained Gas-

[39] See Popkin, *History of Scepticism,* 17–43, on the impact of Pyrrhonian skepticism.

[40] Gassendi, *Exercitationes, Opera,* 3:192.

[41] The question of Gassendi's skepticism is complicated and has been addressed extensively in the scholarly literature. See especially, Tullio Gregory, *Scetticismo ed empirismo. Studio su Gassendi* (Bari, 1961); Popkin, *History of Scepticism,* 143–49; Bloch, *La Philosophie de Gassendi,* 75–109; Jones, *Institutio Logica,* x–xii, xlv–xlvii; Ralph Walker, "Gassendi and Skepticism," in *Skeptical Tradition,* 319–34; Egan, *Gassendi's View of Knowledge,* 108–10.

[42] Gassendi, "Physics," in *SP, Opera,* 1:132. William A. Wallace, "Traditional natural philosophy," 202, points out that during the middle ages, natural philosophy based on the senses was credited with a lesser degree of certainty than the certain proofs of mathematics and metaphysics.

sendi. "Reason, which is the same thing as intellect and mind, is directed not only toward speculations, but also toward actions."[43] Thus, judgment leads to conclusions in matters of speculation and to ethical choice in matters of action.

Judgment in both ethics and physics depends on sense perceptions, corrected by judgment, but in both cases the resulting action or knowledge is less than perfect. Particularly in ethical judgments, because of the "imbecility of our minds" and our human frailties, we often mistake the apparent good for the real good and make poor choices. Gassendi believed that ethics is especially vulnerable to such miscalculation, because as Aristotle pointed out, in ethics "the object is contingent matters," which may be realized or not.[44]

However, just as Gassendi thought that in physics, man could at least discover the truth of appearances, so he believed that ethics could provide sufficient knowledge for a person to be able to plan and manage his life on a day-to-day basis. Gassendi wrote, "in the arts, prudence, industry, and labor play such a part, so that the proposed and desired event usually follows, and when it happens, the cause is not hidden."[45] In other words, in art, the artist *usually* controls and understands his artifact, because he made it himself. In ethics, the artifact the individual makes is the good and happy life. This situation differs from that of physics because the physicist does not make the universe, which is an artifact only from the point of view of the divine artisan, God, the only one who can truly understand and control it.[46]

This realization teaches philosophers humility and awe when they recognize that "all their perspicacity and sagacity lacks that of the divine and inimitable artisan of nature by an insurmountable interval."[47] Here one is reminded of the "learned ignorance" of Nicholas of Cusa, who taught that learning served to show us the abyss between God and man, which could only be overcome by a leap of faith.[48]

Nevertheless, Gassendi contended—once again conflating his ideas about science and art—that we still may be inspired by nature to try to

[43] Gassendi, "Ethics," in *SP, Opera*, 2:831.
[44] Ibid., 2:743. Gassendi's ethical probabilism differs from casuistry, the Jesuits' discipline of ethical probabilism, where any action could be morally defended if only one example of its moral acceptability was found. Gassendi was constructing not an ethics vindicating moral ambiguity, but one which recognized the role of reason and calculation in seeking the good and virtuous life. On casuistry, see Brockliss, *French Higher Education*, 226.
[45] Gassendi, "Physics," in *SP, Opera*, 1:731.
[46] Ibid., 1:731; 1:132.
[47] Ibid., 1:132.
[48] Cassirer, *Individual and Cosmos in Renaissance Philosophy*, 7–45.

imitate its workings and decipher its causes, as we do with a watch or a bridge "which we do not make, nor do we affect to make; but we wish to know of what and how they were constructed." Thus, in the search for probable knowledge of the universe, the scientist becomes like an artist, who uses instruments and constructs models.[49]

In fact, Gassendi's notion of both the artist and the scientist comes close to the Renaissance ideal of the virtuoso who could construct both himself and his environment. In that ideal, the wise man is an active agent seeking to understand, master, and control his moral and physical universe.[50] The humanists located this power in human rationality and the ability of the will to make a choice. While Gassendi acknowledged the role of reason, he also emphasized the role of the senses, which made choice more problematical—but also more free.

Probabilism

Gassendi's epistemological ideas not only resulted in a redefinition of moral and natural philosophy, they also necessitated a reevaluation of the process of reasoning itself. While accepting some aspects of Aristotelian logic, Gassendi rejected its ultimate claim: that a demonstrative knowledge of essences or *scientia* could be attained. Instead, like many of his contemporaries, Gassendi was attracted to new forms of argumentation, which led to probable rather than certain knowledge. In his moral philosophy, this kind of thought-process was integral to moral decisions, not just as a process, but also as a kind of moral act itself. In natural philosophy, such reasoning allowed Gassendi to argue for a mechanistic cosmology as a very probable—if not completely certain—explanation of natural phenomena.

Barbara Shapiro has argued that the terms "certainty" and "probability" were experiencing a metamorphosis of meaning by the seventeenth century, with the distinction between them becoming blurred. All knowledge was judged according to a continuum from " 'mere probability,' through 'high probability,' to 'moral certainty.' " Gassendi's use of

---

[49] Gassendi, "Physics," in *SP, Opera,* 1:126.
[50] Alistair C. Crombie, "Science and the Arts in the Renaissance: The Search for Truth and Certainty, Old and New," in *Science and the Arts in the Renaissance,* ed. John W. Shirley and F. David Hoeniger (London, 1985), 15, comments, "The concept of the virtuoso, the rational artist aiming at reasoned and examined control alike of his own thoughts and intentions and actions and his surroundings, seems to me the essence of European morality, meaning both habits and ethics, out of which the European scientific movement was generated and engineered."

probabilistic reasoning contributed, later in the century, to the empirical and probabilistic program of the Royal Society.[51]

Gassendi's logic and his epistemology were heavily influenced by two important, closely related trends in early modern thought: the revival of rhetoric and the rediscovery of Academic skepticism. Since antiquity, rhetoric had been associated with *opinio*—probable knowledge based on persuasive argument and the method of argumentation *ad utramque partem*, arguing both sides of a question to the most probable conclusion. This methodology was associated with humanist redefinitions of the proper way to produce effective arguments—a new form of logic identified with the term dialectic.

The fusion of dialectic and rhetoric, which began during the Italian Quattrocenco and culminated in the work of Lorenzo Valla, Rudolf Agricola, and Peter Ramus, taught that knowledge was acquired by rational argument. Dialecticians of the new school dismissed the commitment to formal validity of Aristotelian logic and its use of "fixed patterns of argumentation which guarantee that from any true premise whatsoever one can only infer a true conclusion."[52] While the new dialectic shared the traditional aim of logic—the art of reasoning well—dialectical logic aimed only at providing good arguments whose validity was problematic. The aim of dialectic was to prove, but not demonstratively.

Thus, Ramus argued for a unified art of discourse, which embraced different kinds of arguments, and which could employ the same kinds of techniques.[53] Ramus associated this form of discourse with rhetoric. The five parts of rhetoric are *inventio*, finding or discovering persuasive arguments, *dispositio*, the structure of the speech or writing, *elocutio*, the oratorial devices used to bring pleasure to an audience, *memoria*, the skill of speaking from memory, and *pronunciaio*, the gestures and style to be used during delivery. Ramus preempted "*inventio*," and "*dispositio*," for his new dialectical logic and associated them with dialectic, a general way of discoursing which reflected nature.[54] Ramist dialectic, therefore, separated the content-oriented and the stylistic aspects of rhetoric.

Such dialectical forms of argumentation lacked the demonstrative rigor of Aristotelian syllogistic logic, but could persuade the listener or

---

[51] Shapiro, *Probability and Certainty*, 16–17; 38–39.
[52] Lisa Jardine, "Humanistic Logic," in *Cambridge History of Renaissance Philosophy*, 175.
[53] Jardine, *Francis Bacon*, 26.
[54] Brockliss, *French Higher Education*, 128–29; Jardine, "Humanistic Logic," 184–86.

reader to adopt a course of moral action or to accept a provisional statement about the natural world. Consequently, rhetorically informed dialectical reasoning gave a wide field to human freedom, because it always
presented alternatives and the possibility of free choice.[55] It did not compel, it persuaded.

Rhetoric itself was influenced by the revival of Academic skepticism
in the late Renaissance. Academic skepticism, most fully developed in
the second-century B.C. by the philosopher Carneades, taught that it was
impossible to know anything—a form of dogmatism criticized by the
Pyrrhonists, who felt one could not even know that one knew nothing—
but that one could reach probable conclusions though *ad utramque partem* argumentation. Reasoned debate on both sides of an issue, taught
Carneades, could allow judgments about probable truth rather than the
suspension of judgment altogether. The philosophy of Academic skepticism was adopted by Cicero and subsequently influenced the Renaissance; a humanist such as Lorenzo Valla could feel that "Orator and
Academic share a common purpose and pursue the most probable point
of view using an identical method."[56] The Ciceronian method of arguing pro and con became assimilated into basic humanist pedagogical
techniques; most students of rhetoric who studied and used this tech-
nique were probably unaware that it shared a common methodology
with Academic skepticism.[57]

Peter Dear has shown how Marin Mersenne, Gassendi's friend and
fellow "mitigated skeptic," was influenced by the union of rhetoric, dialectic, and Academic skepticism, and by changing views of probability
and certainty.[58] While Gassendi had been originally influenced by
Pyrrhonism skepticism in developing his epistemological ideas, he was
also influenced by academic forms of skepticism. He often used the *ad
utramque partem* method of reasoning in the *Syntagma Philosophicum* in
order to arrive at probable conclusions.[59] As early as the *Exercitationes*
(1624), Gassendi charged,

---

[55] Vickers, "Rhetoric and Poetics," 731; and Kahn, *Rhetoric, Prudence, and Skepticism*, 66.
[56] Jardine, "Lorenzo Valla," 262.
[57] I wish to thank Barbara Shapiro for pointing this out to me and also for her other
comments on this chapter.
[58] Dear, *Mersenne*, 12–35. Dear connects Mersenne's mitigated skepticism to his education
by the Jesuits. The Jesuits use of *ad utramque partem* arguments in casuistry has led some
authors to identify this form of moral theology with the increase of probabilistic arguments in areas outside of morality. See Brockliss, *French Higher Education*, 258–60.
[59] Popkin, *History of Scepticism*, 142–46. See also Ian Hacking, *Emergence of Probability*, 45–
47.

[The Aristotelians] think they are committing a sacrilege if they defend an opinion opposed to his or set forth both sides of a question fairly. But as Cicero testifies in his *Orator*, 'Aristotle trained his young students in their school exercises not to discuss subtly in the manner of philosophers, but with the richness of the rhetoricians, both for and against, so that they could speak more elegantly and more richly.'[60]

Taken together, both the new dialectical rhetoric and Academic skepticism validated Gassendi's philosophic probabilism as it pertained to the logical process. Nevertheless, Gassendi did not entirely repudiate the goal of demonstrative knowledge; he thought that true statements could be discovered through syllogistic reasoning, especially in logic itself and mathematics, although even in these cases, no essential knowledge would be revealed.[61]

Thus, in the "Logic," he identified the first of a number of syllogisms as those "whose premises are necessary or clearly true," and which is therefore called an "apodeictic, demonstrative, or scientific syllogism . . . on account of the import of the conclusion, which it demonstrates to be true in such a way that it deserves the title knowledge (that is *scientia*)."[62] In this definition, knowledge, or *scientia*, is a characteristic of the conclusions drawn in the mind, and not a reflection of essential truths outside of the mind. Neither the art of ethics nor the science of physics allows for this degree of certitude, because of their extramental status.[63]

Even within the domain of logic itself, Gassendi highlighted a form of reasoning that was more congenial to his skeptical outlook than demonstrative logic. Also coming from Aristotle, this form was defined as a "suasory, probable, or conjectural syllogism," so called because "of the import of the conclusion which persuades and proves in such a fashion that although it leans more toward clearness than obscurity it still leaves a degree of doubt and for this reason merits the title 'opinion'." This kind of syllogism lacks the necessity of a demonstrative syllogism because there is no necessary agreement between subject or middle term or between the middle term and the predicate, nor is there necessary dis-

---

[60] Gassendi, "Preface to the *Exercises against the Aristotelians*," in *Selected Works*, 20.
[61] Walker, "Gassendi and Skepticism," 331, argues that Gassendi denied the demonstrability of even logic and mathematics because of the pervasiveness of his radical empiricism.
[62] Jones, *Institutio Logica*, 144–45.
[63] This attitude is not unusual. Lisa Jardine shows that Valla and Agricola also denied that ethics and natural philosophy could be known demonstrably (Jardine, "Lorenzo Valla," 259).

agreement. Such problematic syllogisms were often associated with rhetoric, as Gassendi mentioned, "on the grounds that it persuades, which is the business of the orator; but as for assent, it does not compel or demand it, which is the business of the demonstrator." The force of such a syllogism comes from the authority of those who support it, and such authority does not compel. That can be done only by divine authority, because God is "absolutely truthful."[64]

Gassendi offers many examples of suasory syllogisms, taken from law, medicine, the arts of poetry and painting, and natural philosophy. One example, concerning the movement of the earth, shows the approach. Gassendi stated that while a probable syllogism could argue that the earth is at rest, based on the authority of "learned men, and these of the highest reputation," it nevertheless "can be accepted only with some caution" because famous men in the past and in the present believe the earth "moves, either in its own orbit so as to produce day and night, or around a centre so as to create a year."[65] At the bottom of Gassendi's probabilistic reasoning is the sense that all statements about the world are based on some form of human authority, which—unlike the divine—is based only on fallible sense impressions. Gassendi of course was not unique in his understanding of the Aristotelian suasory or contingent syllogism, with which all logicians and rhetoricians were familiar. What is unusual is the extent that probabilistic reasoning, whether syllogistic or purely rhetorical, underlies his natural philosophy and ethics.

Another example of a suasory syllogism concerns rhetoric itself:

> It will be persuasively argued that rhetoric is useful to life from its genus: "Rhetoric is an art; but every art is useful to life; therefore rhetoric is useful to life." In this syllogism the middle term is the genus of the subject—art the genus of rhetoric— but "to be useful" is the predicate; it is not the genus of art nor a property pertaining to every kind of art, nor anything attaching to art necessarily; it is rather a contingent adjunct or common quality.[66]

Consequently, one assents to this conclusion with hesitation because rhetoric may be helpful or harmful or merely neutral.

This argument is interesting not only for the way it demonstrates the suasory syllogism, but also for what it says about Gassendi's view of rhe-

---

[64] Jones, *Institutio Logica*, 148–49.
[65] Ibid., 151–52.
[66] Ibid., 150.

toric. While he admitted a rhetorical syllogism, and the probabilistic reasoning it entailed, the art of rhetoric is a different matter entirely. Gassendi, like many before him, recognized that while rhetoric could be beneficial, it could also be used for morally ambiguous purposes. This is particularly so once the stylistic parts of rhetoric were divorced from its other aspects which were preempted into the new dialectic. Thus, although rhetorical methodology was basic to his philosophy, Gassendi did not openly admit to being a rhetorician, whose art is morally ambiguous.

On the other hand, Gassendi knew that ethics and some forms of rhetoric had been tightly linked since antiquity, and in a manner that emphasized their closeness rather than their divergence. Aristotle had taught that the rhetorician must know what will bring his listeners goodness or happiness, and urge a course of action leading to good and virtuous living. Likewise, Cicero linked epideictic rhetoric, the speech of praise or blame, with ethics.[67]

During the Renaissance, rhetoric became the most important part of the humanist educational program, because of its emphasis on human communication and the centrality of man and its immediate relevance to the *vita activa*.[68] The close connection between rhetoric and ethics continued into early modern times, particularly when ethics was equated with prudence, or ethical action.[69]

Thus, when Gassendi used rhetorical forms of argumentation in the "Ethics," his approach was validated by a long tradition in moral philosophy. Nevertheless, the persistent attempt by some to equate rhetoric with sophistry made its utilization somewhat suspect.

Thus, Gassendi was repeatedly attacked for being a rhetorician. The astrologer Jean-Baptiste Morin called him one because he did not use the style of the schools. Gassendi excused Morin's accusation on the grounds that the astrologer "was ignorant of the matter and unaware how the different liberal arts differ or connect with each other; while he divorces wisdom and eloquence, they are very much joined together."[70]

Likewise, in his "Reply" to Gassendi's "Objection" to his *Meditations*,

---

[67] Brian Vickers, *In Defence of Rhetoric* (Oxford, 1988), 22–23; 54–58.
[68] Cesare Vasoli, "The Renaissance Concept of Philosophy," 62.
[69] Kahn, *Rhetoric, Prudence, and Skepticism*, 9–11.
[70] Pierre Gassendi, "De motu impresso. Epistola III," in *Opera* 3:526. Samuel Sorbière states that Gassendi taught rhetoric when he was a young man in Digne (Sorbière, "in his introduction to the *Opera*," 1:ii–iii unnumbered in text). Jean-Baptiste Morin makes the charge that Gassendi was a rhetorician repeatedly. See, for example, Morin, *Astrologia Gallica principiis et rationibus propis stabilita, atque in XXVI Libros distributa* (The Hague, 1661), ix.

Descartes charged Gassendi with using "various debating skills," "rhetorical display," and "rhetorical tricks," in short of being a rhetorician
rather than a philosopher.[71] Anyone reading Gassendi will sympathize
with Descartes.

In addition to using *ad utramque partem* argumentation, Gassendi used
implicit and explicit dialogues to argue his points, and he embellished
his arguments with copious quotations used for his own purposes. The
result can lead the reader to despair, requiring a determined effort to
keep in mind Gassendi's ultimate purpose: the effort to find the most
probable truth about moral and natural philosophy possible for fallible
human beings. In presenting his argument and material in such a manner, Gassendi gave the reader the freedom to choose the likeliest conclusion, although his own preference for Epicurean solutions is always
clear.[72]

A few of many examples display the approach. In the first part of the
"Ethics," Gassendi considered both historiographical and substantive
questions concerning Epicurus and his view of pleasure. He presented
every possible piece of evidence from antiquity concerning Epicurus's
notion of pleasure and whether it was obscene or virtuous. Example
follows example, and quotation follows quotation, both for and against
Epicurus, but with the ultimate aim of persuading the reader of a positive view of Epicurus and Epicurean hedonism.[73]

Later, in his discussion of the characteristics of pleasure itself, Gassendi considered whether pleasure and virtue are connected. He gave
both sides, but concluded that Epicurus seems to be right in arguing
they are indistinguishable.[74] Likewise, when examining whether piety is
pursued because of pure, altruistic love or rather because it can bring
considerable long-term benefits, Gassendi concluded, "it seems to be
established, and may not be disproved, if someone hopes for these eternal, future delights, he will love, worship, and delight in God."[75] In

---

[71] René Descartes, "Author's Replies to the Fifth Set of Objections," *The Philosophical Writings of Descartes*, 3 vols., trans. John Cottingham, Robert Stoothoff, and Dugald Murdoch (Cambridge, 1984), 2:241–43.

[72] Gassendi expressly links the liberty to philosophize to the ability to judge the probability of different philosophies. See "Concerning Philosophy in General," in *SP, Opera*, 1:30. My discussion in this paragraph owes much to the interpretation of the relationship of ethics and rhetoric in Kahn, *Rhetoric, Prudence, and Skepticism*, 1–78. On the liberty of philosophizing, also see Sylvia Murr, "Foi religieuse et *libertas philosophandi* chez Gassendi," *Revue des sciences philosophique et théologique* 76 (1992): 85–100.

[73] Gassendi, "Ethics," in *SP, Opera*, 2:678–92.

[74] Ibid., 2:702–3.

[75] Ibid., 2:710.

much of his ethical writings, Gassendi seems to shy away from the declarative mode; the word *"videtur,"* "it seems," pockmarks his work and turns it from a dogmatic system into an exercise in probability.

In ethics, especially, probabilism becomes not only a premise of Gassendi's discursive style, but also a necessary adjunct to his cardinal ethical principle. The calculation of pleasure and pain, when a rational individual weighs the pros and cons of an action in order to determine what will bring the greatest amount of pleasure in the long run, is *ad utramque partem* reasoning in its most moral and prudential manifestation.

For Gassendi, the key to leading an ethical or tranquil life becomes the active pursuit of probable knowledge of natural philosophy. Gassendi approvingly quotes Seneca's dictum, "the life of pleasure, contemplation, and action are indivisible."[76] A tranquil man and a man of science are one and the same: the true philosopher. This union of the contemplative and active life in the wise man is by no means original to Gassendi, but he does give this Renaissance commonplace a different meaning when he merges contemplation and the empirical investigation of nature.[77] At the beginning of the *Syntagma*, Gassendi stated this very clearly:

> A philosopher does not seek profit or glory, but his zeal is only in finding and esteeming the truth . . . and he argues from no authority, by no enigmas, by no ironies, but by naked reason, by simple, open, and indubitable experiments, which are repeated many times. He is never exhausted in meditating, in searching, and in exploring. He is not obstinate, and if he is forced to change his opinions, he does so in good faith and quickly to avoid the less probable opinion and admit the more probable. . . . He has a sincere love of honesty . . . and he is tranquil and circumspect, and thus loving calm, he is innocent, and as much as he can he does good to everyone and injures no one.[78]

The characteristics of the philosopher according to Gassendi encapsulate the argument of this chapter. A philosopher is an empirical investigator of truth, constantly seeking for the most probable explanation of things without ever becoming dogmatic. He is honest and tranquil and a friend to all. An empirical natural philosophy, conjoined with a probabilistic form of reasoning, results in a humane and benevolent person.

[76] Ibid., 2:716.
[77] Rice, *Renaissance Idea of Wisdom*, 47–49, 55–57.
[78] Gassendi, "Concerning Philosophy in General," in *SP, Opera*, 1:10.

Not surprisingly, Gassendi contended that it is the contemplation of the universe itself which brings the greatest amount of happiness: "We will speak of this delight not only in the 'Physics,' but also in the 'Ethics,' when we reach the discussion of pleasure, which is furnished from the knowledge and contemplation of things, and makes the greatest part of happiness."[79]

The reason for this connection between ethics and physics goes back to the very subject of the philosophical discipline itself. Ethics studies humanity, while physics studies the nature of the universe. It is the special gift of God's providence that human beings possess free choice, while the universe, completely contingent on God's will, is governed by law. Humans must be free, while the universe is determined by God's providential plan.

Ethics and physics are inextricably linked in the thought of Gassendi, tied together by his methodological and epistemological premises; no section of his philosophical magnum opus is complete, or indeed completely understandable, without the others. Yet, Gassendi did not follow Epicurus in simply making physics an appendage of ethics; nor did he follow what may be his own basic inclination, and make ethics subsidiary to physics. Although the way we investigate nature and the way we make moral decisions are essentially the same—and even though the knowledge we achieve in both physics and ethics, founded in observation and mediated by reason, is probable rather than certain—the different categories of philosophy must be examined separately. The study of ethics and the study of physics must be complementary, but also autonomous.

Thus, before the mediating link between ethics and physics can be found, it is necessary to understand Gassendi's ethical system, and to see how it relates to his natural philosophy. Gassendi perceived the dangers to the possibility of human freedom implicit in the new mechanistic universe. One of the aims of his ethical philosophy was to establish a privileged place for human liberty in a universe which operated mechanistically, according to God's plan. Paradoxically, Gassendi's concept of freedom grew out of an analogical understanding of the new mechanistic principles of motion. Gassendi's new ethics reflected the new physics of the seventeenth century.

[79] Ibid., 1:5.

CHAPTER THREE

The Ethics of
Pleasure and Freedom

The Epicurean Background

In the preface to the *Exercitationes paradoxicae adversus Aristoteleos* (1624), Gassendi outlined the contents of eight proposed books criticizing Aristotle. He would complete only the first two, but the outline shows his early interest in Epicureanism, particularly in the ancient philosopher's ethical teachings. Gassendi wrote, "Finally, Book VII deals with moral philosophy. . . . It hardly requires a lengthy capitulation. In one word, it teaches Epicurus's doctrine of pleasure by showing in what way the greatest good consists of pleasure and how the reward of human deed and virtues is based upon this principle."[1]

Several persistent themes, adopted and adapted from Epicurus, animated Gassendi's ethical writings. He accepted the claim of the ancient hedonist that pleasure is the highest good. He also agreed with Epicurus that virtue is a necessary adjunct to pleasure and that, consequently, the pleasurable life is ascetic rather than profligate. Finally, for both Epicurus and Gassendi, pleasure motivates choices made in life, whether one seeks immediate pleasure or the best possible pleasure, a state of tranquillity.[2]

Ultimately, Gassendi identified four different kinds of pleasure, at

---

[1] Pierre Gassendi, *Exercitationes, Opera*, 3:102; "Exercises against the Aristotelians," in *Selected Works*, 72. When *Selected Works* is cited, the translation is taken from it.
[2] Epicurus's various statements concerning pleasure can be found in Epicurus, *Extant Remains*, 327–74, and A. A. Long and D. N. Sedley, *The Hellenistic Philosophers*, 2 vols. (Cambridge, 1987), 1:112–24.

least implicitly, in his moral philosophy: there is the instinctive desire for pleasure that characterizes even irrational creatures, and then there is the calculated search for ever more physical pleasure, which is the motivating force of rational but unenlightened individuals. Wise human beings reach a third level of pleasure when they understand that true pleasure is tranquillity or lack of pain, and make decisions to achieve this aim. Finally, the last level of pleasure, and one not to be achieved while we live, is the unutterably sublime pleasure of the beatific vision of God.[3]

Like Epicurus, Gassendi linked pleasure directly with freedom. Epicurus taught that the human mind possessed the rationality and flexibility that enable it to calculate what would bring the greatest pleasure over time. This ability of the mind frees the individual from the necessity of unthinkingly pursuing the nearest pleasure unremittingly, and makes choice and avoidance a self-directed—and therefore free—decision.[4]

Gassendi retained the free rationality of Epicurus, where choice results in what Gassendi named *libertas,* or true freedom for the individual. He contrasted it with willingness or spontaneity—*libentia*—which makes an individual voluntarily but unavoidably pursue a good out of a necessity of his own nature or will. Gassendi located *libertas* in the intellect, which is indifferent before a decision is made, and can weigh and judge alternatives.[5]

In addition, Gassendi, the early modern priest and philosopher, welded Epicurean concepts of pleasure and freedom to God's providential design, and to his own probabilistic epistemology. Human fallibility, or the human incapacity to know the essential truth of things, will become a crucial element in God's creation of free human beings.[6] Gassendi formulated an ethical system that preserved Epicurean ethical ideals, but reinterpreted them in Christian terms—not just nominally, but in a complex and subtle structure. Just as Marsilio Ficino had joined Platonic love and Christian charity in the fifteenth century, and the neo-Stoics

---

[3] Gassendi's doctrine of pleasure is located in Part One of the "Ethics," which is entitled "De Felicitate," in *SP, Opera,* 2:659–735.
[4] On rationality and flexibility in the Epicurean account of freedom, see Mitsis, *Epicurus' Ethical Theory,* 119–37. Much of my account of Epicurean ethics follows Mitsis in his recent work on the subject. While some of Mitsis's arguments are controversial, his interpretation makes sense in terms of the Epicurean texts we retain. Moreover, Gassendi's own interpretation of Epicurean ethics comes close to Mitsis's reading. On the reaction to Mitsis, see Gisela Striker, "Commentary on Mitsis," in *Proceedings of the Boston Area Colloquium in Ancient Philosophy,* ed. J. J. Cleary, vol. 4 (New York, 1988), 315–20.
[5] Gassendi, "Ethics," in *SP, Opera,* 2:822–24.
[6] Ibid., 2:823–24.

attempted to equate Stoic and Christian virtue in the sixteenth century, Gassendi thought Epicurean pleasure could be reformulated as a Christian concept.[7]

In addition, the mechanical philosophy's understanding of nature opened a new level of discourse to Gassendi, the natural and moral philosopher. Gassendi used analogies drawn from the new science of motion to explain human choice and action, and to coordinate divine providence with natural and human action. The concept of inertial motion provided a link between the behavior of matter and human action—a way of construing a determined world inhabited by free creatures.[8] Humanist, philosopher, natural philosopher, and priest—Gassendi's diverse roles could be reconciled in the moral and physical universe he constructed.

Given the deep roots of Gassendi's thought, it is impossible to understand him without beginning with Epicurus.[9] Epicureanism is a philosophy of the individual, concerned with procuring individual happiness and tranquillity. As Cicero noted in *De Finibus*, the Epicureans believed that pleasure is the *telos*, or the end of life.[10] They further based their emphasis on pleasure on the observation of the newborn child, who instinctively seeks pleasure and shirks pain.[11]

But pleasure, according to Epicurus, is often misunderstood: "When, therefore, we maintain that pleasure is the end, we do not mean the pleasures of profligates and those that consist in sensuality . . . but freedom from pain in the body (*aponia*) and from trouble in the mind (*ataraxia*)."[12]

The highest pleasure, what Epicurus calls the pleasure of rest—or katastematic pleasure—is the passive pleasure associated with the absence of anxiety and physical pain, equivalent to tranquillity (*ataraxia*) in the soul. It is a continuous and indefinite state of being—in short, the state

---

[7] On Renaissance neo-Platonism, see Copenhaver and Schmitt, *Renaissance Philosophy*, 127–42. On neo-Stoicism, see Jill Kraye, "Moral philosophy," 370–74.

[8] Gassendi's doctrine of inertia can be found in the first letter of *De motu impresso a motore translato*, *Opera*, 3:478–499. This work consists of three letters and was written between 1640 and 1643. The first letter was originally published in 1642.

[9] For an account of Epicurus's ethical doctrines, see Cyril Bailey, *The Greek Atomists and Epicurus* (Oxford, 1926); Frederick Vaughan, *The Tradition of Political Hedonism from Hobbes to J. S. Mill* (New York, 1982); Robert M. Strozier, *Epicurus and Hellenistic Philosophy* (Lanham, Md., 1985); and Mitsis, *Epicurus' Ethical Theory*.

[10] Cicero, *On Ends* [*De finibus*], in *The Hellenistic Philosophers*, 1:112.

[11] Plutarch, *Plutarch's Moralia*, trans. B. Einarson and P. H. De Lacy, vol. 14 (Cambridge, Mass., 1967), 283.

[12] Epicurus, *Extant Remains*, 87.

of being satisfied.[13] But it is linked with the pleasures of motion, or kinetic pleasures, that fulfill physical needs—sometimes elaborately—and cease once the need is filled.[14]

Epicurus, in making pleasure the universal *telos*, had to make it accessible to every individual.[15] To that end, he stripped pleasure of any content which would make it difficult to achieve: "We must consider that of desires some are natural, others vain, and of the natural some are necessary and others merely natural; and of the necessary some are necessary for happiness, others for the repose of the body, and others for very life." The only real necessities in life are those which release us from pain, such as food and shelter.[16] Other natural desires that are not for necessities might be a desire for a luxurious diet or the gratification of sexual desires. Vain desires include the desires for wealth and power.

Epicurus ranked desires on a scale of self-sufficiency. Those things most easily obtainable leave the individual most self-sufficient, independent, and free. "Again, we regard independence of outward things as a great good. . . ," he explained, "they have the sweetest enjoyment of luxury who stand in least need of it."[17] The outward things that Epicurus rejected included marriage, children, any sort of political involvement—in short, everything associated with society rather than the individual—with the notable exception of friendship.

For Epicurus, "The greatest fruit of self-sufficiency is freedom."[18] Freedom from all external ties allows a man to pursue the highest aim in life, his own pleasure, without the need to care or worry about any being other than himself.

Phillip Mitsis, a recent commentator on Epicurus, locates the Epicurean theory of pleasure in the tradition of Greek eudaemonism, or theories that happiness is the greatest good.[19] Aristotle in particular taught this; he regarded happiness as self-sufficiency, invulnerability, and completeness, allowing the individual to satisfy his needs himself with no fear of chance or contingency disrupting his life.[20] Aristotelian happiness is a kind of balanced equilibrium or harmony where desires have

[13] Mitsis, *Epicurus' Ethical Theory*, 30–31.
[14] P. H. De Lacy, "Epicurus," in *Encyclopedia of Philosophy*, 3:4–5.
[15] On this aspect of Epicurean ethics, see J. M. Guyau, *La Morale d'Épicure et ses rapport avec les doctrines contemporaines* (Paris, 1917), 45.
[16] Epicurus, *Extant Remains*, 87, 99.
[17] Quoted in Diogenes Laertius, *Lives of Eminent Philosophers*, trans. R. D. Hicks, 2 vols. (Cambridge, Mass., 1925), 2:655.
[18] Epicurus, *Extant Remains*, 119.
[19] Mitsis, *Epicurus' Ethical Theory*, 17.
[20] Aristotle, *Nicomachean Ethics*, 208–9 (vii:13).

been satisfied and the person is content. This idea is close to the Epicurean idea of katastematic pleasure or tranquillity.

But Epicurus was not totally consistent in this view of pleasure. When Epicurus himself stated that pleasure motivates all actions in life, he seemed to anticipate utilitarian hedonism, that choices are made because something is pleasurable, not because it is useful: "For we recognize pleasure as that which is primary and congenital;" wrote Epicurus, "from it we begin every choice and avoidance, and we come back to it, using the feeling as the yardstick for judging every good thing." Here, pleasure seems to be a positive good rather than a kind of balance: it is not an ultimate end, but a current guide to living life most happily. And while Epicurus stated, "No pleasure is a bad thing in itself," he also claimed that some pleasures should be avoided and some pains embraced.[21] An additional criterion is needed to help determine what to pursue and what to forego. That criterion is human rationality.

Human rationality enters Epicurus's system with the principle of the calculation of pleasure and pain.[22] It seemed obvious to Epicurus that some pleasures, in the long run, will lead to an increase in pain, while some pains will eventually lead to pleasure—particularly since the pleasure aimed at is human contentment.[23] Thus, in conducting our lives we must consider the ultimate end—tranquillity and lack of pain in the body—and calculate our means accordingly. This calculation leads to opting for an ascetic and virtuous life, because there is more pleasure to be obtained by abstinence and conformity than by profligate behavior.[24]

Ultimately, Epicurus, in his desire to make pleasure accessible to anyone, without sacrifice of self-sufficiency, equated pleasure with the absence of pain. This pleasure cannot be intensified either by duration or by additional pleasures of motion. Once obtained, it contains eternity within itself.[25]

Epicurus invoked this idea in his battle against fear of death. There is no necessity for long life, he argued, for once pleasure is obtained, a

---

[21] Epicurus, *Extant Remains*, 87, 89.
[22] Mitsis, *Epicurus' Ethical Theory*, 22–30. This concept of the calculus of pleasure and pain differs from the Benthamite version because the concept is attached to the idea of pleasure as the end where all desires have been satisfied rather than viewing pleasure as a sensation or feeling which can be continually increased. There are other scholars who think that Epicurus more closely anticipates Bentham and the British utilitarians. See Cyril B. Bailey, *The Greek Atomists and Epicurus* (Oxford, 1928), 526–28, and more recently, Gisela Striker, "Ataraxia: Happiness as Tranquillity," *Monist* 73 (1990), 97–110.
[23] Epicurus, *Extant Remains*, 89.
[24] Ibid., 87–89.
[25] Ibid., 99.

person has reached the ultimate experience and needs nothing else—
not even life. Pleasure makes a human being self-sufficient in the face
of death. "Infinite time contains no pleasure greater than limited time,"
Epicurus assured his disciples, "if one measures by reason the limits of
the flesh."[26]

Fear of death and fear of the arbitrary actions of the gods, explained
Epicurus, are the two major sources of mental turmoil. The only cure
for these anxieties is an understanding of the nature of the universe.
Such an understanding will also alleviate fear of punishment after death,
because we will understand that the body reverts to its atomistic parts,
and therefore the individual simply becomes no more. Likewise once
the nature of the universe is explored, we will understand that the gods
are not necessary to explain its functioning.[27] Thus, Epicurus developed
a detailed natural philosophy to support his ethical teachings.

The Epicurean universe, like the Epicurean man, is self-sufficient. It
has no need of principles outside itself. The universe is composed of
atoms and void and nothing else. For all eternity, according to the cosmology Epicurus borrowed from Democritus, eternally moving matter
interacts with other matter, and fortuitously produces worlds as a byproduct. The idea of divine providence is unnecessary and unthinkable
in such a world.[28]

Although Epicurus eagerly accepted Democritus's denial of teleology,
the idea of natural necessity, or inescapable laws of nature, horrified
him: "For, indeed, it were better to follow the myths about the gods than
to become a slave to the destiny of the natural philosophers: for the
former suggests a hope of placating the gods by worship, whereas the
latter involves a necessity which knows no placation."[29]

It is crucial to the Epicurean ethical system that the individual remain
a free agent. Natural necessity destroys man's self-sufficiency and control
over his own destiny. In order to avoid natural necessity's determinism,
Epicurus introduced the concept of the swerve, or *clinamen*. Repudiating
the eternal erratic motion of Democritus, Epicurus postulated that
atoms naturally fall downward in parallel lines, like rain, because of their
weight.[30] At some time, for no particular reason, an atom swerves, a
chain reaction ensues, and world-building commences.

---

[26] Ibid., 96, 99.
[27] Ibid., 41–55.
[28] Ibid., 19–53.
[29] Ibid., 91.
[30] On the differences between Democritus and Epicurus, see Cyril Bailey, *Greek Atomists*, 117–37.

The swerve serves both as an explanation for free will and a necessary part of Epicurean physics. Without the swerve, the individual atoms would never meet and collide, and the cosmos could never take shape. Likewise, this element of fortuitous behavior on the part of the atom is the explanation of human free will, which also originates in the fortuitous swerves of the atoms that compose the soul.

According to Lucretius, who provides the only surviving Epicurean discussion of the problem, the proof for free will is a posteriori. Since we know that man possesses free will, there must be an element of indeterminism in nature.[31] Without an element of chance in the universe, free will in human beings would be impossible.

Recently, Mitsis has argued against the accepted modern interpretation of Epicurean chance and randomness. He argues that Epicurus could not have given such a wide role to self-sufficiency and free will in decision-making if everything we do ultimately can be reduced to the random and unpredictable movements of microscopic pieces of matter. This state of affairs would ultimately destroy human freedom, the core of Epicurean ethics, because action would not reflect rational choice. According to Mitsis, the actual relationship between atomic events and human action is somewhat vague and problematical, but certainly human rationality proves there is more to conscious life than atomic motion: macroscopic action is not determined by microscopic movement.[32]

An argument that might confirm Mitsis's interpretation can be found in the Epicurean account of the gods. Epicurean theology supports the notion of rational and self-sufficient gods, whose existence presumably is not undermined by random swerves in their atomic makeup: "The blessed and immortal nature knows no trouble itself nor causes trouble to any other, so that it is never constrained by anger or favor. For all such things exist only in the weak."[33]

The Epicurean gods are rational and free, if not very busy. Although Epicureanism was often considered an atheistic philosophy, it accepts the existence of the gods as self-evident.[34] However, the indolence of the gods means that they will not take the trouble to make trouble for anyone else.

Thus, more accurately, Epicureanism is an antiprovidential theology.

[31] Lucretius, *On the Nature of the Universe*, trans. J. H. Mantinband (New York, 1965), 41.
[32] Mitsis, *Epicurus' Ethical Theory*, 130–41.
[33] Epicurus, *Extant Remains*, 95.
[34] Ibid., 83. On Epicurean theology, see A. J. Festugière, *Epicurus and His Gods*, trans. C. W. Chilton (Oxford, 1955).

Its gods did not make the earth or human beings, nor do they guide the earth or reward and punish human beings, who are collections of atoms that disperse after death as if the individuals had never existed. A person, therefore, has nothing to fear from the gods or death, but can remain content and tranquil while alive.

Whether one locates freedom in atomic motion or human rationality, Epicureanism, of all the philosophies of the ancient world, most assertively secures an independent and self-sufficient place for the individual in this world. Freed from fear of death and fear of the gods, a person can happily live his life pursuing pleasure and avoiding pain, confident in his own power to control the decisions he freely makes.

The Rehabilitation of Epicurean Physics and Theology

Before Gassendi could transform Epicurean philosophy into an acceptable basis for his own system, he had to rid the ancient philosophy of the negative connotations which had haunted it since antiquity. Many pagan philosophers, led vehemently by Cicero, had attacked both the physical and moral tenets of Epicureanism.[35] They most bitterly castigated Epicurus's doctrine that pleasure is the highest good, and they would have seconded the later critique of the Church fathers that Epicureanism was materialistic and atheistic, and would result in social chaos—because there would be no reason to obey laws or uphold society. For the Christians, Epicurus's denial of divine providence and the immortality of the soul was particularly intolerable.[36]

The condemnation of the ancient Church fathers resounded through the ages, even landing Epicurus in the sixth circle of Dante's Hell.[37] A

[35] See, for example, Marcus Tullius Cicero, *Tusculun Disputations*, trans. J. E. King (Cambridge, Mass., 1945), 531–35, and Plutarch, *Moralia*, 302.

[36] The third century Christian apologists Arnobius and Lactantius were particularly concerned with refuting Epicurus. By the fourth century, however, Epicureanism had ceased to be a vital force in the western world. Augustine noted, the Epicureans' "ashes are so cold that not a single spark can be struck from them" (quoted in Jones, *The Epicurean Tradition*, 94). Epicureanism lingered in the middle ages almost entirely only a synonym for debauchery until the Italian humanist Poggio rediscovered Lucretius' *De Rerum Natura* in 1417. The tenth book of Diogenes Laertius was printed for the first time in 1533. On Epicureanism in the middle ages and the Renaissance, see Kurd Lasswitz, *Geschichte der atomistik vom mittalter bis Newton*, 2 vols. (Hildesheim, 1963; originally published 1890); Trinkaus, *In Our Image*, 1:103–70; and Jones, *The Epicurean Tradition*, 117–65.

[37] In Canto 6 of *The Inferno*, while describing the fate of the heretics, Dante wrote, "In this dark corner of the morgue of wrath/ lie Epicurus and his followers,/ who make the soul share in the body's death" (Dante Aligheri, *The Inferno*, trans. J. Chiari [Princeton, 1954], 96).

1632 letter to Gassendi from the philosopher Tomasso Campanella shows its endurance.[38] The Spaniard, who himself had been imprisoned for twenty-seven years by the Inquisition, expressed his displeasure at Gassendi's espousal of Epicureanism, particularly because it denied divine providence.[39] This criticism drew a soothing response from Gassendi, who assured Campanella, "You insist upon providence, and I argue the same thing against Epicurus, and if he errs about anything, I do not want to defend him. . . . I must remember what is suitable for a Christian and a priest."[40]

Providence was only one of the problems Gassendi faced in rehabilitating the philosophy of Epicurus and transforming it to his own use. Ironically, Gassendi found that atomistic physics, whether in the Democritean or Epicurean formulation, was in actuality more amenable to Christian rehabilitation than was the Epicurean moral system. Into an Epicurean universe of indivisible atoms, Gassendi simply introduced God as its creator and maintainer, who had providentially ordered the motion of matter to suit his divine plan.[41]

While Democritus and Epicurus had made motion intrinsic to matter, Gassendi suggested that it was infused into atoms at their creation: "It may be supposed that the individual atoms received from God . . . the force requisite to moving, and to imparting motion to others. . . . All this to the degree that he foresaw what would be necessary for every purpose for which he had destined them."[42]

This infused motion changes both the physics and the philosophy of atomism. It obviates the necessity for the *clinamen* in the Epicurean system, since world building becomes part of God's providential plan and operates according to the second causes he instituted.[43] And since God is the originator of this motion, Gassendi avoided the atheistic implications of Democritean atomism, where the ubiquitous, eternal motion of the atoms determines all natural events.

Gassendi argued that the functioning of the atoms does not contradict God's role as first cause, because as an absolutely powerful deity, he can always change nature's actions. Normally, however, he will not intervene directly in the universe, because the regularity of the processes of nature proves his existence, omnipotence and providence better than

---

[38] Tomasso Campanella to Gassendi, May 7, 1632, "Letters," *Opera*, 6:407.
[39] Campanella to Gassendi, July 4, 1632, ibid., 6:408.
[40] Gassendi to Campanella, November 2, 1642, ibid, 6:54.
[41] Pierre Gassendi, "Physics," in *SP*, *Opera*, 1:283–87.
[42] Ibid., 1:280; *Selected Works*, 400–401.
[43] Gassendi, "Physics," in *SP*, *Opera*, 1:283–371.

any miracle: the order of nature is "incomparably more marvelous to observe."[44]

The inertial motion of the atoms becomes God's device for providentially guiding the world; God infuses a force into the atoms "by means of which this indefinite motion is maintained, and it has been a principle of the world that will last until the end. Certainly this is sufficient to explain the causes of things."[45]

While God could have created things instantaneously—and can intervene in natural processes at any time he wishes—he uses moving atoms as the vehicle of his divine plan, his divine concourse as Gassendi called it. God rules the universe through his general providence, which is sometimes called fate: "fate is nothing other in itself, than those natural causes, to the extent that they act through themselves and in accordance with the force implanted by God."[46]

God's general providence rules the natural world, but Gassendi maintained that there is another kind of providence—God's "special providence"—which rules human beings. The thing that distinguishes the natural and the human is freedom, which human beings possess and natural entities lack. Human liberty, therefore, must be understood in terms of the context of a universe governed by God who impresses a kind of natural necessity on his creation, but always excepting rational beings.[47]

The Ethical Theory

In Gassendi's ethics, the instinctive search for pleasure and avoidance of pain—an instinct implanted by God—plays the same role in guiding human action as the infused motion of the atoms does in determining physical action. The concept of matter in motion functions as a paradigm, which allows Gassendi to develop his own ethical system in a most complex manner. Motion provides the metaphor for understanding the free actions of individuals and the divinely determined action of natural things.

[44] Ibid., 1:315, 318. Gassendi's notion of God is voluntarist. See Osler, "Providence, Divine Will, and the Theological Background to Gassendi's Views on Scientific Knowledge," 549–60, and *Divine Will and the Mechanical Philosophy*, 48–58.
[45] Gassendi, "De motu impresso," *Opera*, 3:487–88; *Selected Works*, 126–27; and "Physics," in *SP, Opera*, 1:417, 493–94.
[46] Gassendi, "Ethics," in *SP, Opera*, 1:282, 315–21, 337.
[47] Ibid., 1:310. Gassendi made the analogy between the universe and a huge machine, which was constructed by an all-powerful artisan ("Physics," 1:317).

In addition, Gassendi incorporated Greek eudaemonist theory in its Epicurean form with an anticipation of Benthamite hedonism.[48] Pleasure served two roles in Gassendi's thought: both as a spur to immediate action and as final goal of prudential calculation. The desire for pleasure impels human movement, while the experience of pleasure is a state of constant and uniform contentment.

Before he could develop his own understanding of pleasure and motion, Gassendi had to justify Epicurus's doctrine that pleasure is the highest good. He explained that "Epicurus felt that no other pleasure is the end, than that [pleasure] which consists in stability, somewhat like repose, namely tranquillity and freedom from pain."[49] While one feels pleasure while satisfying a desire, true pleasure consists in remaining in a state of satisfaction. Virtue is the surest way to achieve this state of satisfaction. So, reiterating the arguments of Epicurus and Lucretius, and adding some of his own, Gassendi showed that Epicurean pleasure is connected with morality and leads to an ascetic way of life.[50]

This notion of ascetic pleasure and its connection with the virtues became the key to Gassendi's vindication of Epicurean morality. Gassendi followed Aristotle in his definition of virtue as a habit which inclines us to do just and honorable things and in the doctrine that the cardinal virtues themselves are wisdom or prudence, fortitude, temperance, and justice. Temperance and prudence, in Gassendi's adaptation, become essential to the Epicurean ethical code. They lead the wise man to understand that most human desires are vain and mistaken: "The wealth demanded by nature is both limited and easily procured; that demanded by idle imaginings stretches on to infinity."[51] A correct understanding of human needs is vital for self-sufficiency. Otherwise, all chance of freedom and pleasure vanishes, as one is caught on a hopeless treadmill of desire.

Thus, virtue is the only sure way to secure tranquillity of the mind and lack of pain in the body: "virtue alone is called inseparable from pleasure, because . . . it is the necessary cause of pleasure, that is, when virtue has been posited, pleasure and felicity follow." Although the virtues may

---

[48] Bentham taught that all men seek pleasure and avoid pain, although he interpreted pleasure, according to J. H. Burton, as "what it pleases a man to do is simply what he wills to do" (quoted in D. H. Monro, "Jeremy Bentham," in *Encyclopedia of Philosophy*, 282). Bentham also articulated a "calculus" of pleasure and pain, where an individual makes a utilitarian calculation of whether an action will bring more or less pain or pleasure in the long run.

[49] Gassendi, "Ethics," in *SP, Opera*, 2:682.

[50] Ibid., 2:692–94.

[51] Ibid., 2:736, 699.

be desired for themselves, they cannot but bring pleasure to the person who enjoys them. And pleasure, or happiness (the terms are used interchangeably), is the end of life—as taught by Epicurus—and the most perfect condition we can attain.[52]

Gassendi's own theory of pleasure is considerably more nuanced than the Epicurean version. Epicurus's dual interpretation of the meaning of pleasure—that it is both kinetic (the fulfillment of desires) and katastematic (the attainment of tranquillity and the absence of pain)—informed Gassendi's discussion, and influenced his interpretation of the Epicurean calculus of pleasure and pain. Even the calculus itself, for Gassendi, contains an element of ambiguity. It can, on the one hand, mean simply any rational being's desire to maximize long-term pleasure and avoid long-term pain. Or, on the other hand, it can more narrowly mean the wise man's prudence—which leads him to calculate what will result in tranquillity or lack of pain.

The first indication of Gassendi's use of this principle comes from a source other than the "Ethics." In September 1642, Gassendi wrote to his patron, Louis of Valois, that the last criterion Epicurus used in his logic was "passion," which is nothing else in this context but the pleasure-pain principle:

> There are four canons concerning this matter, which I give as certain general rules of all human actions: I. That pleasure, which has no pain connected to it, ought to be embraced. II. That pain which has no pleasure attached to it ought to be avoided. III. That pleasure, which impedes a greater pleasure, or furnishes a greater pain, ought to be avoided. IV. That pain, which either averts a greater pain, or creates a later pleasure, ought to be embraced.[53]

Furthermore, Gassendi continued, pleasure and pain can be used as criteria for action by Christians. He did not describe how these feelings could be connected with Christianity, which usually took a dim view of a normative system based on rational calculation of hedonic self-interest, but he promised to return to the subject when he discussed moral philosophy, which "is not what is said by many."[54]

This passage is significant, because it shows that Gassendi was aware of the long debate about the nature of the passions and their relation-

---

[52] Ibid., 2:692–93.
[53] Gassendi to Valois, August 29, 1642, "Letters," *Opera*, 6:153.
[54] Ibid.

ship to human action. It was perhaps inevitable that a proponent of Epicureanism would be interested in this subject, because neo-Stoicism was in vogue during the late sixteenth century and early seventeenth century in France.[55] The neo-Stoics, like their ancient predecessors, who were the bitter opponents of Epicureanism, believed that the passions were the enemies of reason and the virtuous life. The passions, or any emotional excesses, were seen as essentially destructive for human beings: living the good life required their repression.[56]

Gassendi recognized that "passion" could mean the single-minded pursuit of pleasure, in the sense of maximizing a sensation or a feeling of exceptional delight. Like the Stoics and neo-Stoics, he viewed sensual pleasure with suspicion. He conceded that most human beings will mistake the transitory kinetic pleasures of the appetite for the ultimate pleasure of remaining in a constant state of tranquillity, and will value the former above the latter. Gassendi stated, "I understand assuredly that this (immoderate) desire is natural; consequently, it is discovered to thrive also in boys and even in brutes; and there is no one, who, however much he pretends that he shuns it, does not recognize that he is always held by his appetite, so that he could not lay it aside if he wanted to." If a man does not realize that tranquillity is a finite and final good, his pursuit of pleasure will agitate him continuously, "Since . . . those things that he possesses already, count for nothing, . . . he searches for delight in procuring those things he thinks he lacks."[57]

But this misconception about the nature of pleasure is not necessarily bad. Gassendi took Epicurus's cradle argument—that the first thing a newborn seeks is pleasure, and the first thing it flees from is pain—and converted it into one of the most crucial elements of his ethical system. According to Gassendi, God uses pleasure and pain as the providential devices for carrying out his eternal designs without having to interfere miraculously in the natural process:

> Rather it is suitable that we regard with wonder that cunning of the most wise Artificer of nature; for as every action was going to be wearisome in itself, even natural actions. . . , he therefore seasoned every action with a

---

[55] On neo-Stoicism, see Chap. 1.
[56] On the changes in attitudes toward the passions in the seventeenth century, see A. J. Krailsheimer, *Studies in Self-Interest from Descartes to La Bruyère* (Oxford, 1962); Levi, *French Moralists*, 299–328; and Albert O. Hirschman, *The Passions and the Interests: Political Arguments for Capitalism before its Triumph* (Princeton, 1977). I will return to the subject of the passions in Chap. 6, when I discuss how Gassendi and Hobbes viewed pleasure and pain.
[57] Gassendi, "Ethics," in *SP, Opera*, 2:661, 706, 703.

certain allurement of pleasure; and the more necessary the particular act was to be, either for the preservation of the entire race or for the preservation of each individual being, the greater he willed the pleasure to be.[58]

Gassendi insisted that animate beings would do nothing for their own preservation if it were not for the instinctive desire for pleasure implanted by God. Thus, Gassendi has introduced God's providence into the Epicurean system by means of a fundamental hedonistic principle. The natural desire for pleasure and aversion to pain becomes the "invisible hand" of God, guiding people along ordained paths while not denying them the use of free will. Gassendi's claim to have converted the pleasure-pain principle into a usable criterion for Christians thus becomes more explicable.

The desire for pleasure continues to function as a spur to action throughout life. Most men, since their wisdom is not perfected, create their lives in a continuous search for pleasure. The pursuit of pleasure functions as a kind of motivational work ethic in Gassendi's system, just as it did for Epicurus's. Even the desire for transitory pleasures leads human beings to develop their social natures and underlies the formation of political states and group activity.[59]

Still, Gassendi emphasized, for many human beings the pursuit of pleasure may go awry. In seeking momentary pleasures, they may lose their ultimate goal.[60] In this sense, passion leads man away from rational behavior. Individuals clearly use their reason to determine what will bring them the greatest amount of pleasure and the least amount of pain, but such calculation is suspect if they do not have a correct understanding of the nature of pleasure. Most people use rationality for an irrational end.

It is at this point that the other sense of pleasure comes into play. The wise man recognizes this "certain, special kind of pleasure . . . as the most natural, most easily obtainable, most constant, and most lacking in penalties." While nature gave us pleasure in order to promote some necessary actions, like eating, "it is the state of calmness which is established as the final good."[61] Other pleasures are inconstant and perishable, but tranquillity of the mind and lack of pain in the body are stable and easy to maintain, if one recognizes what is truly necessary and that virtue is the best means to achieve happiness.

---

[58] Ibid., 2:701.
[59] Ibid., 2:703, 721. See Chap. 6 below on Gassendi's social theories.
[60] Ibid., 2:706.
[61] Ibid., 2:715.

Katastematic pleasure played a twofold role in Gassendi's moral system. On the one hand, it is a kind of psychological state in which the individual possesses imperturbable happiness, since all pain and anxieties are absent. On the other hand, it is the *telos* or end toward which the wise man aims, constantly choosing those goods which will lead to it and avoiding those evils which will obstruct it.

Gassendi was especially interested in the use of prudence in the calculation of pleasure and pain. Like Epicurus, he viewed prudence as "the prince of morality." Wrote Gassendi, "Prudence is a moral virtue, which moderates all the actions of one's life correctly, and discerning good from evil and useful from harmful, it prescribes what is necessary to follow or avoid, and how to establish men in the good and happy life."[62]

Prudence also defends us from stress due to engendered or social prejudices (*ingenerantia opiniones*) and leads us to a correct understanding of how the world operates. Gassendi argued that prudence teaches us, for example, that there is nothing evil to be feared from God or death, since sense perception ceases after death and we cannot feel pain, although the immortal soul lives on.[63] We should face the future indifferently, and live for today, since happiness is not judged by quantity but by quality. Likewise, the wise man becomes happy because prudence has taught him to value only the natural and necessary.[64]

Clearly, Gassendi's concept of prudence encapsulates his entire theory of ethics, as an active art teaching the rules for leading an honest life. For Gassendi, virtue, honesty, happiness, and utility are bound together, "A person desires something not because it is useful but because it brings pleasure."[65]

Two meanings of pleasure are, therefore, conjoined in Gassendi's ethical thought. While the desire for ephemeral pleasure spurs instinctive human activity—or the actions of a person who may misunderstand the real nature of pleasure—it is the satisfaction of desire and the resulting tranquillity that order the choices of the wise man. He will use his prudence, that capacity Gassendi so admired, to calculate what will bring tranquillity and lack of pain in the long run.

---

[62] Ibid., 2:744.
[63] There are many different views of what happens to the body after death and before the resurrection at the time of the Second Coming. See, Norman T. Burns, *Christian Mortalism from Tyndale to Milton* (Cambridge, Mass., 1972).
[64] Gassendi, "Ethics," in *SP, Opera*, 2:664.
[65] Ibid., 2:703. On the role of utility in Gassendi's ethics, see Gianni Paganini, "Épicurisme et philosophie au XVIIe siècle. Convention, utilité, et droit selon Gassendi," *Studi Filosofici* 12–13 (1989–90), 4–45.

At the very beginning of the "Ethics," Gassendi had emphasized the importance he was going to give the pleasure-pain principle. In the introduction to "De felicitate," which is the first book of the "Ethics," he wrote, "But such happiness while we live mortal life is experienced more as a wish than as a reality; . . . the more or less the condition of our life approaches this ideal, the more or less happy we may be esteemed to be."[66]

An individual strives according to an idea he has of a life happier than his present state. This striving for happiness or pleasure, even if it temporarily brings pain, raises man above the other animate beings, who lack the capacity of forethought. "Certainly," Gassendi also wrote in "De felicitate," "it is this happiness to which alone men seem to be able to aspire to by natural right; since to put it another way, to pursue and promise himself that excellent thing, is to forget his own mortality, and not recognize that he himself is a man, that is a weak animal, and from the condition of his nature liable to innumerable evils and miseries."[67]

Even those human beings who correctly understand the nature of pleasure as rest still only approach happiness; they do not achieve it: "that highest happiness, which is the absence of every perturbation and pain and the accumulation of every pleasure, is God's alone and those whom God transfigured, because of his immense goodness, into a better life."[68] Thus, although a person may perceive true pleasure, he is doomed to a life of striving for it without achieving it.

Thus, theology led Gassendi to part company with Epicurus on the most fundamental characteristic of pleasure: whether complete pleasure may be attained by anyone who correctly understands its nature. Gassendi reserved this ultimate pleasure for God and for those he saves. Like Valla, Gassendi equated the highest form of pleasure with the beatific vision of God, a divine sweetness that leads us and links us to God.[69]

In other words, Gassendi superimposed a fourth level of pleasure on the three postulated by Epicurus and other hedonists. Pleasure is not only satisfying a desire, through instinct or calculation, or being satisfied and contented, but also a final transfiguration into beatified existence. The highest form of pleasure, in this case, is not tranquillity, but divine ecstasy.

[66] Gassendi, "Ethics," in *SP, Opera*, 2:662.
[67] Ibid., 2:662.
[68] Ibid., 2:717.
[69] Ibid., 2:710.

Why does Gassendi believe that God denies man the ability to attain complete happiness while he lives? The answer lies in Gassendi's doctrine of free will. Along with both Epicurus and the Catholic church, Gassendi utterly condemned fate: "Because if our souls, when they are established in the material world, are ruled by fate; if our souls are destitute of liberty, if they are immobilized by necessity, [if] they do everything unavoidably and inevitably, the reason for human life perishes; nor can there be any place for deliberations. . . . Hence prudence will be utterly in vain; the study of wisdom will be in vain."[70]

The final result of a belief in fate or determinism is that no person can be praised or blamed according to his actions. In particular, prudence, or the ability of man to reason and act, is lost, and the whole human creation becomes pointless. Freedom becomes meaningless in a deterministic universe.

Gassendi's defense of human freedom is based on his understanding of the faculties of the mind and on his radical empiricism.[71] According to Gassendi, liberty is primarily in the intellect and secondarily in the will, although both depend on sense impressions which are perceived directly and unmistakably by the faculty of the imagination.[72] The imagination always presents true images of the appearances of material objects to the intellect, but it is up to the intellect to make a judgment about these appearances, whether, for instance, something is true gold, or false gold, but true brass.[73] A judgment is an affirmation or denial of the ideas provided by the imagination, and it can be correct or incorrect: "the truth of a pronouncement or the truth of a thought . . . is truth to which falsity can be opposed, inasmuch as the mind is open to error and is able to think or pronounce something equally to be or not to be as it really is."[74]

Our intellect must always remain indifferent—that is, not committed to any judgment—before accepting an idea as true. A person must make

---

[70] Ibid., 2:831.
[71] Bloch has also emphasized Gassendi's doctrine of freedom which he connects with the sixteenth-century humanistic and skeptical desire to be free of authority. He accurately credits the elucidation of this doctrine to Gassendi's polemic with Descartes, although I argue that Gassendi's relationship with Hobbes was equally important for the development of his moral premises. See Bloch, *Philosophie de Gassendi*, 60–67.
[72] Gassendi, "Ethics," in *SP, Opera*, 2:822–25. I explore Gassendi's theory of the faculties in more detail in Chap. 4.
[73] Gassendi, "Logic," in *SP, Opera*, 1:93. On Gassendi's theory of judgment and its relation to his empiricism, see Jones's "Introduction" to his translation, *Institutio Logica*, xxix–xxxix.
[74] Jones, *Institutio Logica*, 105.

sure that he is not deceived by any preconception or prejudice, whether from external beliefs or internal predispositions, before deciding about an idea. He must be sure that "the mind is free and neutral in determining what idea it will hold to be true."[75]

Free choice or *libertas* depends on the ability of the mind to make judgments and evaluate evidence indifferently: It is the ability to choose or reject an alternative, or to change one's mind when weightier reasons appear.[76] A free person is "not liable to external forces," that is, his reason or intellect is to some extent independent of its environment. The intellect must always choose the course that seems best to it (as a balance must incline to the heavier side), but the evaluation of evidence is entirely in the power of the individual's intellect. The metaphor of "a balance" does seem to introduce an element of necessity into the intellect's judgment. However, Gassendi argued that a free individual is not determined by what is best as a passive subject, but himself determines what is best as the discriminating agent.[77] Once the intellect has decided what action to take, the will must necessarily follow to accomplish the action.[78] If the intellect acts freely, it always pursues a course of considering all options, that is both sides of the question—*ad utramque partem*—before coming to a decision.

Gassendi's ethical doctrines about freedom depend on his epistemology, which, as the last chapter showed, concludes that humans can have only probable rather than certain knowledge. Since no certain knowledge of essences is possible, people are constantly making, revising, rejecting, and changing judgments.[79] Our judgments are fallible at best, although we always choose the most probable truth, which guides the will to pursue those objects most likely to give us pleasure and flee from those most likely to give us pain. This is similar to the aim of deliberative rhetoric, where the orator, according to Cicero, directs his audience toward "things to be sought and . . . avoided."[80]

Gassendi, in a sense, made every man his own orator, who in the manner of an Academic skeptic and a rhetorician examines all sides before

---

[75] Ibid., 94. The Latin of the last sentence is the following: "Mens indifferens, ac libera fiat ad expendendum, deligendumque, quamnam ut germanam habiturus sit" (Jones, 13). The fact that Gassendi associates "indifferens" and "libera" should be noted.
[76] Gassendi, "Ethics," in *SP, Opera,* 2:821.
[77] On the problem of the seemingly mechanical elements of Gassendi's theory of judgment, see Chap. 6 below.
[78] Gassendi, "Ethics," in *SP, Opera,* 2:822–25.
[79] Ibid., 2:824.
[80] Quoted in Vickers, *In Defence of Rhetoric,* 57.

choosing a course of action.[81] It would not be far-fetched to suppose that Gassendi had the three aims of the orator in mind when he developed his probabilistic ethics. The orator needs to move and carry away his audience (*movere et flectere*), to teach them (*docere*), and in the end to please them (*delectare*) in order to persuade them to do something. The personal, self-directed oration functions in the same way: The intellect teaches what is to be sought or avoided, the will is moved, and the result is pleasure of both act and thought.[82]

Human action, according to Gassendi, is characterized according to whether or not it follows a free act of judgment. Gassendi distinguished between a "willing action" (*spontaneam*), and a "free action" (*liberum*). A willing action is like an involuntary impulse of nature: It is common to stones, brutes, and boys, all creatures without the ability to reason. Thus, a stone will fall to the ground willingly, but not freely, because there was not a prior indifference during which it decided to fall. Likewise, the instinctive impulse of any animate being, who does not possess full rationality, to pursue the good or pleasure is involuntary, because all appetites are inclined toward pleasure from their own nature.[83]

Willingness (*libentia*) characterizes the saints as well, because they know and understand the highest good completely and therefore cannot forsake it.[84] Therefore, according to Gassendi, complete happiness is equivalent to the loss of free will, because no indifference remains in the soul, no element of deliberation persists.

In other words, two of the forms of pleasure Gassendi recognized—immediate pleasure of sensation and the pleasure of beatification—preclude human freedom because they preclude choice. Only the search for long-term pleasure, and especially tranquillity, allows for human freedom, because the choice of what to seek and what to avoid remains self-directed.

---

[81] Gassendi makes an interesting distinction in a letter to Louis of Valois: "Epicurus considers philosophy as *the art of life*, and while the rest of the arts certainly demand a great deal of exertion, this is not for their own end, as when . . . an orator prepares an oration by means of which he persuades another person" (Gassendi to Valois, February 6, 1642, "Letters," *Opera*, 6:131). This might be a distinction without a difference if the orator is the object of his own persuasion.

[82] On the three aims of the orator, see Peter France, *Rhetoric and Truth in France: Descartes to Diderot* (Oxford, 1972), 9; Brian Vickers, "Rhetoric and Poetics," 736–37; and *In Defence of Rhetoric*, 24, 50, 74. It is the terminology of rhetoric which most strongly suggests rhetorical influences on Gassendi. The term *flectere* is particularly significant, and will be analyzed in Chap. 6.

[83] Gassendi, "Ethics," in *SP, Opera*, 2:824.

[84] Ibid., 2:822–23.

Thus, man is a constantly striving creature, striving after a goal—pleasure or complete happiness—that he cannot reach because he is a human being, whose freedom ultimately consists in the ability mistakenly to choose the lesser and more immediate good rather than the ultimate good. Human fallibility is the essence of human freedom.

An individual's destiny remains in his own hands. Although there are some elements of fate and fortune that remain beyond his grasp, he himself is within his own power, and he can so order his life as to obtain the maximum of pleasure possible for a person. God's power and providence remain unimpaired by human free will; indeed, pleasure becomes the device God uses for providentially directing man toward the good, just as he uses motion for directing the actions of the natural world.

Motion and Morality

The use of metaphors and analogies drawn from motion to explicate God's providential relationship toward the human and physical spheres affects Gassendi's thought even more deeply. He describes the human search for pleasure and the pleasure of tranquillity itself in metaphors derived from a mechanistic understanding of motion.

Thus, the pursuit of pleasure becomes like a kind of motion: "the soul is furnished with two parts, intellect or mind and will or appetite; so that the intellect directs itself to the truth, as much as permitted; the will indeed tends to honesty by an indeflectable path."[85] The intellect can hesitate—indeed it must hesitate, since it can know only problematic truths of appearances and since it has the ability to remain neutral—but the will, like a stone, contains a principle of infused motion which makes it continue in its course. The will's desire for any kind of pleasure is the efficient cause of action in the human sphere, just as the motion God infused into the atoms is the efficient cause of change and interaction in the mechanistic universe.

Margaret Osler has pointed out that Gassendi believed the animal soul, which is the same as the *anima*, or irrational, vegetative, and sensitive soul in human beings, is "in constant motion." The motion of the *anima* is the same as the motion of physical matter according to a passage in the "Physics":

> For when a boy runs to an apple offered to him, what is needed to account for the apple's attraction to the boy is not just a metaphorical motion, but

---

[85] Gassendi, "Concerning Philosophy in General," in *SP, Opera*, 1:1.

also most of all there must be a physical, or natural, power inside the boy by which he is directed or impelled toward the apple. . . . The prime cause of motion in natural things is the atoms, for they provide motion for all things when they move themselves through their own agency and in accord with the power they received from their author in the beginning; and they are consequently the origin, and principle, and cause of all the motion that exists in nature.[86]

Here Gassendi seems very close to the materialism of ancient Epicureanism. He used a microscopic and materialistic explanation of some human actions, while leaving room for nonatomistic, macroscopic explanations. The atomistic, unifying natural motion Gassendi described is the motion of a boy, not a rational creature. Boys possess spontaneity, but not the freedom to evaluate indifferently and make a judgment: "boys and brutes, to which are attributed the use neither of reason nor of freedom, do many things willingly (*sponte*), but also inanimate things, like a rock falls willingly, or fire ascends willingly; therefore it seems that to happen willingly is the same thing as to happen naturally."[87] Stones and boys have to do what they have to do. But even rational men contain elements in their souls that impel them to seek pleasure, because the will always pursues the good.

It is in the description of katastematic pleasure that Gassendi most consistently used metaphors of motion. Katastematic pleasure is a "continuing state," as opposed to kinetic pleasures, which are transient. It is very "natural" and very "lasting," but other pleasures pass away in a moment, and they are inconstant, "whereas tranquillity continues in an uninterrupted course, unless it is interrupted and perishes by our own defects."[88] One might say that when a person pursues kinetic pleasures, he is acted upon by other forces—the lures of other kinds of pleasure— just as a stone, while moving inertially, can be knocked off its course by other pieces of matter. In both cases the result is a change in direction. But in a state of katastematic pleasure, motion never varies and the person never abandons the true good.

---

[86] Gassendi, "Physics," in *SP, Opera,* 1:337; *Selected Works,* 421–22. Cited in Margaret J. Osler, "Baptizing Epicurean Atomism: Pierre Gassendi on the Immortality of the Soul," in *Religion, Science, and Worldview: Essays in Honor of Richard S. Westfall,* ed. Margaret J. Osler and Paul L. Farber (Cambridge, 1985), 169, 169n.

[87] Gassendi, "Ethics," in *SP* in *Opera,* 2:824. Gassendi in this passage was clearly using Aristotelian terminology to explain the motion of the elements. He does occasionally lapse into Aristotelianism when he is speaking loosely about natural processes, but this does not contradict the fact that he still understood motion in the sense of the mechanical philosophy, as the great bulk of his work shows.

[88] Gassendi, "Ethics," in *SP, Opera,* 2:686, 715.

It is apparent that the pleasure of rest or katastematic pleasure is itself a kind of constant and uniform motion—it is itself not "rest" in the sense of not moving, but rest in the sense of remaining in perpetual motion without agitation. In fact, Gassendi draws an analogy between the tranquil motion of a boat, which is calm and placid not only when it is becalmed, but "especially when it is blown by a favorable wind" and the tranquillity of the soul, which retains its calm whether one is at leisure or whether one is active and toiling. The tranquil soul "always maintains a consistent course, and it is always similar to itself, and it is moved neither by exultant joy, nor depressed sorrow."[89]

Gassendi, who was the first natural philosopher to publish the correct formulation of the principle of inertia in his treatise, *De motu impresso* (1642), described inertial motion as "natural" and "uniform and perpetual in its nature." He argued that in a void "a stone would be moved eternally by its motion and in the same direction that the hand directed it" unless a perpendicular motion intervened.[90] Moreover, just as he had in his discussion of tranquillity, Gassendi used the analogy of a ship's motion to support his arguments for the possibility of inertial motion.[91]

Thus, on the one hand, the desire for pleasure functions like the infused motion of the atoms; it is a dynamic principle of movement. On the other hand, tranquillity or complete pleasure is like the state of inertial motion. It is, in fact, the limiting case of earthly pleasure—the way pleasure would be if one were absolutely wise—just as a stone or atom moving in the void is the limiting case of inertial motion.

Gassendi wrote *De motu impresso* and the "Ethics" at approximately the same time.[92] Whether he used analogous language consciously or unconsciously to describe a physical principle and a psychological state is difficult to determine. Did his physics inform and shape his ethics or vice versa?

There is no definite answer to this question, but Gassendi certainly was aware of the far-reaching implications of infusing physical concepts or metaphors into his ethical philosophy. The two ancient atomists, Democritus and Epicurus, had faced the same issue. Democritus had con-

---

[89] Ibid., 2:718.
[90] Gassendi, *De motu impresso, Opera,* 3:493–96; *Selected Works,* 137–41. Gassendi imagined a space completely empty of matter except for the moving rock. Thus, his uniform motion would be straight, not circular as in the case of Galileo, since there is no circumference in reference to which the rock moves. On Gassendi's correct formulation of the principle of inertia, see Alexandre Koyré, *Newtonian Studies* (Cambridge, Mass., 1965), 185–87.
[91] Gassendi, *De motu impresso, Opera,* 3:480–83; *Selected Works,* 120–22.
[92] On the dating of *De motu impresso* see Bloch, *Philosophie de Gassendi,* xxix.

cluded that the universe and humanity were ruled by fate, or the eternal motion of the atoms. Epicurus had introduced the swerve to liberate the universe and human beings through the spontaneity and contingency of atomic motion. For Epicurus, the indeterminate motion of the soul was like the indeterminate action of the atoms. Gassendi could accept neither Democritean determinism nor Epicurean chance, because his universe was Christian and Catholic, and God had endowed man with reason and freedom.

The importing of metaphors of motion into Gassendi's ethical philosophy is also demonstrated in the language he used in another related theme he developed in the "Ethics" and in a series of letters written to his patron Louis of Valois, also in the early 1640s. Gassendi was wrestling with the question of whether it was possible for a person to achieve tranquillity not only when he withdraws from the world of affairs, but also when he is part of it.

Gassendi advised Valois to "maintain the placid state of the soul constantly, among these public storms."[93] He told him that it is possible to "obtain leisure (*otium in negotio*) in business, tranquility in the middle of the storm, serenity in a state of very agitated affairs" if one fixes on a goal, anticipates problems, and does not fluctuate.[94] In another letter Gassendi argued that the virtue of a wise man is a kind of motion: "Therefore, virtue is certainly immobile, but . . . it ought not to be quiescent. . . . Indeed virtue will be similar to the governor, who sits quietly in the stern of the ship holding the rudder, nor does he [pursue transitory things] like young men, but he does many things greater and better."[95]

A wise man can be happy, and maintain leisure in the midst of business—"*otium in negotio*" were the terms used in the Renaissance debate about the active versus the contemplative life—if he remains constant in his pursuit of a goal, is not misled by ephemeral desires and remains in a state of mind of "active" tranquillity. In short, the motion of a person involved in business can duplicate the inertial motion of a wise man if he does not deviate from a true understanding of katastemic pleasure or tranquillity.

Tranquillity, rather than divorcing a man from affairs, becomes a tool for success in the world: "the soul is called tranquil, not only when one lives in leisure, but also, especially, when one undertakes great and ex-

---

[93] Gassendi to Valois, July 18, 1646, "Letters," *Opera*, 6:252.
[94] Gassendi to Valois, December 29, 1644, ibid., 6:214.
[95] Gassendi to Valois, August 25, 1641, ibid., 6:113.

cellent things, without internal agitation and with an even tempera-ment." A wise man will use the faculty of prudence to judge his own abilities in any matter, to weigh the capacities of others, and to utilize his past experiences to help current enterprises.[96] In short, he will be prepared for any contingency; and if by some chance, he does fail, he will not be destroyed, because he always retains his inner tranquillity and the knowledge that he did the best he could.

Thus, Gassendi believed he had found a prescription for a life of happy calm within the turmoil of public affairs. Metaphors of motion become the means of constructing a work ethic for the wise man. Does this mean that he had abandoned the Epicurean ideal of withdrawal from the world into a life of private happiness spent with friends of like mind? By no means. Also in the "Ethics," he asked, "Do you see any courtier, anyone full of dignities, and the managing of affairs, who is not disgusted by this kind of life? Do these men not envy the quiet of those who they observe resting in a tranquil port, having escaped from the troubled sea?"[97] In this case, motion becomes relative, and the motion of the wise man who has escaped the tumult is more desirable than a course of life constantly threatened by external forces.

Gassendi formulated a Christianized Epicurean ethical system, which maintained that pleasure is the highest good and human beings are free. In the Gassendist revision, the meanings of pleasure multiply. The desire for immediate gratification results in instinctive action for irratio-nal creatures, while the search for long-term pleasures, a surfeit of plea-sure over pain, results in a continuing pursuit of goods for those who calculate what will bring pleasure without realizing the true characteris-tics of pleasure. While an element of rationality is evident in the search for intense pleasure, it contains a mistaken estimation of what the best pleasure is. Pleasure for the wise man, quite differently, is the recogni-tion that tranquil calm is the happiest state possible for human beings whether involved in this world or withdrawn from it. But even this kind of pleasure pales before the truly ultimate pleasure, the beatific vision of God. Liberty or freedom of movement is the legacy of God to the wise man, because his choices are self-directed and self-corrected.

In his own unique synthesis, Gassendi reconciled God and Epicurus, man and nature, and freedom and necessity. His universe is cohesive, with each part of the creation operating—and moving—according to

---

[96] Gassendi, "Ethics," in *SP, Opera*, 2:717, 745–46.
[97] Ibid., 2:763.

the imperatives of God's providential plan. Even within the confines of a mechanistic universe there is room for human liberty and free choice. Man escapes from fate or natural necessity, because while God made the natural world bound and determined, he created human beings free.

Gassendi, Descartes, and Their Predecessors on the Liberty of Indifference

Freedom and Theology

When Gassendi discussed freedom and necessity, he knew that the metaphysical problems were infused with theological dimensions. The discussion raised the question of destiny or fate, and the relationship of human action to divine providence. According to Gassendi, destiny or fate is the decree of the Divine Will; fate that involves human beings is simply predestination.[1] Predestination and freedom are the opposing boundaries of the human moral horizon. Thus, Gassendi contended,

> As much as fate, fortune, or free will are admitted or rejected, there will be virtues in men, or no virtues, there will be vices, or no vices. Consequently there will be either actions which ought to be praised or condemned, or no actions to be praised or condemned, or no rewards or punishments merited. For it is agreed that there is praise or blame, only when things are done with deliberation or freely, and there is no praise and blame if something happens by fortune or necessity.[2]

Gassendi's ethical thought reflected the explosive theological debates inflaming both Catholic and Protestant Europe in the sixteenth and early seventeenth centuries.[3] His terminology was straight from the trea-

---

[1] Gassendi, "Ethics," in *SP, Opera*, 2:840.
[2] Ibid., 2:821.
[3] On this debate, see Jaroslav Pelikan, *Reformation of Church and Doctrine (1300–1700)*, vol. 4 of *The Christian Tradition: A History of the Development of Doctrine* (Chicago, 1984).

tises of Saint Thomas Aquinas, Duns Scotus, and particularly the sixteenth-century Spanish Jesuit theologian, Luis de Molina, a more controversial source. In 1640, during the same period that Gassendi was writing or rewriting the "Ethics," Molina's doctrines were most vehemently attacked by Cornelius Jansen (1585–1638) in the *Augustinus* (1640). In it, Jansen joined an ongoing French debate on predestination, spurred by the appearance in 1630 of a defense of traditional Augustinian theories by the Oratorian, Father Guillaume Gibieuf (1591–1650).

Descartes, Étienne Gilson has shown, was particularly influenced by the teachings of Gibieuf, and in the early 1640s, he engaged in a heated controversy with Gassendi.[4] They debated the meaning and status of the "liberty of indifference"—a concept associated most strongly with Molina—and whether human beings could be praised or blamed for moral or immoral choices, or errors, if choice was itself in some measure determined by God. Both Gassendi and Descartes followed prior thinkers in developing theories of the relationship of will and intellect to solve intractable problems about judgment, error, and indifference.

Molina (1535–1600) was one of the most important post-Reformation Catholic thinkers, whose theological writings are extraordinarily complex and difficult.[5] He was intensely concerned with the problem of reconciling human freedom with God's omniscience and the related problem of the relationships of providence, grace, predestination, and human salvation.[6] In every instance, Molina took the most radical position possible in the defense of liberty, arguing against the positions of Aquinas and other scholastics, and explicitly against the doctrines of Luther and Calvin.

Molina especially held two theological doctrines: the liberty of indifference and the *scientia media*, or middle knowledge of God. In his own philosophy, Gassendi adapted the first and approved of the second.

Molina rejected all previous ideas on free will and its relationship to

---

[4] Étienne Gilson, *La liberté chez Descartes et la théologie* (Paris, 1913), 296–330. There are several scholars who disagree with this identification. See especially Anthony Kenny, "Descartes on the Will," in *Cartesian Studies*, ed. R. J. Butler (Oxford, 1972), 6–7.

[5] His doctrines are expounded in the treatise *Concordia liberi arbitrii cum gratia donis, divini praesciendi, providentia praedestinatione et reprobatione* (Lisbon, 1588; reprint Paris, 1876). All translations by author unless otherwise noted.

[6] On Molina, see Anton C. Pegis, "Molina and Human Liberty," in *Jesuit Thinkers of the Renaissance*, ed. Gerard Smith (Milwaukee, 1939), 76–131; Antonio Queralt, *Libertad Humana en Luis de Molina* (Granada, 1977); and Freddoso's introduction to Molina's *On Divine Foreknowledge (Part 4 of the* Concordia), translated with an Introduction and Notes by Alfred J. Freddoso (Ithaca, 1988), 1–81.

God, from Augustine onward, because he felt they all retained an unacceptable element of determinism. As Gassendi would do a half-century later, Molina distinguished different kinds of freedom.

Even though all Catholic theologians believed that liberty meant freedom from coercion or constraint, many accepted the coexistence of freedom and causal necessity. From this outlook, free actions included not only willing and spontaneous ones, but also those driven by natural necessity. As long as someone or something follows its own nature, it is considered to be free, in both the natural world and human actions.[7] The Oratorians, Dominicans, Jansenists, and others, as well as the Protestants, accepted the idea that determination by necessity—that is, by the love of God or sin—does not destroy human freedom.

But Molina argued that this view of freedom left no power of choice to the individual, and that it characterized boys, madmen, and beasts as well as rational souls.[8] This "sort of spontaneity is not unlike that which is found in a mule being led by a halter in one or another direction," Molina asserted, "it destroys the choice's freedom and without a doubt effects in it a fatal necessity."[9]

In opposition to the more deterministic views, Molina contended that human freedom requires both lack of restraint or physical coercion and lack of determination by any outside force or agent. Indifference is absolutely necessary to freedom. In the case of grace itself, salvation is dependent upon the free action of the individual—an action that God foresees, but in no way determines.[10]

A truly free agent is free, "because having everything requisite to acting, he can act or not act, or he can do one thing, or he can also do the opposite." This is Molina's definition of the liberty of indifference, "Because if simultaneously one may choose indifferently either this, or the opposite, liberty is discerned in that act because it is the kind of act, as they say, which possesses a full and perfect liberty." This definition is repeated elsewhere in the text: "Since a free power is no other thing than to be able to choose indifferently this or that, and not to choose an act, as to be able to choose and not choose the opposite, then there is a liberty not only of contradiction, but also of contriety."[11]

Clearly Gassendi adopted the distinction between true liberty and quasi-liberty, or willingness, from Molina. In the "Ethics," Gassendi

[7] Richard Taylor, "Determinism," in *Encyclopedia of Philosophy*, 2:359–72.
[8] Molina, *Concordia*, 11.
[9] Luis de Molina, *On Divine Foreknowledge*, 136.
[10] Gilson, *Liberté chez Descartes*, 292–308.
[11] Molina, *Concordia*, 471.

stated: "Liberty especially consists in indifference, by means of which the faculty called free can incline or not incline to something (as *they* call the liberty of contradiction), or can incline to one thing as much as it can incline to the opposite, as *they* call the liberty of contriety" (my emphasis). This radical lack of determination is contrasted with voluntary or spontaneous actions,

> Great men are not absent, who think the will is especially free when it is so determined toward one thing, as if it is the highest good, so that it can not be deflected toward another (that is, to evil); because the choice, the pursuit, the enjoyment of this kind of good is highly voluntary and for this reason must be called highly free. But still, I do not know if *they* sufficiently notice the difference between a voluntary action (*spontaneam*), and a free action (*liberam*).[12]

Gassendi was reacting to an entire history of theological debate on free will, including the work of Molina himself. His use of the indefinite pronoun *they* clearly reflected this tradition. Gassendi would have learned the arguments of this controversy during his university education; he studied in the years immediately after a ten-year papal commission finished examining both Molina's doctrines and the charges of heresy levelled by the Dominicans.[13] While Molina's doctrines were approved, allowing the young priest to adopt them, the dispute also taught Gassendi the alternative theories on freedom and determinism, theories going back to the Fathers of the Church.

For example, Saint Augustine had taught that God "has only to control the attractiveness of the object (the *delectatio*) in order for the will to be moved as he foresaw that it would, without his interference in the will's essential (but relative) freedom." This position is causal determinism, and for those theologians who believed the will hopelessly corrupted by the Fall, the inclination to evil was an equally determining cause of human action.[14]

For Gassendi, who made the pursuit of pleasure and the avoidance of pain a central part of his ethical system, ideas that seemed to make the passions determinative had explosive impact. He embraced Molina's theory of indifference because it allowed him to maintain a appetitive ethic without sacrificing a core element of freedom.

---

[12] Gassendi, "Ethics," in *SP, Opera*, 2:822.
[13] On the controversy between Molina, his follower, Francisco Suarez, and the Dominicans, led by Domingo Bañez, see Molina, *On Divine Foreknowledge*, vii–viii.
[14] Miel, *Pascal and Theology*, 57–58.

Nevertheless, human beings are bounded; they live in a universe created and governed by God through his providence and grace. In fact, Gassendi, in his "Physics," advocated a complete theological voluntarism, making the entire created world contingent on God's will. "Truly God is free," argued Gassendi, "since he is neither confined by anything nor imposes any laws on himself which he cannot violate if he pleases. . . . Therefore God . . . is the most free, and he is not bound as he can do whatever . . . he wishes."[15]

The omnipotence of God includes his general providence, by which he rules his creation.[16] While God uses second causes in establishing the course of nature, his continuous and pervasive concourse is necessary for the operation of the world. Gassendi compared the role of God, the source of the created world, to the action of the sun, the source of light.[17]

The idea of God's general concourse is probably taken directly from Molina, although it was a common theological premise. Molina has also used the sun/God analogy to explicate God's relationship to the world. He maintained, moreover, that God's general concourse is usually funneled through specific second causes—although Molina seems to make his second causes somewhat more autonomous than does Gassendi, who argues that God could (but usually does not) dispense with second causes.[18]

In the debate between Molina and his Dominican foes, the question of God's causal influence on the world was focused closely on the relationship between God's providence and human freedom. If God is the continuous causal agent of all that happens, how can this causation be reconciled with human freedom and the liberty of indifference? The question is essentially that of predestination and reprobation: What role, if any, does human freedom of choice play, if humans are saved or damned according to God's providential plan and inexorable decree?

Gassendi spent several pages in the third chapter of Book 3 of the "Ethics" discussing the two alternative explanations of predestination. He was not comfortable dealing with the problem, and his discussion is

---

[15] Quoted in Margaret J. Osler, "Fortune, Fate, and Divination: Gassendi's Voluntarist Theology and the Baptism of Epicureanism," in *Atoms,* Pneuma, *and Tranquillity: Epicurean and Stoic Themes in European Thought,* 160 (Gassendi, "Physics," in *SP, Opera,* 1:309).

[16] Gassendi, "Physics," in *SP, Opera,* 1:330.

[17] Osler, "Fortune, Fate, and Divination," 159.

[18] Ibid. On God's use of second causes, also see Chap. 3 above and Chap. 5 below. On Molina's concept of secondary causation in the natural world, see Molina, *On Divine Foreknowledge,* 18–9, 178–9.

hedged with qualifiers. He summarized the two most pronounced theological positions on predestination: Either "God has damned and saved arbitrarily in the beginning without reference to good deeds and bad," or "God, foreseeing good and bad deeds, saves and damns accordingly." Gassendi favored the second position, because "it allows freedom to man, while it is difficult to see how this first does, since whatever man does is fruitless."[19] In fact, in a very simplified version, the second position is Molina's doctrine of the "scientia media," or middle knowledge of God. By this view, God foresees what a person would do in any conceivable circumstances (free conditional futures), but his conditional knowledge does not determine the action of the individual—whose salvation depends on his freely accepting the grace of God.[20]

According to Gassendi, "God foresaw the state you are now in. With the aid of his sufficient grace and from your own works, you will do either good or evil as he foresaw. Consequently God has predestined or reprobated from this foreseeing." God's grace is necessary to salvation, but like Molina, Gassendi denied that the intrinsic, efficacious grace of God determines human actions, "it is difficult to preserve liberty in those, who, by an efficacious decree of God, are predestined, without any regard to their good works."[21]

Rather, both Gassendi and Molina distinguished between God's sufficient and efficacious grace. God knows what humans will do in a situation, through his divine foreknowledge, and he creates the necessary conditions for meritorious choice and offers his sufficient grace to the individual, who through his free decision to cooperate with God accepts this grace and is saved. Thus, God's providence, grace, and foreknowledge are maintained, without human liberty being diminished.[22]

Even though Gassendi was influenced by Molina's doctrines of the freedom of indifference and the middle knowledge of God, there was, however, a crucial difference in their doctrines of human liberty. Molina had located freedom in the radical independence of the faculty of the will. Gassendi believed the intellect was the faculty which made human freedom possible.

Molina's theory of faculties was influenced by the doctrines of Duns Scotus, who had defended the primacy of the will and who distinguished

[19] Gassendi, "Ethics," in *SP, Opera*, 2:843.
[20] H. Francis Davis, Aidan Williams, Ivo Thomas, Joseph Crehan, eds., *A Catholic Dictionary of Theology*, 3 vols. to date (London, 1962–), 3:293.
[21] Gassendi, "Ethics," in *SP, Opera*, 2:843. Molina, *On Divine Foreknowledge*, 178–80.
[22] On the concept of sufficient grace in Molina, see John A. Mourant, "Scientia Media and Molinism," in *Encyclopedia of Philosophy*, 7:338.

"between the will as simple 'appetitus naturalis,' passively and necessarily directed towards happiness, and the 'voluntas libera,' or the will in its essential freedom. This essential free will has the freedom of contriety (to choose one of two opposing acts) and the freedom of specification (to choose between possible acts and objects.)"[23]

The freedom of contriety became part of the systems of both Molina and Gassendi, but Gassendi did not follow Molina and Duns Scotus in fully rejecting the system of Thomas Aquinas. Aquinas was an intellectualist, who emphasized the importance of the intellect in his theory of human liberty. Gassendi adopted Aquinas's intellectualism, combined it with Molina's doctrine of indifference, based it all on Epicurean epistemology—rejecting all other forms of determinism along the way—and synthesized his own doctrine of human freedom.

Gassendi commended Aquinas's belief that God creates both necessary and free causes, a position Molina also held. Aquinas's basic doctrine of free choice (an expression he uses instead of free will) is found in the *Summa Theologica*, Question 83, Article 1. The response to this question was very important in the formulation of Gassendi's ethical thought. Aquinas argued that,

> Man has free choice, or otherwise counsels, exhortations, commands, prohibitions, rewards, and punishments would be in vain. In order to make this evident, we must observe that some things act without judgment, as a stone moves downwards; and in like manner all things which lack knowledge. And some act from judgment, but not a free judgment; as brute animals. For the sheep, seeing the wolf, judges it a thing to be shunned, from a natural and not a free judgment; because it judges, not from deliberation, but from natural instinct. . . . But man acts from judgment, because by his apprehensive power he judges that something should be avoided or sought. But because this judgment, in the case of some particular act, is not from a natural instinct, but from some act of comparison in the reason, therefore he acts from free judgment and retains the power of being inclined to various things. . . . Now particular operations are contingent, and therefore in such matters the judgment of reason may follow opposite courses, and is not determinate to one. And in that man is rational, it is necessary that he have free choice.[24]

[23] Pegis, "Molina and Human Liberty," 113–20.
[24] St. Thomas Aquinas, *Summa Theologica*, trans. Fathers of the English Dominican Province, 5 vols. (New York, 1948; reprint Westminster, Md., 1981), 1:87.

As this passage shows, Aquinas provided much of Gassendi's normative system. Gassendi paraphrased Aquinas when he wrote, "if our souls
are destitute of liberty. . . . Hence Prudence will be in vain. . . , all com-
mands and exhortations become ridiculous and superfluous. Thus there
is no virtue, no vice, and all praise and condemnation is unwarranted."[25]
Likewise, the analogy of a rock falling downward, in a natural but unfree
action—an image that figured so importantly in Gassendi's psychology—originated in this passage from Saint Thomas. Even the calculus
of pleasure and pain, although developed more specifically by Epicurus,
is implied in Aquinas's analysis of the free choice of the judgment. In
addition, both Aquinas and Gassendi endorsed the liberty of contriety,
the ability to choose the opposite (*potestas ad opposita*). And both characterized this ability to choose the opposite as an indifference in the intellect about the object of choice.[26]

Aquinas also believed that the intellect determines the will: "Now the
first formal principle is universal being and truth, which is the object of
the intellect. And therefore by this kind of motion the intellect moves
the will, as presenting its object to it."[27] Gassendi similarly stressed the
intellect's power over the will: "In a word, that common opinion is from
every point excellent, which holds the will to be a blind power, or one
which tends toward no aim and manifests no repugnance, unless the
intellect carries the flame before it."[28]

But at this point Gassendi started to move away from a strictly Thomistic interpretation of the relationship of will and intellect. The medieval
theologian gave a far wider scope to the will than Gassendi did. While
Aquinas had taught that the intellect was the formal principle of action,
he also believed that the will was the efficient cause of action, and that
since the object of the will was the universal good—in its most absolute
sense, God—the will was the first motivator of action in its pursuit of the
good. Once activated by the object of the will, the intellect chooses the

[25] Gassendi, "Ethics," in *SP, Opera*, 2:831–32.
[26] St. Thomas Aquinas, *Summa Theologica*, 11: 251–65. According to Gilson's analysis of
Aquinas, "The man, on the contrary, acts after having determined by judgment what he
ought to choose or avoid, and this judgment is free because it does not result from a
natural instinct leading in such a case to a determined action; it results from an examination of the reason" (*Liberté chez Descartes*, 249). For Aquinas, the reason can always chose
otherwise, "potestas ad opposita," upon the determination of the intellect (Miel, *Pascal
and Theology*, 59).
[27] Aquinas, *Summa Theologica*, 2:251.
[28] Pierre Gassendi, *Disquisitio metaphysica seu dubitationes et instantiae adversus Renati Cartesii,
Opera*, 3:438. This work will be referred to as *DM* in the notes.

means to a particular good; this choice of means is indeterminate, since humans can know only partial or particular goods.[29]

The difference between Aquinas's position and Gassendi's is clear from the text of Gassendi's "Ethics." He argued that the intellect not only judges the true—its province in scholastic philosophy—but also decides what is good, and in doing so it is the primary faculty. In no real sense does the desire of the will for the good motivate the action of the intellect:

> . . . the Intellect inclines, or establishes, concerning goods and evils, by pronouncing that this is evil, and that this is good; or less good or less evil; and so when the will is said to be averted from one, and inclined to another, this happens to the degree that the judgment is now for one, and now for another; and the will is influenced as the intellect is influenced.[30]

The intellect thus possesses the power of judgment concerning true and false and good and evil. The will is a passive power that simply implements the decision of the intellect.

Molina would deny that Gassendi had saved human freedom by transferring the powers of the will to the intellect. The Spanish theologian had rejected Aquinas because Molina thought if there is an antecedent cause of choice in the intellect, that choice is predetermined.[31] The absolute contingency of the will depends on the absence of all causal determination. How could Gassendi defend himself from the charge that in developing a completely intellectualist account of human choice, he had foundered more deeply in the sea of determinism than even Saint Thomas?

Gassendi found his answer by making the intellect indifferent. He certainly agreed with Aquinas that the intellect must choose the true if it knows the true, just as the will must choose what the intellect presents to it as good. Gassendi wrote: "although the intellect is indifferent, so that it follows one or another judgment, still it is not indifferent, so that it leaves a manifest truth to follow one less true. . . . Thus it may never happen, that the assent of the intellect, having been made by experience or reason, will change unless weightier reasons and more excellent experiences are perceived."[32]

[29] Ralph McInerny, *Ethica Thomistica: The Moral Philosophy of Thomas Aquinas* (Washington, D.C., 1982), 63–78.
[30] Gassendi, "Ethics," in *SP, Opera*, 2:823.
[31] Pegis, *Molina and Human Liberty*, 113, 117.
[32] Gassendi, "Ethics," in *SP, Opera*, 2:824.

This being the case, how can error, and with it lack of determination, creep in? "Sometimes the intellect leaves the true for the false," Gassendi contended, "but that which moves the intellect is the appearance of truth."[33] We can be misled by the appearance of truth, and the reason that the false can seem to be true is that we are dependent on our senses for all knowledge.

The empiricist epistemology that Gassendi adopted from Epicurus allowed a far greater range to error, and thus freedom, than even Saint Thomas would have permitted. Although Aquinas too felt that our knowledge was based on sense perception and operations of the intellect using the data of sense, the medieval philosopher accepted the reality of substantial forms and first principles. Since Gassendi felt all knowledge was at best probable, and that we can never know essences, he repudiated any doctrine that seemed to admit of any kind of evident knowledge. Thus he avoided the trap of causal necessity, which Molina felt destroyed the doctrine of free choice in Aquinas's system, without embracing Aquinas's doctrine of the will.

Molina had argued that the will is so absolutely free that it can even choose the object presented as less good.[34] His concept of the liberty of indifference was more encompassing than Gassendi's, and he seemed not to be bothered by the fact that error, while being necessary to freedom, also could result in sin and damnation. Certainly, he did not blame God for this consequence of freedom: "But you should not infer that He is in any way a cause of sins; for as far as their fault and defectiveness are concerned, sins are traced back to created free choice alone as to their cause."[35]

Molina was satisfied with this solution, but Gassendi was less sanguine. He asked why God could not have made all men so that they would have delighted to cooperate with God's grace, and thus be saved. God could have made the enabling conditions for knowledge, and consequently salvation, more possible for human beings, within a providential system that allowed for human participation in attaining salvation, even at the possible expense of their freedom. But it seems that God has created a universe where due to a lack in their natures—the natures made by God—some humans are ultimately damned: "Man accomplishes things only through grace, but it is in his choice to seek grace or not. . . . This does not answer the question of why God destined some men to glory

---

[33] Ibid., 825.
[34] Queralt, *Libertad Humana*, 125.
[35] Molina, *On Divine Foreknowledge*, 179.

and some to dishonor or why he has allowed them to misunderstand the appearance of things and thus do wrong, although they would willingly do right. This remains a divine mystery."[36]

In the last analysis, the problem of salvation and damnation becomes an epistemological puzzle. Sin is directly related to error. If we knew correctly, we would not choose the wrong, and we would be saved. Gassendi was anxious and perturbed by this problem, and the result was a definite ambivalence in his attitude toward freedom and spontaneity, an unease that occasionally manifests itself in his writing:

> It is agreed then, while we live, we are foolish. The intellect and the will cannot be constant, but can mistake the good for the bad. It is only in the afterlife that indifference of this kind will end, because in it the Highest Good is known and recognized clearly; nor can anything more true occur to the intellect, nor anything better to the will, which might deflect it, and thus it adheres most constantly and invariably, and by the highest necessity and willingness [*libentia*].[37]

Gassendi and Descartes on Error and Sin

In dealing with the problem of error—or its theological counterpart, sin—Gassendi not only commented on his theological predecessors, but also battled the philosophical giant of his own time, René Descartes. Their relationship can be captured in the two epithets with which they addressed each other: "mind" and "flesh." Descartes was the supreme example of the rationalist school, while Gassendi trumpeted the empiricist cause. Inevitably, they collided.

There was no reciprocity of influence between Gassendi and Descartes; whatever Gassendi gained from the debate came from philosophic antagonism rather than agreement.[38] Marjorie Grene argues that Gassendi was one of Descartes's most perceptive critics, and she gives seven examples of their profound disagreement, extending from their different attitudes toward humanism, the degree of their skepticism and

---

[36] Gassendi, "Ethics," in *SP, Opera,* 2:844.

[37] Ibid., 2:825.

[38] The following studies analyze Gassendi's relationship with Descartes: René Pintard, "Descartes et Gassendi," in *Travaux du IXe Congrès de Philosophie—Congrès Descartes II* (Paris, 1937); Bernard Rochot, "Les vérités éternelles dans la querelle entre Descartes et Gassendi," *Revue philosophique de la France et l'étranger* 141 (1951):288–98, and "Gassendi et la 'logique' de Descartes," *Revue philosophique de la France et de l'étranger,* 80 (1955): 300–308; Olivier René Bloch, "Gassendi critique de Descartes," *Revue philosophique de la France et de l'étranger,* 91 (1966), 217–36.

their attitude toward certainty and the possibility of reaching essential knowledge, to the relationship they posited between essence and existence. Grene's analysis is fine, but as she readily admits she is dependent on Lynn Joy and Bloch for her understanding of Gassendi, whom she has not read extensively. Consequently, like theirs, her discussion of the controversy lacks a theological and ethical dimension.[39]

Margaret Osler, on the other hand, argues that the fundamental difference between Gassendi and Descartes was that Descartes was an theological intellectualist and Gassendi was a voluntarist. Descartes's realist ontology depended on his conception of God's creation of necessary truths which were necessary because of God's immutability. Gassendi's nominalism and empiricism, on the contrary, rested on God's will, which integrated an element of complete contingency into the created universe. There are no necessary truths because of God's absolute power.[40] While my study of Gassendi begins with human freedom, and its relationship to a probabilistic epistemology, Osler starts from God's action and its consequences for the creation. The two views are complementary, and differ largely in emphasis. It should be noted also that when I refer to Gassendi as an intellectualist I mean the emphasis he placed on the human intellect; in terms of the divine, he emphasized the will.

Gassendi's critique of Descartes's doctrine of error, and the development of his own theory of error, based on a different theory of the faculties, had implications for Gassendi's concept of human freedom, itself a comment on the problem of God's relationship to humankind. Relevant here is Gassendi's reaction to what he thought Descartes was saying, rather than what the latter might have actually maintained. Descartes himself was in no way influenced by Gassendi.[41]

[39] Marjorie Grene, *Descartes* (Minneapolis, 1985), 139–68. Henri Gouhier is another Cartesian scholar who considers Gassendi at length, *La pensée metaphysique de Descartes* (Paris, 1962).

[40] Osler, "Providence, Divine Will, and the Theological Background to Gassendi's Views on Scientific Knowledge," 549–60; "Eternal Truths and the Laws of Nature: The Theological Foundations of Descartes' Philosophy of Nature," *Journal of the History of Ideas* 46 (1985), 349–362, and *Divine Will and the Mechanical Philosophy*, 153–70. Osler's interpretation of Descartes differs from most other commentators. See, for example, Amos Funkenstein, *Theology and the Scientific Imagination from the Middle Ages to the Seventeenth Century* (Princeton, 1986), 117, 179–92, who emphasizes the voluntaristic content of Descartes's thought.

[41] The literature on Descartes is vast. I am most interested in the problem of error and the concept of free will in Cartesian thought. These topics are treated most fully in the following recent scholarship: Anthony Kenny, "Descartes on the Will," 1–31; E. M. Curley, "Descartes, Spinoza, and the Ethics of Belief," in *Spinoza: Essays in Interpretation* (La Salle, Ill., 1975), 164–67; Bernard Williams, *Descartes: The Project of Pure Enquiry* (Hamondsworth,

Gassendi and Descartes shared much in common. Both were Copernicans and proponents of the new science. They were equally adamant
in their desire for tranquillity and political noninvolvement. They both
advocated forms of corpuscularianism, although Descartes did not accept the notion of a void. Still, Descartes borrowed some of his ideas
from atomism, particularly the concept of circular vortices, which figured in the system of Democritus.[42] Descartes and Gassendi agreed that
the initial creation and subsequent functioning of the world is due to
God's action.

The two philosophers probably did not meet until the late 1640s, but
they knew of each other's work from at least 1637. At that time, they
became involved in their first altercation, when Descartes neglected to
acknowledge Gassendi's work on the perihelion of the sun.[43] But there
was little contact until the spring of 1641, when Descartes asked their
mutual friend, Mersenne, to circulate the manuscript of the *Meditations*
among the philosophically able of his friends in order to elicit comments and objections.[44] Mersenne quickly complied with Descartes's request, writing an objection himself, and soliciting comments from
Gassendi and Hobbes, among others. These various opinions were
printed at the end of the 1641 edition of the *Meditations* as the "Objections," with Descartes's replies following. Gassendi wrote the fifth set of
objections. Descartes's reply to Gassendi was particularly bitter, evoking
a heated response in his usually gentle adversary, and provoking comment in the intellectual world of the time.[45]

The "Fifth Objections" were completed by May 1641. By October
1641, Gassendi was once again working on his Epicurean philosophy.
At the same time, he must have been writing his "Instances," or Doubts,
a lengthy response to Descartes and an elaboration of his original objections. The "Fifth Objections," Descartes's "Responses," and Gassendi's
"Instances" together formed the *Disquisitio metaphysica*, which was completed by March 1642, but not published until two years later.[46] The

---

1978), 163–83; Margaret Dualer Wilson, *Descartes* (London, 1978), 139–50; David M.
Rosenthal, "Descartes on the Will," in *Essays on Descartes' Meditations* (Berkeley, 1986),
405–32.
42 Thomas S. Kuhn, *The Copernican Revolution* (New York, 1957, 1959), 238–40.
43 Sortais, *Philosophie moderne*, 2:11–5, gives a detailed biographical account of their relationship.
44 Descartes to Mersenne, November 11, 1640, and March 4, 1641, in Mersenne, *Correspondance*, 9:232–34, 530–32.
45 For reactions to this controversy, see ibid., 10:728–29; 11:50.
46 On the dating of these works, see Craig Brush's introduction to his translation of por-
tions of the *Disquisitio* in *Selected Works*, 153.

Instantia, or Doubt, directed against Descartes's Fourth Meditation contains many ideas that are found in Book 3 of the "Ethics."[47]

Gassendi and Descartes disagreed most vehemently on epistemological issues. In the introductory letter to the "Fifth Objections," Gassendi commended Descartes's aim of proving the existence of God and the immortality of the soul. He then added, "And so I advance these arguments . . . not against the things themselves that you undertook to prove, but against your method and the strength of your proofs."[48] In short, Gassendi believed that Descartes's method of systematic doubt contributed nothing to knowledge of essences, and he rejected the idea that inferences from mental concepts could lead to knowledge about what really exists.

Descartes believed that he could use his method of systematic doubt to reveal clear and evident truth. For Descartes, the only evident knowledge is what the thinking being discovers in himself and then applies to external things, its validity being guaranteed by the fact that God is not a deceiver.[49] Gassendi's empiricist response was that "all ideas seem to be adventitious—to proceed from things which exist outside the mind and come under one of our senses."[50]

Gassendi argued that it was absurd for Descartes to suggest that anyone could divest himself of all prejudices engendered by prior perceptions, or that the attempt to do so was even worthwhile.[51] In fact, this method of inquiry would divorce us from God: "Furthermore, you say not only that 'the senses hinder the mind in many ways,' but also that 'they do not help in any way to grasp ideas of God and the mind,' you

---

[47] Bloch has shown that Chap. 1 of Bk. 3 of the "Ethics" ("Quid libertas, seu liberum arbitrium?") "reprise en substance, ou pour une part littéralement" several pages of the Instances written against Descartes in 1641 (*DM, Opera,* 3:367–71) and reproduces "du reste purement et simplement un passage des *Animadversiones* de 1649, pour lesquelles il doit été redigé specialement, ou tout au moins, sans doute, postérieurement à la *Disquisitio*" (*Philosophie de Gassendi,* 64).

[48] Gassendi, *Selected Works,* 158 (*DM,* in *SP, Opera,* 3:273).

[49] See Willis Doney, *Eternal Truths and the Cartesian Circle* (New York, 1987) for a list of the most important articles published on these themes in the last twenty-five years. Gassendi was the first critic to point out the circularity of Descartes's argument about clear and distinct ideas.

[50] Gassendi, "Fifth Set of Objections," in Descartes, *Philosophical Writings of Descartes,* 2:195 (*AT,* 7: 279–80). *AT* refers to René Descartes, *Oeuvres de Descartes,* ed. Charles Adam and Paul Tannery, 12 vols. (Paris: J. Vrin, 1964–76), the standard text of Descartes's works. The reference to *AT* follows the citation from *Philosophical Writings.*

[51] Bloch argues that Gassendi, in rejecting the Cogito and Descartes's entire theory of knowledge, is repudiating the "intuition intellectuelle, la saisie d'une essence par l'intermédiaire de la pure apprehension intérieure de la conscience" (*Philosophie de Gassendi,* 123).

seem to be accusing all wisdom, both divine and human, which urges us
to use our sight so that we may rise from the perfections observed in
things to the understanding of the perfections of God."[52]

Thus, observation of the creation is the best way to know the creator.
Not surprisingly, Gassendi is the only one of Descartes's critics to defend
final causation and the argument from design against Descartes's attack
in the Fourth Meditation:

> it is wholly appropriate and laudable to consider the end . . . since either
> the thought that the universe is uncaused and governs itself or the
> thought it was made by chance and is ruled by the same chance could
> occur to someone, then in what way will the conviction arise either that
> the world was really created by some cause or that it is governed and ruled
> by some moderator unless we observe the wisdom with which all things in
> it are disposed?[53]

That is, a passive, contemplative glance at the universe would not necessarily lead to a belief in a creator God. Instead it might result in the
belief in an autonomous, self-directed, and eternal nature or a universe
ruled by chance. Only an investigation of the teleological characteristics
of the world reveals its cause. Thus, empiricism is inseparable from the
search for and belief in the existence of God.

Gassendi's embrace of teleology was not the only ground for his rejection of Descartes's image of clear and evident ideas, supposedly war-
ranted by God. First of all, he asked, how do we know that God will not
deceive us? Who can penetrate the divine mind? Furthermore, in the
elaboration of his critique in the "Instances," he questioned Descartes's
claim that we have in ourselves the power from God not to err, and thus
the ability to perceive the truth. If God has given us a fallible faculty, the
knowledge gained through that faculty can never be infallible.[54]

Descartes himself first emphasized the problem of error. He argued
in the Fourth Meditation that God is not a deceiver; therefore, he must
have given man all the abilities he needs not to err; consequently, "I
should . . . never make a mistake."[55] Obviously, sometimes human be-

---

[52] Gassendi, *Selected Works*, 240 (*DM*, in *SP*, *Opera*, 3:362).
[53] Ibid., 234 (*DM*, in *SP*, *Opera*, 3:361).
[54] Ibid., 230 (*DM*, in *SP*, *Opera*, 3: 359–60). Ira Wade remarks about the difference between Gassendi and Descartes, "Thus, while Descartes hold to the unity of systematic
thought, Gassendi is more inclined to support the erring, unsystematic, free-thinking
mind" (*The Intellectual Origins of the French Enlightenment* [Princeton, 1971], 219).
[55] Descartes, *Philosophical Writings*, 42 (*AT*, 7:61).

ings are mistaken. It is imperative at this point for Descartes to argue that error is not an unavoidable burden. If we are doomed to err, our perceptions of clear and distinct ideas would be false, and it would not be possible to construct an evident science.

Descartes had many suggestions to account for the existence of error. It is, in the first place, a product of our finite being, reflecting that part of us which partakes in nothingness, rather than God. As such, it has no positive reality and cannot be attributed to God. In any case, Descartes argued, all of this is a divine mystery impenetrable to man. What may seem a lack in an individual may in fact contribute to the perfection of the whole.[56]

Gassendi had only one reply to all of these arguments, which he reiterated constantly throughout the "Fifth Objections": "The difficulty, you see, is not so much why God did not give you a greater faculty of knowledge, but why he gave you a faculty subject to error. The question is not why the supreme craftsman did not want to bestow all the perfections on all his works, but why he wished to bestow imperfections on some of them?"[57]

Descartes refused to accept Gassendi's criticism as valid. He elaborated his theory of error in the Reply to the Fifth Objection.[58] According to Descartes, error does not exist in the positive faculties God has given us, but rather is the result of the province of the will being infinitely greater than the province of the finite intellect.[59] Error results when the will passes judgments on things the intellect does not fully understand. Thus, error is the product of the interaction of the two faculties, not any lack inherent in them. Furthermore, while human knowledge is different in kind from the divine, human will is similar: "For although God's will is incomparably greater than mine, both in virtue of the knowledge and power that accompany it and make it more firm and efficacious, and also in virtue of its object, in that it ranges over a greater number of items, nevertheless, it does not seem any greater than mine when considered as will in the essential and strict sense."[60]

Like God's will, human will is free because there is no restraint on its

[56] Ibid., 38–39 (*AT*, 7:55–56).
[57] Gassendi, "Fifth Set of Objections," in Descartes, *Philosophical Writings*, 217 (*AT*, 7:312–33).
[58] Descartes, *Philosophical Writings*, 258–60 (*AT*, 7:376–379).
[59] The relationship of the intellect and the will and their role in human freedom was an integral part of the ethics part of the philosophy curriculum in the seventeenth-century university, where both Gassendi and Descartes initially were exposed to these themes. See Brockliss, *French Higher Education*, 220–22.
[60] Descartes, *Philosophical Writings*, 40–41 (*AT*, 7:57–58).

ability to assent and deny. Error itself will result when the will, indifferent because of a paucity of knowledge, makes a judgment about something. Indifference itself is not a mark of liberty, as some have urged, but rather "a defect in knowledge or a kind of negation." Descartes believed that human liberty consists primarily in clearly perceiving the good and the true, either through one's natural light or through God's grace, and freely following this as the end of man. In this case, liberty is the absence of indifference, not the mark of its presence. Descartes described the liberty of indifference as "the lowest grade of freedom" and the source of error—because a person errs when the will is not determined by clear and distinct ideas, and assents to confused perceptions rather than suspending judgment.[61]

Gassendi believed that Descartes was a determinist. But modern scholars usually consider Descartes an advocate of free will, or "indetermination," because he believed that man's will is utterly free "with respect to the voluntary operations of the mind." In his *Meditations* he described such freedom as infinite, meaning that no limitation is put on the mind's power of choice."[62] Freedom, however, is confined to choice in the physical world. When it becomes a question of freedom of action in relation to God and the choice or avoidance of a known good, a person is determined in his actions by constraining factors. In scholastic terms, he is determined by necessity. God himself does not make a human being do something, rather he does it out of love of God. In this sense he is determined by God.

Moreover, even in this world, clear and distinct ideas limit our choices because they remove all possibilities of indifference or prevarication in the operations of the faculties of the mind. In Gassendi's terms, this is causal determinism, but Descartes believed that men are most free when they are most determined by their clear and distinct ideas: "For if I always saw clearly what was true and good, I should never have to deliberate about the right judgement or choice; in that case, although I should be wholly free, it would be impossible for me to ever be in a state of indifference."[63]

---

[61] Ibid., 40–41 (*AT*, 7:58–60). On Descartes and the liberty of indifference, see Wilson, *Descartes*, 140, and Curley, "Ethics of Belief," 166. Kenny, "Descartes on the Will," in contradiction to other interpretations, believes Descartes does associate free will with the liberty of indifference, but also thinks it consists only of the liberty of spontaneity (18).

[62] Richard Taylor, "Determinism," 2:365, and Descartes, *Philosophical Writings*, 40 (*AT*, 7:57).

[63] Descartes, *Philosophical Writings*, 40 (*AT*, 7:58). See Curley, "Ethics of Belief," 165, who writes, "For Descartes deliberately defines freedom in such a way that it will be consistent both with the will being determined by the intellect and with it being determined by

In 1640, Mersenne strongly advised Descartes to modify his doctrine on the liberty of indifference because of the controversy created by the publication of the works of Jansen and Gibieuf. Gilson argues that it was obvious to anyone reading the *Meditations* in 1640 or 1641 that Descartes was antagonistic to Molinist theology.[64] It would have been equally obvious to anyone reading Gassendi's "Ethics" and his critique of Descartes in the 1640s that Gassendi was influenced by, and sympathetic to, some of the doctrines of the sixteenth-century Jesuit defender of human liberty.

Gassendi had a different conception of error and the indifference of the will than Descartes. The empiricist began with his belief that the intellect is the dominating faculty in choice and judgment, and the will merely follows its decisions.[65] The will must always follow the understanding, remaining itself indifferent until the understanding perceives some reason to move it. Once these reasons are perceived, judgment will be passed "with a certain amount of insecurity and hesitation." The will can never decide on an opposite conclusion unless the understanding first apprehends reasons for this other conclusion. Even so, the judgment is often wrong because of its fallibility. Error is not in the incorrect use of free will, declared Gassendi, "so much as in the disparity between our judgement and the thing which is the object of judgement. And it seems that error arises when our intellectual apprehension of the thing does not correspond with the way the thing really is."[66]

In his Reply, Descartes charged Gassendi with making the will follow the determination of the intellect: "You refuse to allow that the will can be directed to anything which is not determined by the intellect." If the will were totally dependent on the intellect, which is dependent on sense impressions, we would not only be unable to guard against error, but we would be unable to refrain from persisting in error. There could be nothing like free will which could turn us aside from error.[67]

Descartes believed we may always wish for something we do not under-

---

God. Freedom in judging does not consist in our being able to either affirm of deny, but in our being so moved to affirming and denying that we aware of no external force which determines us. When we perceive something clearly and distinctly we are drawn irresistibly but freely to believe it." This is precisely the same as Gassendi's understanding of Descartes.

[64] Gilson, *Liberté chez Descartes*, 320–21, 356.

[65] On the place of Gassendi's concept of the will and intellect and their relationship to the soul, see Margaret J. Osler, "Baptizing Epicurean Atomism: Pierre Gassendi on the Immortality of the Soul," in *Religion, Science, and World-View*, 172–73.

[66] Gassendi, "Fifth Set of Objections," in *Philosophical Writings*, 220 (*AT*, 7:317).

[67] Ibid., 260 (*AT*, 7:378).

stand. He gives the example of desiring an apple that has been poisoned, and deciding it is a suitable food because of its pleasant qualities. One passes a judgment because of pressing desires, not a cold examination of the facts. Once again, error in this case is not in the faculties themselves, but in their faulty interaction. For Descartes, Gassendi's theory of the faculties would destroy human liberty: "O flesh, do not seem to attend to the actions the mind performs within itself. You may be unfree, if you wish; but I am certainly very pleased with my freedom since I experience it within myself. What is more, you have produced no arguments to attack it, but merely bald denials."[68]

Gassendi was deeply offended at Descartes's imputation that he denied human liberty, and in the "Instances" of the *Disquisitio metaphysica*, replying to the Fourth Meditation, he once again defended the primacy of the intellect over the will. Gassendi described in great detail how every choice we make is based on a prior apprehension or enunciation of apprehensions by the intellect. Thus, when we decide an object is animate, it is because we have seen it move from place to place, and we know from prior observations that the mark of an animate body is the power of self-movement.[69] In a case where the will is involved, as for example when we decide to eat a fruit, we do so because the understanding perceives that the fruit is sweet, and is therefore desirable. The act of will is the result of judgment but does not contribute to judgment.

In another case, after perceiving the presence of poison in the fruit, the intellect, because it knows that poison is harmful, decides to reject the fruit although it is sweet. However, there may be even another operation of the intellect, whereby it realizes from other previous knowledge that the poison in the fruit can "deliver one from intolerable suffering." The intellect therefore reasons, "That which can deliver one from intolerable suffering, although it is poisoned, must be sought; this fruit can do it, therefore it is necessary to take it." Once the intellect has made a judgment, an act of will results: "the will does not make choice of the poison rather than being turned away from it if the intellect has not previously judged that to the poison is joined the deliverance from evils, and that it is necessary to seek a lesser evil, that is to consider it a good because it delivers from a greater evil."[70] Clearly, this analysis of the relationship of will and intellect contributed to the idea of the calculation of pleasure and pain found in the "Ethics," or perhaps was even inspired by it.

[68] Ibid., 259 (*AT*, 7:377).
[69] Gassendi, *DM*, *Opera*, 3:367.
[70] Ibid., 3:368.

Gassendi then elevated his discussion of error into the moral context: "The intellect apprehends how a thing is true in its own terms, but also how it is esteemed to be good by someone else. To the extent that the intellect judges something to be good, so it is desired by the will."[71] Thus, we judge the appearance of what is true and what is good through a perception of the intellect: goodness and truth fuse through the operation of the cognitive faculty. Ultimately, it is the free intellect that evaluates the worth of a thing and directs the will to desire it.

But both the will and the intellect deal in possible rather than absolute truth and goodness. Gassendi sees an innumerable field of probabilities available to the intellect, where the degree of truth and goodness varies but is still somewhat "similar" to absolute truth and goodness. The intellect will never reject the more probable for the less probable truth, nor will it deviate from the more good to the less good. But we are the perceiving subjects, and we control our perceptions to the degree that we can reevaluate our judgments or redirect our attention. In this sense, we are masters of ourselves and our environment.[72]

Two key passages by Descartes and Gassendi show that both philosophers were aware of the probabilistic tradition, and its links with rhetorical concepts and moral decision. In the Fourth Meditation, Descartes stated, "There is no need for me to be impelled both ways in order to be free; on the contrary, the more I am inclined one way—either because I clearly understand it under the aspect of truth and goodness, or because God has so disposed my inmost consciousness—the more freely do I choose that way."[73]

In this passage, Descartes used the Latin phrase *in utramque partem* in the first sentence, "to be impelled both ways," *in utramque partem ferre posse*. This usage evokes Gassendi's similar statement in the "Ethics": The soul "is constituted like the place where two roads meet, and it is placed as if in the middle of two ways, and it is indifferent to both ways, because it is free." In the Latin, the soul is *adeo ut, a priore deflectans, constituatur quasi in bivio a & ad utramque partem indifferens sit; quod sane est liberum esse.*[74] The language here suggests that Gassendi was responding to Descartes directly, at least in this part of the "Ethics."

Thus, both Gassendi and Descartes connected rhetorical forms of reasoning with the liberty of indifference, whether they believed indiffer-

---

[71] Ibid.
[72] Ibid., 3:370–71.
[73] Descartes, *Philosophical Writings*, 40 (*AT*, 7:57–8).
[74] Gassendi, "Ethics," in *SP, Opera*, 2:838–39. See Chap. 6 below for more on this analogy.

ence was necessary for free choice or not. Descartes had rejected the
rhetorical tradition explicitly in his philosophy from his earliest writings.
Henri Gouhier has argued that Descartes repudiated both rhetoric and
dialectic, which he paired together.[75] Nevertheless, it has been argued
that rhetoric, which Descartes studied at La Fleche, pervaded the philosopher's work in both his use of metaphor and his eloquence and even
as a philosophic tool.[76]

Consequently, it may be that his use of the phrase *in utramque partem*
was self-conscious, as it certainly was with Gassendi, so that his statement
was not only limited to the denial of the liberty of indifference, but was
also a negative comment on the probabilistic tradition itself. He used a
metaphor dialectically to establish his evidential philosophy. The irony
here is that Gassendi fastened on just this phrase to work out the content
of his liberty of motion, where probable knowledge allows us the freedom to move in either of two ways.

Gassendi, in his debate with Descartes, did finally admit that it is possible to reach absolute knowledge, or movement in one direction only,
once we reach a different state of being. His ambivalent attitude toward
ultimate determination is as apparent in the *Disquisitio* as it is in the
"Ethics." The blessed in heaven have a clear knowledge of the sovereign
good, and know God: When this is the case, all indifference vanishes,
because the intellect cannot conceive anything more true, or the will
love anything better. Even in this supreme instance, it is the intellect
that determines the will to love the good. Gassendi acknowledged that
this kind of determination is not a forced or constrained determination:

[75] Gouhier, *Pensée metaphysique,* 95–103. On Descartes's use of rhetoric, see Thomas M.
Carr, *Descartes and the Resilience of Rhetoric: Varieties of Cartesian Rhetorical Theory* (Carbondale,
Ill., 1990), 28–32. Carr argues that Descartes did not seek for *scientia* in every field of
knowledge. In particular, in moral matters, he was content with the probable. If this is so,
differences in epistemologies and ontologies would not make an impact on Gassendi and
Descartes's ethical theories. My argument is that they do.

[76] Pierre-Alain Cahné, *Un autre Descartes: Le Philosophe et son langage* (Paris, 1980), 96. See
Carr, *Resilience of Rhetoric,* 1–2, for a historiographical account of this question. Carr himself makes the argument that Descartes invents a "notion of attention": "Descartes'
method leaves room for rhetoric if it is considered not in terms of its outward form—the
geometric chains of proof—but in terms of its vivifying core, the notion of attention.
Attention enjoys a privileged status in Descartes' epistemology. It unites the mind's two
chief faculties (the will and the understanding) as the will focuses the gaze of the mind's
eye ever more sharply on ideas perceived in the understanding. The process of distinguishing clear and distinct ideas leads to the judgment of *evidence,* in which the unity of the
mind's active and passive dimensions as a single thinking substance is affirmed" (4). Descartes is then able to develop a "rhetoric of philosophic discourse to get from self-evident
to evident to others" (31–32). This is an interesting interpretation and contributes to the
idea that evident knowledge, once achieved, results in causal determination.

It is conceived rather as entirely made of content, of accord, and of agreement, and it is consequently especially spontaneous, most sweet, and most desirable; such a necessity [of determination] appears therefore to many people as liberty and even as the most high liberty, but it still seems one can rather call it "libentia" or what one wished most willingly. . . . It is still not doubtful that all notions of liberty seem to disappear if one suppresses indifference.

Still, if we are led to the true either by God or by natural knowledge, "liberty itself must be less considered as diminished as brought to its finished perfection, so that a tendency is produced toward the true and not toward the appearance, and toward the greatest good rather than toward the least."[77] Thus, error is routed when we perceive the true and the good; epistemological uncertainty disappears when we are saved. Gassendi seems to force himself to the conclusion that this is the uttermost form of freedom, rather than its opposite; clearly he preferred liberty in his usual sense of the freedom of indifference.

For Gassendi the essence of free will is the ability to be indifferent, to be able to make mistakes. Error, therefore, which is an evil in itself, seems to be a good taken in the perspective of the whole man. Error is a positive and necessary part of man's being. This paradoxical reality is in fact God's gift to man. It is what makes human beings human, for if man were determined in the Cartesian sense, or in the Augustinian sense, or even in the Thomistic sense, either by the natural light or by grace, he would cease to be human because a human must be free. But freedom as an arbitrary act of will, as Molina would have it, would sacrifice man's rational faculty.

The answer is the indifference of the intellect, but it is an answer that fails fully to satisfy: The Catch-22 quality of human liberty remains a mystery only God can fully understand. But another system popular in Gassendi's time tried to explain God's actions and human destiny. For many people, astrology provided the answers theologians had failed to find about the ultimate relationship of human and divine interaction. Gassendi further articulated his ethical doctrines in a response to a system he considered dangerous, impious, and absurd.

---

[77] Gassendi, *DM*, in *SP, Opera*, 3:371.

CHAPTER FIVE

The Astrological Threat
to Freedom

Tommaso Campanella, the Spanish natural philosopher who warned Gassendi about the dangers of Epicureanism's denial of divine providence, had what he considered excellent evidence of divine design. Campanella was deeply involved in astrological magic and believed that the movement of the sun, according to God's plan, heralded the approach of the millennium in the near future.[1]

In the Middle Ages and the Renaissance, the action of the stars was often linked to God's providential design.[2] The prominent English astrologer William Lilly began his 1647 treatise on astrology by advising the neophyte never to "neglect that Divine Providence, by whose all-seeing order and appointment all things heavenly and earthly have their constant motion."[3] If God worked in mysterious ways, the stars seemed a plausible avenue, and many astrologers found a ready audience for their services among the great of their time. Campanella himself advised Pope Urban VIII and Louis XIII, and during the English Civil War, Lilly found favor with the Parliamentary forces.[4]

---

[1] On Campanella and astrology, see D. P. Walker, *Spiritual and Demonic Magic* (London, 1958; reprint Notre Dame, 1975), 203–12.

[2] Agrippa, a sixteenth-century thinker and former proponent of astrology, remarked in a denunciation of judicial astrology that "it teacheth moreover to foretell, to call backe, to avoide or flee the endes of all thinges that maie happen, and the secrete disposition of Gods providence" (Henry Cornelius Agrippa, *Of the Vanitie and Uncertaintie of Artes and Science*, trans. James Sanford [1569, 1575], ed. Catherine M. Dunn [Northridge, Calif., 1974], 99).

[3] William Lilly, *An Introduction to Astrology* (1647; reprint Hollywood, Calif., 1972), 10.

[4] Lilly's career is discussed in Nicolas H. Nelson, "Astrology, *Hudibras*, and the Puritans," *Journal of the History of Ideas* 37 (1976): 522–23.

Gassendi accepted the idea that God might express his power through the stars or other kinds of suprahuman influences, like angels or even demons. But he denied that astrologers could, therefore, penetrate into God's plan and predict the future.[5] Human fallibility and human freedom precluded knowing what might come; human fate or fortune was beyond astrological divination.

When Gassendi attacked astrology for undermining human liberty, he echoed centuries of prior accusation, going back to Saint Augustine. Christian theologians had long contended that determination by the stars controverted human liberty and ethical choice, as well as implicitly diminishing God's omnipotence.[6] The perceived threat of astrology increased during the Renaissance, according to Eugenio Garin, who writes, "in the astrological problem (and in that of magic) is reflected the exasperating central difficulty of the new humanist culture: if human science is to be valid, iron laws of nature are necessary; but if universal and necessary laws of nature exist, how is free and creative human activity possible?"[7]

The power and pervasiveness of astrology presented a direct challenge to Gassendi's ethical system.[8] Astrology enraged Gassendi for many reasons: it undermined prudence and ethics, it challenged the growing status of physics as a scientific discipline, and it claimed to offer demonstrable knowledge in a probabilistic world. Worst, when the astrologers linked their enterprise to divine actions, they insulted God's prerogatives. Most significantly, Gassendi believed astrology depicted a universe where necessity destroyed all human liberty.

[5] Gassendi, "Physics," in *SP, Opera,* 1:731; "Ethics," in *SP, Opera,* 2:851. Attacks on astrology can be found in three different places in Gassendi's *Opera:* in the "Physics," in *SP,* 1:713–52, at the end of the "Ethics," in *SP,* 2:847–60, and in Book 1 of Gassendi's *Tychonis Brahei, Equitis Dani Astronomorum Coryphaei Vitae,* 5:387–99.

[6] Keith Thomas, *Religion and the Decline of Magic* (New York, 1971), 361. Judicial astrology had been condemned as recently as April 1631, when Urban VIII issued a bull against it. See Lynn Thorndike, *A History of Magic and Experimental Science,* 8 vols. (New York, 1923–58), 7:100.

[7] Garin, *Astrology in the Renaissance,* 26–27.

[8] There has been a great deal of work done on astrology recently. Among the most helpful studies are the following: Keith Thomas, *Religion and the Decline of Magic;* Garin, *Astrology in the Renaissance;* Brian Vickers, ed., *Occult and Scientific Mentalities in the Renaissance* (Cambridge, 1984); Patrick Curry, ed., *Astrology, Science, and Society: Historical Essays* (Woodbridge, 1987), and *Prophecy and Power: Astrology in Early Modern England* (Princeton, 1989); S. J. Tester, *A History of Western Astrology* (Woodbridge, Suffolk, 1987); Richard Kieckhefer, *Magic in the Middle Ages* (Cambridge, 1989). Many of the authors who appear in these volumes address the question of the demarkation of science and magic, or whether astrology was a "pseudo-science" in early modern times. In my discussion, I will limit myself to the way Gassendi perceived astrology and its differences from his conception of science and ethics.

Since antiquity, most astrologers had attempted to deny the deterministic implications of stellar influences, but with limited success. The predictions of astral or natural astrology—which sought to show how the stars affected sublunary occurrences in nature, such as weather and the tides, and how they might influence general human events—were claimed to be probable rather than certain. Nevertheless, as Patrick Curry argues, "The close relation of this astrology to natural philosophy—with its emphasis on causal and law-like determination—is obvious."[9]

While astrologers allowed for an element of contingency in these predictions—for example, regional variations would influence the general effects of the stars—the predictions themselves implied more than mere "weather-forecasts." In the pre-modern age, when events were much more beholden to the exigencies of natural forces, such predictions could affect political and social decisions and actions.[10]

Some astrologers insisted that the forecasts of judicial astrology—which made predictions about the fate of individuals, usually by means of a horoscope or nativity—were highly speculative. The outcome, they argued, could be modified by the character of the person involved or by his foreknowledge of the envisioned event. Divine providence could change the future. Given the complexities of astrological calculations, the prediction itself might be miscalculated.

Ficino, the great Renaissance neo-Platonist and proponent of astrology, was typical in his insistence that astrology did not contradict human freedom. Rather, he argued, it was an aid to free will: "Through the 'election' pertaining to free will celestial things are just so subject to the use of our prudence as plants serve the physician."[11] Thus, "it was a platitude . . . that the stars inclined, but did not compel" in individual cases.[12]

No matter how much the astrologers prevaricated about the necessity imposed on humanity by the positions of the heavens, judicial astrology was repeatedly condemned by the Church because of its deterministic

---

[9] Curry, *Prophecy and Power,* 8.

[10] Thomas, *Religion and the Decline of Magic,* 334. Agrippa remarked, "there is no kinde of men more pestilent to the publicke wealth, than these: which by the starres, by lokinge in handes, by dreames, and such other skilles of divination promise thinges to come" (*Vanitie and Uncertaintie of Artes and Sciences,* 102).

[11] Marsilio Ficino, *Three Books of Life,* ed. and trans. Carol V. Kaske and John R. Clark (Binghamton, N.Y., 1989), 381. Walker, *Spiritual and Demonic Magic,* argues that Pico, Ficino's student, in his condemnation of astrology actually condemned only "superstitious astrology," which denied free will, and not astrology in general (56–57).

[12] Thomas, *Religion and the Decline of Magic,* 135.

implications, while the more general natural astrology was permitted. By the sixteenth and seventeenth centuries, however, the boundaries between natural and judicial astrology had become increasingly unclear. Many opponents of astrology felt that both natural and judicial astrology destroyed contingency, and they rejected the claim that astrology should be viewed as part of natural philosophy.[13] The Italian Aristotelian naturalist Pietro Pompanazzi (1462–1525) particularly demonstrated in his work the dangers of associating astrology and natural philosophy together, with its deleterious implications for free will. Pompanazzi adopted the naturalism of the Stoics concerning fate and freedom and their belief in astrology. He argued that human action is the result of external causes like the stars, and while the will retains some element of freedom, most events are determined by celestial influences.[14]

It was clear by the seventeenth century that the predictability postulated by astrology was similar to the natural necessity of a mechanical universe. Some astrologers even associated their system with the new science; they claimed that their discipline was as much a modern, empirical science as astronomy.[15]

In the "Physics," Gassendi emphasized the element of natural necessity in astrology, which he portrayed as a kind of mechanistic system: "For, the astrologers will have it, that the sidereal bodies . . . when an infant is born, do so act and club their rays together upon him, as that they impress upon him a necessity (nor more nor less) of living in such a condition; of dying at such a time and in such a manner . . . and so of all other accidents in his whole life."[16] Such an interpretation of astrology must have heightened Gassendi's determination to destroy the validity of the entire system. The new natural philosophy of the seventeenth century had to be rescued from the encoiling embrace of astrological determinism.

[13] See Antonio Poppi, "Fate, Fortune, Providence and Human Freedom," in *The Cambridge History of Renaissance Philosophy*, 654–58. Garin, *Astrology in the Renaissance*, also comments on the close links between astrology and natural philosophy in the Renaissance, "If the struggle against a fate determined by the stars seems a valid vindication of man's free action, it is also true that the defenders of the most vigorous determinism show a keen sense of the rationality of natural laws and the unity of nature" (xii). See also Wayne Shumaker, *The Occult Philosophy in the Renaissance* (Berkeley, 1972), 54.

[14] Poppi, "Fate, Fortune, Providence," 655–60.

[15] Nelson, "Astrology, *Hudibras*, and the Puritans," 526–27.

[16] Gassendi, *The Vanity of Judiciary Astrology or Divination by the Stars*, translated by a Person of Quality (London, 1659), 89. This is a contemporary translation of six books of Gassendi's "Physics," in *SP, Opera*, 1:714–52. The translation is quite good and conveys both the sense and feeling of Gassendi's text. Where it is inaccurate, I will substitute my own translation. I have modernized the spelling and some of the punctuation of the 1659 translation.

One of the challenges in attacking astrology was its comprehensiveness. Keith Thomas points out that the very breadth of astrology made it so compelling—it bridged the gap between natural sciences and social sciences in providing an all-embracing explanation of "the baffling variousness of human affairs."[17] To refute such an explanation, Gassendi invoked many of the fundamentals of his philosophical system. Long after his death, he was recognized as one of the most important seventeenth-century opponents of astrology.[18]

Lynn Thorndike has suggested that Gassendi's detailed knowledge of astrology reflected a strong interest in this subject, probably going back to his youth. In the 1620s, Gassendi came under the influence of Peiresc and Mersenne, both of whom regarded astrology with skepticism and, in the case of Mersenne, hostility. Peiresc had printed an attack against astrology by George of Ragusa in 1623. Mersenne had attacked astrology, including Pompanazzi's materialistic system, at length in the *Quaestiones in Genesim* (Paris, 1623), where he both reaffirmed many of the arguments against astrology going back to Giovanni Pico, and anticipated Gassendi's critique, which, Thorndike theorizes, Mersenne also inspired.[19] In his 1623 work, Mersenne declared that astrology was against faith, undermined God's providence, and was antithetical to a belief in human free will: "What is going to happen in the future does not depend on the stars, and especially our freedom does not depend on the stars."[20]

Mersenne denied that the stars are causes of events, although he did concede that they might sometimes, by God's device, be signs of natural events. He found no evidence, through either observation or reason, proving the certain nature of astrology. Mersenne rejected the naturalism of the Renaissance, and in particular the doctrine of the correspondence between the microcosm and the macrocosm. Finally, Mersenne

---

[17] Thomas, *Religion and the Decline of Magic*, 324.

[18] Curry, *Prophecy and Power*, 72; Jacques C. Halbronn, "The Revealing Process of Translation and Criticism in the History of Astrology," in *Astrology, Science and Society*, 212.

[19] Thorndike, *Magic and Experimental Science*, 435–37, 446. Thorndike's treatment of Gassendi is very harsh. While he accurately summarizes Gassendi's arguments, he denies that the Frenchman had any lasting influence or that his own philosophy was free from serious defects. He concludes, Gassendi "sandwiches a skeptical corpuscular philosophy in between slices of superstition and error. This is no doubt due to custom, to the difficulty of shaking off the tradition of the past; and partly to consideration, not entirely unselfish, for his audience. But sometimes it seems due to a lingering interest on his own part in what he rejects or ought to reject, but cannot quite part with" (458). Osler, *Divine Will and the Mechanical Philosophy*, 96–97, argues that Gassendi surely knew Mersenne's work, and particularly targeted Pompanazzi in his own critiques of astrology.

[20] Quoted in Lenoble, *Mersenne*, 130.

sensed the danger of associating physical astronomy and judicial astrology and he sought to distinguish between them strongly, declaring that only astronomy was a true science, and astrology a false "*chimère.*"[21]

Many of these same themes appear in a 1629 letter Gassendi wrote to the Dutch astronomer Henri Reneri. He condemned both natural and judicial astrology, the first because there is no necessary connection between the stars as causes or signs of sublunar events and the events themselves, and the second as an affront to human fortune, religion, and reason.[22]

By 1630, Mersenne had involved Gassendi in an attack against the Christian neo-Platonist Robert Fludd, whose magical system Mersenne and Gassendi found repugnant.[23] While most of Gassendi's treatise against Fludd concerned other issues, at the very end he mentioned astrology. He castigated it as an uncertain discipline relying on ephemerides and astrological toys, rather than on experiment and observation. Consequently, concluded Gassendi, it can provide no knowledge about the physical world, which must come from observation and experiment.[24]

The developed polemic against astrology came in Gassendi's later works, including the *Syntagma*. In Part 4 of the "Ethics," immediately following his discussion of human freedom and God's power, Gassendi turned to the question of divination, which he noted was most vehemently attacked by Epicurus. Gassendi took it as a given that if divination were possible, it would mean that the stars dictated future events without the possibility of future contingents, human freedom would be destroyed.[25]

---

[21] I am dependent on Lenoble for this summary of Mersenne's attitudes toward astrology. See Lenoble, *Mersenne*, 128–31. Thorndike, *Magic and Experimental Science*, also gives an account of Mersenne and astrology, 435–37. See also William L. Hine, "Marin Mersenne: Renaissance Naturalism and Renaissance Magic," in *Occult and Scientific Mentalities in the Renaissance*, 165–76.

[22] Gassendi to Henri Renerius, March 6, 1629, *Parhelia, sive Soles Quatuor spurii, qui circa verum apparerunt Romae anno MDCXXIX. Die XX Martii. Epistola.*, in *Opera*, 3:658–59.

[23] Gassendi's treatise against Fludd was published initially in 1630 in Paris as the *Epistolica exercitatio* and later included in the *Opera* as *Examen Philosophiae Roberti Fluddi Medici, in quo et ad illius Libros adversus R. P. F. Marinum Mersennum Ordinis Minimorum Sancti Francisci de Paula scriptos, respondetur*, 3:213–68. A full analysis of this work is beyond the scope of this book, but it would repay study. Some information on Mersenne and Gassendi's relationship with Fludd can be found in William H. Huffman, *Robert Fludd and the End of the Renaissance* (London, 1988), 62–71. On Fludd, see also Frances A. Yates, *The Rosicrucian Enlightenment* (London, 1972; reprint Boulder, Colo., 1986), and Robert S. Westman, "Nature, Art, and Psyche: Jung, Pauli, and the Kepler-Fludd debate," in *Occult and Scientific Mentalities*, 177–230.

[24] Gassendi, *Examen Philosophiae Fluddi, Opera*, 3:266.

[25] Gassendi, "Ethics," in *SP, Opera*, 2:847.

In the "Physics," Gassendi argued, when astrologers "come to this, that nothing of good and happiness befalls man, but by the disposition and favour of the planets: is anything imaginable more fabulous, more profane? . . . Have they measured with an ell, or weighed in the scales, the forces of the planets . . . to determine the fate of mortals, and their affairs?"[26]

Gassendi, while acknowledging the difference between natural and judicial astrology, discussed them as though they were one and the same. In the introduction to his "Life of Tycho Brahe," Gassendi wrote that the Chaldeans and Egyptians felt that astrology studied both the effects of the stars on the air and on human affairs, and particularly the ways "life is fated" by the positions of the stars.[27] He made a distinction between ways of studying the stars, but it was not between the two branches of astrology. In the "Physics," he argued that the Chaldeans had separated astronomy, "which considers the motions, distance, order, magnitude, light, and other adjuncts of the stars," from astrology, which considers the effects of the stars, ascribing "certain prodigious virtues to heavenly bodies over inferior ones, as if their influences were fatal and inevitable."[28]

In short, Gassendi did not believe the claims of the astrologers that their doctrine did not contradict the doctrine of human liberty. He readily conceded that astrology was full of conjecture, but this did not soften its fundamental characteristic—the prediction of necessary causes for general and specific events. In his condemnation, Gassendi went beyond the Catholic Church itself, blasting both natural and judicial astrology in a sweeping denunciation.[29]

Gassendi argued that only moral prudence, not the advice of astrologers, could aid us in determining our actions. Right in the middle of Gassendi's discussion of astrology in the "Physics," there appears a paraphrase of the principle of the calculation of pleasure and pain:

Nor do we deny that God gave man sagacity and wisdom of mind, in order to his conjecture, what may be beneficial, and what hurtful to him in the future; but we deny that this sagacity is any other but the chief part of moral prudence, or that we ought to conceive it to consist only in the skill

[26] Gassendi, *Vanity of Judiciary Astrology*, 48–49.
[27] Gassendi, *Tychonis Brahei, Opera*, 5:371.
[28] Gassendi, *Vanity of Judiciary Astrology*, 1–2.
[29] Halbronn, "The Revealing Process," 209, points out that for the opponents of astrology, including Gassendi, "From the seventeenth century on, the battle was about the uses of astrology, even medical or agricultural."

of astrology, as they would have it. As if when men stood in doubt, what would be the event of such and such an affair, they ought not to consider the causes, instruments, circumstances, and probabilities of what they design, and so proceed to action, or desist accordingly: but only to have recourse to the papers of the astrologers, and there to enquire whether or no, and how their enterprise should succeed.[30]

Clearly Gassendi believed that astrology challenged the provenance of ethics—that it, in fact, destroyed ethics. To believe in astrology was to give up on ethical choice; without such prudential action human freedom disappears. Furthermore, Gassendi argued that recourse to astrologers brings only misery; happiness can be found only by following "the dictates and rules of moral prudence; and to live in respect to oneself, honestly; in respect to others, justly: and for the rest to commit all to Providence Divine, and to be prepared for all the encounters of fortune."[31]

The argument counterpoising ethics and astrology is the subtext of the rest of Gassendi's specific and voluminous arguments against astrology, many of which deal with criticisms of the methodological errors, epistemological mistakes and fallacious assumptions of the supposed science. Gassendi believed absolutely that once the errors of astrology were exposed, a reasonable man had to dismiss it out of hand: "As if any man of sound judgment could regard the heavens, and behold those seven wandering stars; and yet conceive in his mind, that they should make any impression so manifold, so particular, inevitable, and certain." Such a man could only respond to the claims of astrologers with "laughter at their folly."[32]

Gassendi found this kind of rhetorical argument convincing because of his own unshakable belief in the character of the wise man—one who understands the nature of science and ethics and so confines his speculation to the observation of sidereal motions and his actions to prudence. Thus, "Nor indeed can any man so well reject this art, as the most knowing in celestial matters: because what others admire as great and sacred mysteries, these discover to be only childish, devious, and absurd fictions." Only ignorant or presumptuous men give credit to the predictions of astrologers: "And so well conceited are we of ourselves, that we suffer ourselves to be persuaded, that whatever befall us, cer-

---

[30] Gassendi, *Vanity of Judiciary Astrology*, 77.
[31] Ibid., 87.
[32] Ibid., 89, 41. Halbronn, "The Revealing Process," 210–11, believes this is the most central argument that Gassendi uses against astrology.

tainly the heavens took care for it: and being deluded by this proud credulity we instantly believe whatever is told as from the heavens, as something ordained and inevitable."[33] Belief in astrology is fundamentally an ethical decision—if we accept the inevitability of the stars, we abrogate rational choice. We also lose any chance for wisdom and the possibility of happiness.

, In his denial of the determinism of astrology, Gassendi concentrated on astrological theories of causation. He denied that the stars cause sublunar events: "something true in the effect, can be referred to another cause rather than to this or that part of the first heaven which has been distributed from a mere opinion through the zodiac."[34] When the astrologers argued from the effect of the sun on the earth to the influence of all celestial objects on the earth, Gassendi retorted, "it is odious and detestable to delude men by a manifest paralogism, and from a specious antecedent to draw such a consequence as really is no consequence."[35]

Even if the stars do have some effect on sublunar events, he argued, we should look for the immediate cause of an event, which can be ascertained with some degree of certitude, rather than for some remote cause which can never be established with any likelihood. All natural philosophy is to some degree conjectural, Gassendi conceded, but legitimate natural philosophers at least connected effects with their likely causes through observation and experiment, and advanced their ideas as probabilities rather than certainties.

Astrologers claimed the more traditional attribute of science: *scientia*, or true knowledge. They declared that their discipline was a demonstrative science that offered certain and evident knowledge, the kind of knowledge which was associated with mathematics and logic—although they tempered this claim with the caveat that their predictions were fallible.[36] This spurred Gassendi to establish that astrology was not just fallible, but false.[37]

---

[33] Gassendi, *Vanity of Judiciary Astrology*, 122, 148.
[34] Gassendi, *De motu impresso, Opera*, 3:545.
[35] Gassendi, *Vanity of Judiciary Astrology*, 24–25.
[36] On astrology's claim to be a science, see Garin, *Astrology in the Renaissance*, 49–51. On demonstration in mathematics and the physical sciences, see Nicholas Jardine, "Epistemology of the Sciences," in *The Cambridge History of Renaissance Philosophy*, 687–93.
[37] Nicholas Jardine, "Epistemology in the Sciences," 685, comments, "much of the most innovative debate of the period on the questions of the attainment of knowledge concerns disciplines whose credentials as *scientiae* were conceived as questionable: the 'unorthodox' sciences, astrology, alchemy, natural magic and so on; and the practical and operative disciplines, architecture, cartography, military engineering, and the like."

Astrologers, concluded Gassendi, are not mathematicians—nor are they any other kind of scientist. And just as astrology is not a legitimate science, neither is it a legitimate art. Gassendi had defined an art as a practical disciple whose rules could be taught, and whose aim was probable rather than demonstrative knowledge.[38] Since the rules and claims of astrology were false, it did not meet these criteria.

Gassendi anathematized astrology as "a fallacious and cheating art" and then as a "vain and uncertain" art because "it contains no one fundamental, which is not disallowed of and impugned by some one or more professors themselves" and finally that it is "not so much a true art, as a mere lottery or guessing game."[39] Gassendi here echoed the accusations of Cornelius Agrippa, who charged, "Astrological prophecy does not so much consist in Art, as in a certain diffuse chance of things. . . . Wherefore this Art is nothing else but a false conjecture of superstitious persons."[40]

Gassendi's repeated discrimination between astrology and a genuine art shows the importance he attached to this argument. He contrasted astrology with the true "arts of medicine, rhetoric, and navigation," which contain more of an element of certainty because "human prudence and industry so act their parts that the proposed and desired end does for the most part follow thereupon; and when it does so follow, the cause is not hidden."[41] Astrologers cannot act prudently, he notes, because they lack any methodology which will help them truly accomplish the end they seek: true predictions of future events.

But for Gassendi, the notion of prudence had more than the simple meaning of following a rational procedure. The ability to act prudently is also the defining characteristic of the wise man, and prudence connotes not only rationality, but also virtue. Astrology, therefore, in lacking prudence, consequently also lacked a basic ethical core. Astrology would lead not only to false conclusions but to improper living. Thus, it had to be distinguished from the art of ethics which leads to the proper decisions in life.

Gassendi realized that astrologers would use any excuse to avoid recognizing that their art was invalid, but he particularly objected to their invocation of God when rationalizing their failures. Along with undermining human morality, he complained, astrologers demeaned God's

[38] For a discussion of the arts and sciences in early modern times, see Chap. 1.
[39] Gassendi, *Vanity of Judiciary Astrology*, 2, 56, 76.
[40] Agrippa, *Vanitie and Uncertaintie of Artes and Sciences*, 100.
[41] Gassendi, *Vanity of Judiciary Astrology*, 76.

dignity and power. In using God as an alibi for error, thundered Gassendi,

> they make it as if it were certain, that such an effect would inevitably ensue, as they had foretold; unless God by some special resolve of his providence is pleased to avert it: as if it were better that God should be supposed to pervert the general order of causes and effects, that in his infinite wisdom he ordained and instituted from all eternity; than that their foolish aphorisms should be suspected of uncertainty and deceit: and as if it was more reasonable to recur to a miracle, than to discuss the fallibility of their rules.[42]

Gassendi believed in a voluntaristic God, who could intervene in the natural process if he so desired, but he also argued that God had instituted laws of nature and human nature to let the universe operate by second causes, without his direct interference. To Gassendi, the idea that astrologers used God's omnipotence as a screen for their own incompetence and the imposture of their discipline was intolerable.

Moreover, he charged, when astrology claimed it was a "certain true science," it offended against God, the only being who could have complete knowledge of the stars.[43] Gassendi admitted that the stars affect the earth to some extent, even that God had given the stars certain virtues, but he felt it was impossible for human beings to determine what these effects or virtues are. At most, Gassendi argued, the stars are signs of events, but not causes, and even as signs their import is far from certain, since the things they apparently signify—even the seasons of the years—do not necessarily follow. Thus, Gassendi proposed "this considerable truth. That the certain and infallible prenotion of things to come, whose necessary connections to their particular causes or sign is unknown to man, ought to be ascribed to none but God himself, who made and ordered all causes, signs, and events."[44]

Having derided its epistemological premises, Gassendi argued that astrology's arbitrary and fallacious character was also shown by astrologers' own arguments among themselves. They disagreed in their

---

[42] Ibid., 144–47, 75–76.
[43] Gassendi, "Ethics," in *SP, Opera*, 2:732.
[44] Gassendi, *Vanity of Judiciary Astrology*, 4–5; 21. Osler has argued that any necessary knowledge on the part of human beings would circumscribe God's freedom by limiting his omnipotence. See Osler, "Providence, Divine Will, and the Theological Background to Gassendi's Views on Scientific Knowledge," 546–60, and "Fortune, Fate, and Divination, 155–74.

divisions of the zodiac, and in their analysis of astrological houses and conjunctions.[45]

Gassendi takes many of these arguments from Giovanni Pico, the fifteenth-century champion of human freedom, who attacked astrology in his last work, *Disputationes adversus astrologiam divinatricem* (1494).[46] It is a debt Gassendi readily acknowledges—although he does not follow Pico's defense of natural magic.[47] Gassendi's denial of the causal relationship between the stars and specific human events is found in Pico, who had also anticipated Gassendi in declaring astrology "the most infectious of frauds" which "destroys prudence, pollutes morality, defames heaven, and makes men unhappy, troubled, and uneasy; instead of free, servile, and quite unsuccessful in nearly all their undertakings."[48]

Gassendi, like Pico, believed that complete knowledge of the stars is beyond human comprehension, because unlike those things we can observe directly (and affect), the actions of the stars cannot be ascertained "without either difficulty or shadows."[49] Astrologers had answered this charge by claiming that they reasoned by analogy. Both Pico and Gassendi believed that this kind of analogical knowledge was extremely tentative and open to question.[50] Gassendi argued that analogy is a less than trustworthy guide in establishing precise celestial characteristics: "yet how we should come to determine the several natures of the other five planets, I profess not yet to learn. In particular, because Mars appears reddish; may we therefore conclude that he is a burning, scorching planet? Saturn because pale, is therefore cooling? O this would be an admirable consequence, if a carbuncle would but burn and lime cool that hand that touches it!" All of these suppositions, he concludes, are "mere dreams" and are not supported by any kind of empirical evidence.[51]

It is clear that the kind of analogy Gassendi condemned here is differ-

---

[45] Gassendi, *Vanity of Judiciary Astrology*, 22–57.

[46] On Pico, see Garin, *Astrology in the Renaissance*, 80–133; Shumaker, *Occult Philosophy*, 19–27; Poppi, "Fate, Fortune, Providence," 650–53; and Thorndike, *Magic and Experimental Science*, 4:485–511. Many of the same arguments against astrology can be found in Agrippa, *Vanitie and Uncertaintie of Artes and Sciences*, 93–108, with which Gassendi was also undoubtedly familiar.

[47] Gassendi, *Vanity of Judiciary Astrology*, 71.

[48] Quoted in Shumaker, *Occult Philosophy*, 19; see also 20–22; and Copenhaver, "Astrology and Magic," 270.

[49] Gassendi, *Vanity of Judiciary Astrology*, 116–17.

[50] Gassendi, "Physics," in *SP, Opera*, 1:713.

[51] Gassendi, *Vanity of Judiciary Astrology*, 47–8.

ent in kind from his own use of metaphorical figures and analogical concepts to explain motion and pleasure. Astrologers claimed a reified correspondence between external aspects of the objects and the states they described. Gassendi's usage was linguistic and heuristic. The way a rock falls helped him to understand the way a man pursues pleasure, but he did not conclude from this similarity in movement that a man is rocklike. While an astrologer needed to provide evidence for his assertion, Gassendi, because of the nature of his discourse, did not.

The kind of proof Gassendi most seriously demanded was experimental proof, which, he felt, could provide the highest level of certitude possible for a physical science. Astrologers had long argued that astrology was the most empirical of the sciences, founded on observation and experience. Gassendi certainly has no argument against experience, "since against genuine and certain experience no reason can prevail." However, he argued that astrologers fail to make true observations of "the stars (of which the greatest part of them are wholly ignorant) but consult only Ephemerides and the rules set down in books."[52]

Gassendi was operating with a different concept of "experience" than that of the astrologers he was attacking. Clearly, for him experience had become a matter of direct observation or even performing experiments. Gassendi understood that the very nature of astrology itself precluded the kinds of observations upon which the astrologers claimed to base their conclusions: "it was not possible for them ever to make the same kind of experiment so much as only twice; because the same position of the Heavens cannot return again, not only after many hundreds, but also many millions of years." Likewise, Gassendi argued that it was impossible that the Babylonians and Chaldeans, for example, could ever have made the kind of observations which formed the base of so many astrological calculations, because they investigated the movement of the sun and the moon only to determine the times of eclipses. In fact, he noted, the ancients disagreed so much about the nature of the heavens, they had not even the necessary knowledge to make accurate observations.[53]

Moreover, Gassendi argued, any predictions that astrologers do make,

[52] Ibid., 130–31.
[53] Ibid., 132, 43, 70. Thomas, *Religion and the Decline of Magic*, 329, remarks on the same problem, "But the trouble was that the subject was ill-fitted to become a real experimental science. The careful correlation of past events with the movement of the heavens was key to the whole endeavor, but life moved too slowly for quick results. If the great conjunction of Saturn and Jupiter only occurred once every eight hundred years, observed John Selden, it was going to be difficult to verify or refute any theories relating to it."

based on either their own or ancient observations, are impossible to verify by experiment or even to disprove by experiment: "there is nothing which they can prove by experience; or which may not be disproved by contrary experience: so that their rules become plainly arbitrary." Gassendi, with an early sense of the importance of falsification in experimental procedures, argued that since astrological experiments or experiences were impossible to falsify, astrology could not be a legitimate science.[54]

Most astrological observations were also based on the idea that the universe was earth-centered. Such observations, therefore, became problematical with the introduction of heliocentrism, at least in Gassendi's estimation. Thus, in his argument for the impossibility of ascertaining the position of the stars at the moment of birth, he asked how the true time of birth could be known "if the true motion of the sun were not yet known nor the true places of the planets, as it is now manifest they were not known before this our age?"[55]

While early moderns such as Johannes Kepler and Campanella—and many twentieth century advocates of astrology—argued that astrology could coexist with a heliocentric universe, Gassendi dismissed the possibility, and felt that Copernicanism forced astrologers to recalculate their entire system.[56] "Again," Gassendi inquired, "what if those things we have discovered of the planets, and their motions, be such as to require a new [astrological] theory and new precepts concerning them and their periods, different if not contrary to those that have been excogitated and delivered?"[57]

If the astrologers changed their reference points, Gassendi argued, then they would lose any warrant from the authority of the ancients and their observations.[58] Hence, they were damned if they did and damned if they didn't—to Gassendi's great satisfaction.

Gassendi was also aware of other changes going on within natural philosophy. Mathematical and physical astronomy, strictly separated in the middle ages, were developing into an integrated discipline in the sixteenth and seventeenth centuries.[59] Astrology had always been associ-

---

[54] Ibid., 66–67. See Shapin and Schaffer, *Leviathan and the Air-Pump*, 3–21, on the evolution of the concept of experiment in the seventeenth century.
[55] Gassendi, *Vanity of Judiciary Astrology*, 97.
[56] Curry, *Power and Prophecy*, 349, and "Saving Astrology in Restoration England: 'Whig' and 'Tory' Reforms," in *Astrology, Science, and Society*, 246–50.
[57] Gassendi, *Vanity of Judiciary Astrology*, 53–4.
[58] Ibid., 132.
[59] Nicholas Jardine, "Epistemology of the Sciences," 698.

ated with mathematical astronomy, and thus found itself in an even closer relationship with physical astronomy by the time Gassendi was developing his critique.[60] Gassendi fought to preserve the independence of both astronomy and mathematics from the claims of the astrologers:

> Astrology was called, by way of excellency, the Mathematics; as being that art, which the Chaldeans professing with great ostentation, arrogated to themselves the proud title of Mathematicians: which I the rather take notice of, to intimate with how little reason, and ridiculous authority, the prophetic astrologers of our age usurp that noble attribute to themselves.[61]

In the 1640s and 1650s, Gassendi engaged in a polemic with an astrologer who made large claims for a reformulated astrology, Jean-Baptiste Morin (1583–1656). Morin also came from Southern France, and like Gassendi, had attended the University of Aix and studied astronomy with Jacques Gaultier, Gassendi's earliest teacher in natural philosophy. He had abandoned a medical career for astrology, because it promised more "certainty" than medicine. He rose to become one of the most famous astrologers of his age, advising kings and cardinals.[62]

In the 1620s and early 1630s, Morin remained a friend and correspondent of Gassendi's, but his addiction to astrology and denunciation of Copernican astronomy brought them into open conflict in the 1640s and 1650s. Each charged the other with heretical and unchristian beliefs; Gassendi emphasized the fact that astrology had been condemned repeatedly by the Church, and Morin attacked Gassendi's Epicurean-

---

[60] Robert S. Westman, "The Astronomer's Role in the Sixteenth Century: A Preliminary Study," *History of Science* 18 (1980): 105–47, has emphasized the importance of mathematics in the growing disciplinary self-consciousness of the early Copernicans of the sixteenth century. He argues that mathematics and natural philosophy had often been linked by a connection both had with astrological medicine, but that this connection did not lead to innovation of the part of the astrologer, "The astrologer who calculated horoscopes or sought improved tables of mean motions never tried to challenge the explanatory fundamentals of his discipline. He was, in short, parasitic on astronomy for his calculational tools and on natural philosophy for his concepts of force and cosmological order (119)." On the growth of disciplines, see also Charles B. Schmitt, "The Rise of the Philosophical Textbook," 102.

[61] Gassendi, *Vanity of Judiciary Astrology*, 2. Brian Vickers, in his introduction to *Occult and Scientific Mentalities*, 9–10, comments, "The controversies between the occult and the experimental sciences (for each was aware of the threat to its existence posed by the other) undoubtedly had the effect of making the new science more conscious of itself."

[62] Tronson, *La Vie de Maistre Jean Baptiste Morin* (Paris, 1660), 5–11, and Jean-Baptiste Morin, *Astrologia Gallica*, v. For more on Morin, see Mersenne, *Correspondance*, 3:70n.

ism.[63] André Rivet, a mathematician, wrote to Mersenne, "If it was nothing but a battle in philosophy and astronomy, we could be patient and allow them to have at each other. But the interest passes to other things approaching impiety, and it would not be astonishing if God struck them both."[64]

Morin argued that although the fundamentals of astrology had not been known until his own time, nevertheless that did not mean it was not a science: "All the other sciences, even mathematics," were accused of being less than true "before the discoveries of these times."[65] Morin claimed that he was the modern discoverer of astrology, who as one of the "professeurs" of the "most high and divine science" could be admired as a prophet "of future things, by the natural way."[66]

Morin believed he had discovered, through reason, the fundamental principles of his discipline. He was one of a number of astrologers in the seventeenth century who responded to the new natural philosophy by claiming that their discipline was also a science, even a demonstrable science—just the claim that Gassendi found so intolerable.[67]

Morin's astrological system was essentially founded on a new way of dividing the heavens into astrological houses, based on the meetings of the celestial equator, the meridian, and the ecliptic, which he insisted were real rather than imaginary circles. In his system, the relationships of the planets to each other largely determine their influence. Morin believed the stars and the planets influence the earth by means of "an efflux of virtue," which has the attributes of a quasi-material body and is sometimes equated to rays and sometimes to the light of bodies.[68] These rays even obey the laws of optics as they fall toward the earth.[69]

---

[63] Gassendi, *De motu impresso, Opera*, 3:530–31; Morin, *Remarques Astrologiques* (Paris, 1654), 52–59; Morin, *Astrologia Gallica*, ix.
[64] André Rivet to Mersenne, March 28, 1944, in *Correspondance*, 13:90.
[65] Morin, *Astrologia Gallica*, v.
[66] Morin, *Remarques Astrologiques*, 7; *Astrologia Gallica*, iii.
[67] Curry, "Saving Astrology in Restoration England," 247–49; See also Thomas, *Religion and the Decline of Magic*, 351, who writes, "The mid-seventeenth century saw a determined effort to bring the subject [astrology] up to date. . . . The Frenchman J.-B. Morin attempted a thoroughgoing reform, and his ideas had some influence in England." Even Bacon felt that some true principles of astrology could be found, given the proper method of investigation. Cesare Vasoli, "The Renaissance Concept of Philosophy," 73, notes that during the seventeenth century there was an effort to recreate a new "*ordo scientiarum*," combining both tradition and innovation. Morin's attempt at reforming astrology should be seen in this context.
[68] Morin, *Astrologia Gallica*, xii–xiii; *Remarques Astrologiques*, 43–44. Gassendi accused Morin of taking refuge in "an asylum of the ignorant" when he employs "occult and magnetic effluvia" (*De motu impresso, Opera*, 3:539).
[69] This notion is by no means original to Morin. Many fifteenth- and sixteenth-century

Accepting the traditional association of astrology with natural philosophy, Morin studied the new physics. He felt that he had to discuss exten-
sion, optics, place, and motion, and even action at a distance in order
to find the natural principles of his science.[70]

Morin's new astrology was associated with an attack on heliocentrism,
which figured prominently in his work.[71] The astrologer's later works in
the 1640s include a diatribe against Gassendi's arguments for Copernicanism and his Epicureanism. In 1643, Gassendi replied to his critic
specifically in the third letter of his treatise, *De motu impresso*.[72] Most of
his arguments against astrology in the "Physics" probably were also written with Morin in mind.

Gassendi spends the first part of the third letter of *De motu impresso*
denying that Copernicanism has been entirely condemned by the
Church: The immobility of the earth is not an article of faith.[73] What
has been condemned, Gassendi declares, is the belief in judicial astrology, which the Church has anathematized repeatedly in both past and
present: "For the sake of judicial astrology, the astrologers . . . have
betrayed the passion of contemplating the stars, to give themselves to
the supposition that they will announce what is going to happen to men;
and both the holy Fathers, and the pagans, and . . . recent papal decrees
have condemned judicial astrology . . . as an art most damned and pro-
hibited by the Church."[74] The implicit argument here is that legitimate
astronomers, who still contemplate the stars and accept Copernicanism,
are truer Christians than false astrologers who believe that human fate
is determined by the stars. It seems that ethics and religion agree with
Copernicanism better than with astrology.

The other major theme of Gassendi's attack on Morin is also intro-

---

astrologers attributed the influence of the stars to some form of astral rays, and even
argued for its scientific validity thereby. John Dee wrote, "for Astrologie is an Art Mathe-
maticall, which demonstrateth reasonably the operations and effects of the naturall beams
of light and the secret influence of the Stars and Planets in every element and elementall
body at all times in any Horizon assigned" (quoted in Don Cameron Allen, *The Star-Crossed
Renaissance* [New York, 1956], 53–54). I should emphasize here that most astrologers
did not adopt a mechanistic world-view, but that the ideas of some could be interpreted
mechanistically.

[70] Morin, *Astrologia Gallica*, 145.

[71] Two early treatises, *Famosi problematis de telluris motu vel quiete* (Paris, 1631) and *Responsio
pro telluris quiete* (1634) began the tirade, which continued in 1643 in the treatise *Alae
telluris fractae.*

[72] Mersenne, *Correspondance*, 12: 280n.

[73] Gassendi, *De motu impresso*, 530–31. On this subject, see my article, "French Reaction
to the Condemnation of Galileo," 34–54.

[74] Gassendi, *De motu impresso*, 3:530–31.

duced at the beginning: Morin "thinks that he alone knows the truth, that he only grasps something and proves it by a demonstration, so that he thinks that those people who disagree with him are stupid."[75] Morin claimed that his arguments allowed him to demonstrate the immobility of the earth. Such evident arguments were considered an impossibility by Gassendi for epistemological and ethical reasons. The Third Letter of *De motu impresso* therefore concentrated on destroying Morin's arguments for the demonstrability of his attack on Copernicanism. Since several of Morin's most crucial arguments depended on his astrological reasonings, Gassendi also attacked the notion that astrology is a demonstrable science.[76]

Gassendi began with a general attack on the demonstrability of Morin's arguments: "The question is only whether there is a demonstration or convincing reason which proves that the earth is immobile or at rest in the center of the universe."[77] Then he asked, "does Morin understand what may be called a demonstration?" A demonstration must be clear and evident and so overwhelmingly convincing that no one can deny it. If Morin's reasonings are demonstrated, "if they are therefore evident, why do they not compel everyone who reads them and understands them to assent to them?" The answer of course is that they are not demonstrative, and that in fact no physical science is demonstrable.[78] Therefore, these arguments lead to *"opinio"* not to *"scientia."*

In the following section of *De motu impresso*, Gassendi recounts an experiment Morin performed to show that his predictions were accurate, which he believed confirmed his entire rational astrology. The astrologer had sent Gassendi his prediction concerning the death of Louis XIII on May 9, 1643, which he characterized to him as a "most brilliant experiment" (*perillustre experimentum*). Gassendi flatly dismissed Morin's claim, because "the matter might happen from a medical prognosis or from chance" and the uncertain health of the king could result in his death at any time. When the king finally died on May 14, Morin charged Gassendi with hardness of heart and unbelief for failing to acknowledge

---

[75] Ibid., 3: 520.
[76] Gassendi's method in this letter is to encapsulate many of Morin's arguments within his own work, which he then answered point by point. The result is a wide-ranging defense of Copernicanism on physical and religious grounds, although Gassendi included the necessary caveat that he willingly conceded to the decree of the cardinals (who condemned Galileo) on this issue, but he argued that it is still permissible to pursue these matters as an intellectual exercise and in a hypothetical manner (*De motu impresso*, 542).
[77] Gassendi, *De motu impresso, Opera*, 3:542.
[78] Ibid., 3:542–3, 562–63.

the near-precision of his prediction.[79] But for Gassendi, Morin had still failed to show that events could be predicted by astrology.

Morin defended this and other predictions by emphasizing their conjectural nature. He argued that a proper understanding of the nature of the heavens allows for astrological prediction: "Therefore astrological predictions frequently come true; for the inferior and particular causes clearly are obedient to the power of the superior and universal causes— this is a law of nature—although all predictions are in fact merely conjectural and no one can predict anything with certainty."[80]

Morin was clearly uncomfortable with the ambivalent status of his discipline; he had once been drawn to astrology because of its "certainty." Nevertheless, he could not admit an "inexorable fatalism," because it was against Church law. So, he equivocated: God's intervention, human free will (which he admits as a given), the foreknowledge of probable future events may all turn aside the hand of fate, "but the stars' inclination so strongly incline or predispose the native [or subject of a nativity] that at least the inclination can be asserted with considerable certainty." And indeed, "a wide field arises for making predictions, and if only human ingenuity could be so far refined to be equal to the task it could predict even the smallest events that fate has in store, but since the human intellect is feeble it must err except in the most evident situations."[81]

These are clearly the kind of arguments Gassendi attacked in his war on astrology, although Morin's detailed articulation of them came after Gassendi wrote the "Physics." At the end of his tirade against Morin in *De motu impresso*, Gassendi returned to the fundamental connection between his physics and his ethics. He stated: "it is true in both physics and morality, that often we may think that something is convincing, and on the basis of this we may chose some good action, even if we disapprove of the end which led to that persuasion."[82] It is possible to be mistaken in physics and ethics; freedom to choose permits human freedom, and nondemonstrative science, as Gassendi further argued, allows the Copernican hypothesis. The essential fundamentals of nature are unknowable, and natural philosophers are forced to rely on the most probable arguments in establishing physical hypotheses.

Gassendi was attempting to carve out a place for human freedom

[79] Ibid., 3:546–47.
[80] Jean-Baptiste Morin, *The Morinus System of Horoscope Interpretation*, trans. R. S. Baldwin (Washington, D.C., 1974), 9. This is a translation of Bk. 21 of Morin's *Astrologia Gallica*.
[81] Ibid., 12, 30–31, 89–90.
[82] Gassendi, *De motu impresso*, *Opera*, 3:562.

within the confines of a world regulated and determined by natural laws, themselves instituted by divine degree. Whether this world functioned according to the pattern astrologers postulated, or whether it obeyed mechanistic rules of action and reaction, human beings had to be exempted from any kind of determinism, and allowed freely to pursue their own fates, as God had ordained. An analysis of the role that unceasing (if unavailing) striving for pleasure plays in human development perhaps would reveal why God has made us into what we are. Freedom needs to be contextualized.

During a long and fruitful interchange with Thomas Hobbes, Gassendi tried to do just this.

CHAPTER SIX

The Ethics of the
Mechanical Universe

Gassendi's and Hobbes's Psychological Theories

Pierre Gassendi and Thomas Hobbes shared a fascination with motion, mechanism, and human morality. The result was a relationship far more interdependent than scholars have generally realized, especially in the formation of Hobbes's psychology and Gassendi's ethics.[1] Gassendi was one of the first thinkers to realize the implications of Hobbes's philosophy, particularly of the mechanistic and kinetic assumptions, and to respond to them in the development of his own philosophy.

Quentin Skinner has shown that Hobbes made a lasting impression on the intellectuals he met while in exile in France in the 1640s, several

---

[1] Gianni Paganini, "Épicurisme et philosophie au XVIIème siècle. Convention, utilité et droit selon Gassendi," 5–45, and "Hobbes, Gassendi, e La Psicologia del Meccanicismo," in *Hobbes Oggi* (Milan, 1990), 354–410. I thank Professor Paganini for generously sharing his work and ideas with me. Other scholars dispute any important relationship between Gassendi and Hobbes. Arnold Rogow argues that Gassendi's "clumsy empiricism and crude Epicureanism did not attract Hobbes, and thus when Hobbes placed Gassendi in the first rank of philosophers, we can assume he did so more out of friendship than out of a genuine belief that Gassendi was the intellectual equal of the great thinkers of his time" (Arnold A. Rogow, *Thomas Hobbes: Radical in the Service of Reaction* [New York, 1986], 143–44). I can find no evidence that Rogow has actually read Gassendi. On the other hand, Richard Tuck suggests that Hobbes delayed publication of his work in the 1640s because of his exposure to French philosophy, "and his burgeoning friendship with Pierre Gassendi may be very important in explaining Hobbes's desire to rewrite and modify his work" (Richard Tuck, "Hobbes and Descartes," in *Perspectives on Thomas Hobbes*, ed. G. A. J. Rogers and Alan Ryan [Oxford, 1988], 27). Tuck does not argue for an early influence by Gassendi on Hobbes's work.

of whom became disciples of his system.[2] While Gassendi's younger contemporaries were content to follow Hobbes, Gassendi himself was probably the first thinker to engage in a dialogue with him.

Both Gassendi and Hobbes used motion analogically, linking the physical and the human in kinetic metaphors. Influenced by his knowledge of Gassendi's work or his own reading of Epicurus, Hobbes employed atomistic metaphors to describe how human beings act in the state of nature and in the state. Human psychology, for Hobbes, is the result of physiologically determined motions—the impact of corpuscles, or physical species, on a human receptor who responds with some kind of internal motion toward or away from the object emitting the species.

Gassendi knew about Hobbes's system, and echoed it in some parts of the *Syntagma*. His theory of voluntary action, or *libentia*, essentially duplicates Hobbes's description of all human action. But Hobbes's consistent materialism was too much for the Catholic priest, especially because it destroyed human freedom and degraded human rationality, the individual's *libertas* so fundamental to Gassendi's system. Gassendi walked a tightrope with Hobbes, employing aspects of his thought, but ultimately arguing that human motion is not the same as the motion of the rest of the physical universe. Consequently, Gassendi introduced teleological and metaphysical notions into his discussion of human passion, appetite, and motivation.

Gassendi's relationship with Hobbes must also be viewed in the context of Democritean versus Epicurean atomism, because issues dividing the ancient philosophers still separated their modern revivers. Thus, Gassendi defined his ethics of motion in a dialogue with both the ancient materialist, Democritus, and the modern materialist, Hobbes.

By 1641, when Gassendi recommenced his Epicurean studies after a five-year hiatus, Hobbes was a familiar figure in France. He had made three trips to the continent, in 1610, 1629, and 1634–36, which were apparently crucial to his intellectual development.[3] In 1634, during

[2] Quentin Skinner, "Thomas Hobbes and His Disciples in France and England," *Comparative Studies in Society and History* 8 (1965–66), 154. Skinner is arguing against the point of view expressed by Samuel Mintz, that "The literature against Hobbes is charged with the drama of different world views in collision" (Mintz, *The Hunting of Leviathan: Seventeenth-Century Reactions to the Materialism and Moral Philosophy of Thomas Hobbes* [Cambridge, 1962], viii). Thomas Spragens seconds this conclusion: "Hobbes' own contemporaries reacted to his thought with virtually unanimous horror" (Spragens, *The Politics of Motion: The World of Thomas Hobbes* [London, 1973], 21).
[3] Frithiof Brandt, *Thomas Hobbes' Mechanical Conception of Nature* (Copenhagen, 1927), 50–54. More recent studies have supported the argument that Hobbes's stay in France was vital to his intellectual development. See, for instance, Gary B. Herbert, *Thomas Hobbes: The Unity of Scientific and Moral Wisdom* (Vancouver, 1989), x.

Hobbes's third visit, he became very friendly with Mersenne. Hobbes recalled in his autobiography that he had "applied his vacant hours to the study of natural philosophy, and more especially to the perfect understanding of mechanism, and the causes of animal motion. He had frequent conversations with Father Marin Mersenne, a man of extensive learning . . . whose writings have rendered him deservedly famous."[4]

Hobbes's ties with Mersenne remained strong until the French monk's death in 1648. Mersenne encouraged Hobbes in his philosophical studies: in order to introduce him to the larger intellectual world, Mersenne included the first version of Hobbes's *Tractatus Opticus* within his own *Universae Geometrico* (1644). He also initiated Hobbes's correspondence with Descartes, as well as the "Third Objections" to the *Meditations,* and wrote a highly complimentary prefatory letter to the 1647 edition of *De Cive.*[5]

In 1641, when Hobbes returned to Paris as an exile from the English Civil War, he gravitated to Mersenne's circle, which included the major thinkers of the age: Descartes (at a distance), Gilles Personne de Roberval, and, of course, Gassendi. In his Latin *Vita,* after describing the events of 1640 which prompted his exodus, Hobbes recalled, "he returned again to France, where he could study knowledge more securely with Mersenne, Gassendi, and other men, on account of their erudition and their force in reasoning." He further expanded the account in the second Latin *Vita* (*Vitae Hobbianae Auctarium*), identifying Gassendi as the restorer of Epicureanism.[6]

Hermann Schwarz has suggested that Gassendi and Hobbes first became "acquainted" in 1628, although this date precedes Hobbes's own friendship with Mersenne and even Hobbes' appearance in Paris in 1634.[7] Schwarz advances this view because Hobbes's earliest work on natural philosophy seems to show an influence of atomism, but as Frithiof Brandt comments, "Unfortunately Schwarz does not state whence he has derived this information. We have not been able to find it anywhere."[8] The sources are certainly mute on this point.

---

[4] Thomas Hobbes, *The Moral and Political Works of Thomas Hobbes of Malmesbury* (London, 1750), xi.

[5] Lenoble, *Mersenne,* xxviii, xxxviii; Brandt, *Mechanical Conception,* 91. In 1644, Hobbes also wrote a preface to Mersenne's *Ballista.*

[6] Thomas Hobbes, *Opera philosophica quae Latine scripsit omnia in unum corpus nunc primum collecta studiet labore Gulielmi Molesworth,* ed. W. Molesworth, 4 vols. (London, 1839–44), 1:xiv, xxx. Molesworth reprints three lives of Hobbes, first published together in 1681 by Richard Blackbourne, in the preface to the *Opera philosophica.*

[7] Hermann Leo Schwarz, *Die Unwalzung der Wahrnehmungshypothsen durch die Mechanische Methode* (Leipzig, 1895), 97.

[8] Brandt, *Mechanical Conception,* 388.

Possibly Hobbes met Gassendi in the fall of 1629, after the latter's return from the Low Countries and at the beginning of his substantial work on Epicurus and his participation in the intellectual world of Paris. But at that time, Gassendi was more involved in his *Apology* for Epicurus than in a full-scale revival of Epicureanism. Possibly Gassendi's work on Epicurus inspired Hobbes to look more closely at the doctrine of the ancient philosopher, who had suggested that perception is the result of tiny films of corpuscles produced by objects hitting the sensory organs. This theory may have led to Hobbes's adoption of the doctrines of the emanatory transmission of species and the subjectivity of sensible qualities found in the *Little Treatise*.[9]

Whether or not Hobbes and Gassendi met earlier, 1641 found them both in Paris and both engaged in writing Objections to Descartes's *Meditations*, at Mersenne's request—although Mersenne knew that Descartes distrusted Hobbes, and that Descartes and Gassendi had been involved in an earlier controversy.[10] This labor in the same cause certainly brought Hobbes and Gassendi closer together, and by 1642, Gassendi seems to have been instrumental, with Mersenne, in persuading Hobbes to publish the first Latin edition of *De Cive*.[11]

[9] Ibid., 76–77. Brandt suggests that there may have been some atomistic influence on Hobbes's ideas in the *Little Treatise*, but by and large he discounts the possibility: "A modern reader might be inclined to imagine if Hobbes had known the atomic tradition, then the doctrine of the subjectivity of sensible qualities and mind as the motion of particles might have been obvious to him. This is decidedly non-historical. In none of the revivers of atomism in the 17th century do we meet with such a lucid account of the subjectivity of sense qualities as that given by Hobbes" (75). Brandt was not aware that Gassendi, by 1631, was working on a full-scale revival of Epicureanism, which included an account of the subjectivity of sense qualities and the emission of species, another doctrine Hobbes favored in the *Little Treatise* (see Bernard Rochot, *Travaux de Gassendi*, 43–45). It is possible that when Hobbes met Mersenne in 1634, Mersenne discussed Gassendi's work on Epicurus with him, or even showed him copies of Gassendi's work, which was significantly advanced by that time. If the *Little Treatise* actually was written as late as 1636, rather than 1630, as Brandt maintains, Gassendi's influence may have been significant. In the end, even Brandt admits that "the ultimate result" of atomistic influence on Hobbes "is undecided" (77).

[10] On Descartes's relationship with Gassendi and Hobbes, see Jean Jacquot, "Sir Charles Cavendish and His Learned Friends," *Annals of Science* 8 (1952), 18; Sortais, *Philosophie moderne*, 11–15; and Lenoble, *Mersenne*, 48–51. Descartes's relationship with Hobbes seems no less bitter. Descartes treated Hobbes with the same kind of supercilious disdain as he did Gassendi. He believed that the English philosopher was attempting to steal his ideas in natural philosophy. The animosity they felt toward each other was so deep that Hobbes was afraid in 1646 that Descartes might try to stop publication of the second edition of *De Cive* (Brandt, 129–42).

[11] This is related by Sorbière, who actually saw the book through publication. Samuel Sorbière, *A Voyage to England concerning many Things relating to the State of Learning, Religion, and other curiosities of that Kingdom* (London, 1709), iv.

In 1643, Gassendi mentioned Hobbes for the first time in his correspondence, in a letter to Naudé indicating that Hobbes was then one of his philosophical confidants.[12] The closeness of their relationship is shown conclusively in the correspondence between Charles Cavendish, the brother of Hobbes's patron, the earl of Newcastle, and John Pell in 1644–45. In the first letter, Cavendish wrote the following:

> Manie thankes for your letter and Gassendes his booke. . . . I am of your opinion that Gassendes and De Cartes are of different dispositions, and I perceive Mr Hobbes joins with Gassendes in his dislike of De Cartes his writings, for he utterlie mislikes De Cartes his last newe book of philosophie, which by his leave I highly esteem of. . . . Mr. Hobbes . . . is joined in a greate friendship with Gassendes.[13]

Cavendish strongly wished to heal the breach between Descartes and Hobbes, and this letter seems to imply that Hobbes' friendship with Gassendi was standing in the way of this attempt. In another letter, Cavendish mentioned that Hobbes had joined the very select group of friends who were allowed to read Gassendi's work in manuscript: "Mr. Hobbes writes Gassendes his philosophy is not yet printed, but that he reads it, and it is as big as Aristotle's philosophie, but much truer and excellent Latin."[14] Apparently by 1644, Gassendi had allowed Hobbes to see not just *De Vita et Moribus Epicuri*, but his entire work, which was "as big as Aristotle's philosophie." Evidently, there had grown a close philosophical and personal relationship between Hobbes and Gassendi, which may have had roots in the dispute with Descartes in 1641.[15]

Hobbes's and Gassendi's friendship continued throughout the rest of Hobbes's exile in Paris, and resulted in a laudatory prefatory letter to

---

[12] Gassendi to Naudé, November, 1643, in Marin Mersenne, *Correspondance*, 12:125–26.
[13] Cavendish to Pell, December 1644, in *A Collection of Letters Illustrative of the Progress of Science in England from the Reign of Queen Elizabeth to that of Charles the Second*, ed. J. O. Halliwell (London, 1841), 86–87.
[14] Ibid., October 1644, 85.
[15] In 1647 or 1648 (there is disagreement among scholars), Hobbes, Gassendi, and Descartes were finally brought together through the efforts of the earl of Newcastle. There are many variations of this story, including Gassendi being indisposed for dinner, but meeting with Descartes after dinner, or of another argument between Hobbes and Descartes (about the nature of hardness), which occurred at the dinner. Perhaps there is more than one dinner in question (H. Hervey, "Hobbes and Descartes in the Light of some Unpublished Letters of the Correspondence between Sir Charles Cavendish and Dr. John Pell," *Osiris* 10 [1952], 69–71, and Sortais, *Philosophie moderne*, 15). At any rate, a reconciliation, albeit uneasy, was accomplished between the three men, which lasted until Descartes's death in 1650.

the 1647 edition of *De Cive*, in which Gassendi praised the work highly except "in what pertains to the Catholic religion."[16] After Gassendi's return to Provence in 1647, they corresponded, and Hobbes was greatly concerned when Gassendi fell ill in 1649: "I desire not only that you carry yourself well, but to know that in fact you are well, you who, as much as I am able to penetrate into the interior of a man, surpass all mortals by the science, and by means of virtue surpass the science."[17] Gassendi returned the compliment when he received a copy of *De Corpore Politico* shortly before his death in 1655: "this treatise is indeed small in bulk, but in my judgment it is the very marrow of science."[18]

Gassendi and Hobbes were also bound together by their mutual interest in the new science and, especially, mechanistic modes of motion. Although Gassendi's fascination with motion never took a form as extreme as Hobbes's total preoccupation—which E. A. Burtt described as "Nothing without us but bodies in motion, nothing within us but organic motions"—motion played a major role in Gassendi's physical and ethical theories.[19]

Gassendi believed that the universe is guided by God's infused motion while human beings, analogically, are moved by the pursuit of pleasure. Recent scholarship on Hobbes has focused on the concept of analogy to explain the correspondence between the philosopher's social and scientific ideas. Thomas Spragens argues, following Thomas Kuhn's model, that "conceptual patterns and models developed to deal with natural phenomena became prisms through which he [Hobbes] perceived human and political phenomena." Thus, for Hobbes, the "root-paradigm" of inertial motion analogically penetrated and transformed his understanding of both psychological behavior and political activity, and gave his social theories the status of cosmological realities.[20]

---

[16] Quoted in Sortais, *Philosophie moderne*, 215.

[17] Hobbes to Gassendi, September 22, 1649, in "Letters," *Opera*, 6:522.

[18] Quoted in *Moral and Political Works of Thomas Hobbes*, xv.

[19] Edwin A. Burtt, *The Metaphysical Foundations of Modern Science* (New York, 1954), 129. This line of argument is continued in David P. Gauthier, *The Logic of Leviathan: The Moral and Political Theory of Thomas Hobbes* (Oxford, 1969), 2: "What unifies Hobbes's philosophy, relating his study of politics to his physics, is in fact not the thread of deductive materialism, but the stitch of mechanical explanation. And the name of this stitch is Motion—for motion is Hobbes's conceptual key to the understanding of all reality."

[20] Spragens, *Politics of Motion*, 7. In the debate among modern scholars about the relationship between Hobbes's natural philosophy, psychology, and political theory, I generally follow the views of J. W. N. Watkins that "some of his political ideas are implied by some of his philosophical ideas" (22); for the historiography of this entire debate, see Watkins, *Hobbes's System of Ideas: Study in the Political Significance of Philosophical Theories* (London, 1965), 22–46, and Deborah Baumgold, *Hobbes's Political Theory* (Cambridge, 1988), 5–10. The four most recent philosophical accounts of Hobbes's thought on this issue are the

In particular, Spragens contends, "Hobbes' fundamental psychological model is a human equivalent of the law of inertia." The urge for self-preservation, and self-interest in general, is founded on the "universal tendency" of continual inertial movement.[21] Michel Verdon expands Spragens's analysis, directly connecting it with Hobbes's political theory: In the social environment, humans act like "rectilinear inertially moving individuals" or "inertial egoists." Verdon believes that Hobbes' analogic intuition about inertia and human behavior was the result of his study of Descartes: "the most appropriate model to use in the effort to find a systematic unity between Hobbes' physics and political philosophy is an atomistic version of Cartesian cosmology."[22] But an atomistic cosmology, similar to Descartes's, did exist at the time Hobbes was formulating his philosophy. It is more likely that Hobbes was stimulated by Gassendi directly than by Descartes at several removes.

While Hobbes's first philosophical analysis of motion probably predates his acquaintance with Gassendi in 1641, the full formulation of his psychology in *The Elements of Law* and of his political philosophy in *De Cive* came after he had spent time with Mersenne during 1634–1636. (Gassendi was in Provence at this time.) By 1637, Gassendi had almost completed the first version of his physics, which Mersenne discussed

following: Jean Hampton, *Hobbes and the Social Contract Tradition* (Cambridge, 1986); Gregory S. Kavka, *Hobbesian Moral and Political Theory* (Princeton, 1986); Tom Sorell, *Hobbes* (London, 1986); and David Boonin-Vail, *Thomas Hobbes and the Science of Moral Virtue* (Cambridge, 1994).

[21] Spragens, *Politics of Motion*, 189, 130–33, 178–79. Spragens's interpretation of Hobbesian man pursuing a neverending race is anticipated by Gauthier, *Logic of Leviathan*, who states, "Hobbes's self-maintaining engines are forced into constant activity by the presentation of ever-new objects of desire and aversion in sense-experience" (14). Herbert, *Thomas Hobbes*, 14–19, argues that inertia is not an important part of Hobbes's philosophy; rather the dynamic and dialectical components of conatus or endeavor provided the explanation of natural motions, and indeed of Hobbes's entire political theory and physics.

[22] Michel Verdon, "On the Laws of Physical and Human Nature: Hobbes' Physical and Social Cosmologies," *Journal of the History of Ideas* 43 (1982), 659, 656. Baumgold, *Hobbes's Political Theory*, deemphasizes the individualistic content of Hobbes's thinking, arguing that his discussion in *Leviathan* "manifests a structural, as opposed to individualistic, way of thinking about the performance of civic duties" (5). Baumgold does admit, however, that individualism continues as an important part of Hobbes's philosophy in the context of social structures (14–15). While Baumgold's argument is intriguing, it is not entirely convincing, especially in terms of Hobbes's earlier works, where the link between psychological egoism and political action seems stronger. Alan Ryan also believes there was a strong link between Hobbes's atomism and his individualism: "there is a conceptual affinity between his atomism and his intellectual individualism, but something closer to a logical tie between his intellectual individualism and his political individualism" (Alan Ryan, "Hobbes and Individualism," in *Perspectives on Thomas Hobbes*, 82). Richard Tuck, "Hobbes and Descartes," also argues for the importance of Descartes for the development of Hobbes's thought (16).

widely. And, as Hobbes had written, his main topic of conversation with Mersenne concerned mechanism and motion, topics crucial to Gassendi's atomistic cosmology.

Gassendi's model of the universe was based on the inertial, spontaneous, and continuous mobility of atoms in a void universe. That Gassendi's model was the inspiration for Hobbes's thought cannot be proven, but it is certainly a possibility.[23]

While Hobbes and Gassendi developed independent philosophies in the 1630s, by the end of the decade Gassendi's physical models may have been influencing Hobbes's thought. In turn, by the beginning of the 1640s, Gassendi was modifying the more materialistic aspects of his philosophy, probably in reaction against Hobbes's physical and psychological theories.

In 1637, Gassendi had abruptly halted all his philosophical work, not to resume it until 1641. His reasons were partly personal; his patron and close friend Peiresc had just died, and Gassendi would devote the next few years to writing his biography and working on his own more technical scientific treatises. But he may also have felt that some parts of his neo-Epicurean philosophy could be interpreted as a challenge to traditional Catholic beliefs, that he had strayed from his avowal to Campanella that he could balance his philosophical and theological obligations.[24] This would have been a personal revelation rather than a response to political or religious pressure, which was not a problem for Gassendi at this time.[25] Bloch argues that Gassendi, while writing the chapter, "De caussis, fato, et fortuna," realized how far he had wandered into the path of materialism in his initial physical studies, which are far less modified by theological qualifiers than his later writings.[26]

Certainly, Gassendi believed that the atomic universe he envisioned was the expression of an all-pervasive divine plan, a belief evident in the earliest plan of his philosophic system and in letters to Campanella and others.[27] But when he confined himself to the discussion of the attributes of the atoms themselves, his material philosophy became suspect. In the first part of the "Physics," written before 1637, he proclaimed:

---

[23] On the development of Gassendi's physical theories, see Pintard, *Libertinage érudit*, 42–43; Rochot, *Travaux de Gassendi*, 80–81; and Bloch, *Philosophie de Gassendi*, xviii–xxiii, 359–61.
[24] See Chap. 2 above.
[25] See Chap. 7 below.
[26] Bloch, *Philosophie de Gassendi*, xxix–xxx, 429–77; Howard Jones, *Pierre Gassendi 1592–1655: An Intellectual Biography* (Nieuwkoop, 1981), 40–41. The dating of the various parts of the "Physics" can be found in both these sections of Bloch and Jones.
[27] See Appendix.

It remains now to discuss the weight or gravity of the atoms. This is nothing else than the natural or internal faculty and force, by means of which the atom drives and moves itself through itself. Or, if you prefer, the propensity to motion is innate, original, and inseparable to the atoms, which move by an intrinsic propulsion or impetus. Hence it is that everything is destined to move, and by this motion, everything is bound to be brought forth.[28]

Clearly such a claim for the determining force of motion might be construed as an argument for both natural and human determinism. Gassendi was well aware that Epicurus and others had argued that the parts of the world, due to "constancy of their own nature, and as if from necessity, hold their own course firmly."[29] He acknowledged this possibility in another section of the "Physics," written after 1641, which defends God's providence at length: "Truly there is a question concerning the nature of things, or the force which has been put into seeds of things. But there would not be such a force, and it would not operate so admirably, unless there was someone who at the beginning of the world infused such a force and ordained such an order."[30] Once Gassendi became aware of the materialistic implications of his earlier work, according to Bloch, he suffered a "crisis of conscience," inhibiting any further work on Epicureanism until 1641.[31]

During this period of crisis, Gassendi was confronted by a mechanistic materialism that did deny human liberty. As early as the *Little Treatise* or *Short Tract*, written sometime between 1630 and 1636, Hobbes contended that all aspects of being, from the act of sense (moving bodies impinging on the passive subject) to the instinct for self-preservation itself, happen necessarily. Neither the "animal spirits," the brain, the soul, the appetite, nor the will have any original principle of motion, but rather are completely passive and act only in response to an external agent.[32] Hobbes concluded, "Hence appeares that the definition of a Free Agent, to be that, which, all things requisite to worke being put,

---

[28] Gassendi, "Physics," in *SP, Opera*, 1:273.
[29] Ibid., 1:273, 322.
[30] Ibid., 1:315.
[31] Bloch, *Philosophie de Gassendi*, 477.
[32] Thomas Hobbes, "A Short Tract on First Principles," in *The Elements of Law, Natural and Political*, ed. Ferdinand Tönnies (London, 1929; reprint, New York, 1969), 208–9. I follow Brandt, 48–50, in the dating of the *Little Treatise*. If Tuck's argument that this work was not written by Hobbes, but by either Robert Payne or Sir Charles Cavendish, is correct, obviously my analysis is suspect if I had depended on this work alone rather than *De Cive*.

may work, or not worke, implyes a contradiction."[33] By 1642, in the mature expression of his philosophy in *De Cive*, Hobbes proclaimed, "For every man is desirous of what is good for him, and shuns what is evil, but chiefly the chiefest of natural evils, which is death; and this he does by a certain natural impulsion of nature, no less than that whereby a stone moves downward."[34]

This metaphor is too close to the language Gassendi used in his discussion of freedom to be accidental. When Gassendi described *libentia*— willing, but unavoidable action—he echoed Hobbes:

> just as a stone because it is determined to a downward motion, does not possess indifference toward that motion; so the appetite, because it is determined to the good, is not in the same way indifferent toward good and evil; and the stone by lack of indifference to both motions, is said to move downwards spontaneously (*sponte*), but still not freely; thus, the appetite by lack of indifference to good and evil, is said to be inclined willingly (*sponte*), but still not freely to the good.[35]

Since *De Cive* was written by November 1641, prior to Gassendi's "Ethics," most of which was written after March 1642, the French phi-

---

[33] Ibid., 196.
[34] Thomas Hobbes, *Philosophical Rudiments Concerning Government and Society*, in *The English Works of Thomas Hobbes of Malmesbury*, ed. William Molesworth (London, 1839–1845; reprint, Aalen, Germany, 1962), 2:8. This is Hobbes's own translation of *De Cive*, published in 1651. My analysis of the mutual influences Gassendi and Hobbes may have had on each other is confined to those works Hobbes wrote before returning to England. Thus, the changes and amplification of his doctrines which appear in *Leviathan* are not considered.
[35] Gassendi, "Ethics," in *SP, Opera*, 2:823. The language used here is very important and so I will cite the entire Latin passage: "Unde & sit, ut quemadmodum lapis, quia est determinatus ad motum deorsum, indiffentiam non habet ad ipsum, & ad motum sursum; ita appetitus, quia est determinatus ad bonum, non sit similiter ad ipsum & ad malum indifferens; atque ut quemadmodum lapis defectu indiffertiae ad utramque motum, dicitur quidem *sponte*, at non tamen libere moveri deorsum; ita appetitus defectu indifferentiae ad bonum, & malum, dicatur quidem *sponte*, at non tamen libere ferri ad bonum in commune" (my emphasis). The adverb *sponte* is the same in Latin for the action of both animate and inanimate objects; in English, it is necessary to distinguish between the "willing" action of an animate being, which connotes consciousness, and the spontaneous action of an inanimate object, which is unconscious. Thus, the analogy is even stronger in Latin. In the "Physics," however, Gassendi comes close to endorsing the hylozoic idea that inanimate objects, or at least the "seeds" of things, have some consciousness of their own operations. "Why could not have God imprinted on each thing the notion of its own operation: are we forced to assert that natural things are nothing else than a kind of mere instrument, and God makes them in such a way that they do nothing through themselves?" ("Physics," in *SP, Opera*, 1:285–86). The distinguishing factor between human and other cognition is not necessarily consciousness itself, but rather the freedom to act without being determined to a certain end.

losopher undoubtedly realized the parallels between his concept of voluntary behavior and Hobbes's theories of liberty and natural necessity.[36]

For Hobbes, the striving for self-preservation is basically physiological and necessary because the organism must continue in motion to survive. External objects stimulate the senses by "mechanistic pushes," and the vital, circulatory motion of the heart is either helped or hindered. When the vital motion of the heart is increased, one feels pleasure; when it is diminished one feels pain. The act of deliberation is directly related to our perception of what will cause pleasure and pain, or good and evil. Appetite and fear, stimulated by external causes, alternate during deliberation, which ends in an act of will, either the will to yield (appetite), or the will to abstain (fear).[37] Freedom, or "voluntary action," is merely the ability to act in response to appetite and fear. In other words, one is free whenever there is an absence of impediments to voluntary action; although causally necessitated in one's actions, nothing hinders one's acting.[38]

Thus far, Hobbes and Gassendi agreed about necessary or spontaneous action. But Gassendi maintained, against Hobbes as well as against Descartes, that rational human beings possess another type of freedom. *Libertas* is true freedom, freedom from both coercion and causal determination. It consists in indifference and the ability to choose: "Certainly the intellect is not like those faculties which are determined by one thing, as inanimate objects are by gravity and living things by the generative faculty, etc., but by its own nature is so flexible, so that having the truth as its object, it can now judge one thing and then another of some object, and it can consider now one judgment, and then another judgment as true."[39]

The essence of *libertas*, or the free action of the intellect, is that it is *flexible* and can move in either of two directions. It is just this quality of flexibility which is absent from Hobbes's account of human freedom and Gassendi's notion of spontaneity. *Libertas* is contrasted with *libentia*, or voluntary motion, which is movement in one direction only.

Libertas, or true freedom, is that quality of the human intellect which allows the individual to calculate what will bring us the maximum amount of pleasure and the least amount of pain in the long run, and

[36] On the dating of the "Ethics," see the Appendix.
[37] Hobbes, *Elements of Law*, 63.
[38] Ibid.
[39] Gassendi, "Ethics," in *SP, Opera*, 2:824.

to suit his actions to this perception. But to Gassendi, this calculation is not just an adjunct to the passions of desire and fear. Unlike Hobbes, Gassendi does not relegate reason or deliberation to the internal motion provoked in a subject by contact with the motion of external matter: "reason, which is superior to the senses, can correct the perception of the senses so that it will not accept a sign from the senses unless it has been corrected and at last it deliberates or reaches a judgment of the thing."[40]

For Gassendi, the subject of perception is not passive. Rather, reason has the acutely dynamic role of analyzing sensations before acting. Reason, or freedom of choice, exists when, in deliberation, "a man does not choose one thing, but that he can reject it and choose another."[41] To a certain extent, freedom rests in the fact that an individual is independent of external forces; that is, the intellect is ontologically independent of its environment.

This independence combines with the uncertainty of our judgments to guarantee the indifference and flexibility of the intellect, or *libertas*. Gassendi delineated an ontologically autonomous sphere of action for the exercise of free rationality—something which distinguishes the rational human being from the rest of creation.

For Gassendi, the use of reason in the continual striving for pleasure can produce a wise and tranquil person who, although never achieving complete rest, is content with the few things necessary to life. For Hobbes, at least as Gassendi may have interpreted him, reason is an appendage of the passions rather than a guide to a better life. Human life is a competitive "race" in which we always strive to be the first, and our desire for pleasure results in an ever-increasing demand for power and glory. Hobbesian man cannot escape the pressures of continuous desire, but a Gassendist person can choose to slow down, or turn aside from the pursuit of one kind of pleasure for another.[42]

The differing evaluations of the passions by Hobbes and Gassendi follow from their basic understandings of human nature. Hobbes is ever the pessimist, while Gassendi thought that humans have the potential for virtuous behavior, even while driven by the desire for pleasure. In both cases, the result of the passions—always understood as the desire

[40] Gassendi, "Logic," in *SP, Opera*, 1:81; *Selected Works*, 333.
[41] Gassendi, "Ethics," in *SP, Opera*, 1:822.
[42] Ibid., 2:703–6, 715; Hobbes, *Elements of Law*, 71. See also Watkins, *Hobbes's System of Ideas*, 115, and Spragens, *Politics of Motion*, 175–80.

for pleasure and the aversion to pain—is utilitarian, rational calculation. But the Hobbesian calculates from fear, while the Gassendist follows his hope for happiness.[43]

But to both thinkers, the desire for continual pleasure or continual vital motion to avoid the pain of death, acts as the dynamic impetus to human and social development. In the "Ethics," Gassendi maintained, "Since . . . those things a man possesses already count for nothing . . . he searches for delight in procuring those things he thinks he lacks." Likewise, in *The Elements of Law*, Hobbes argued, "Felicity, therefore (by which we mean continual delight), consisteth not in having prospered, but in prospering."[44]

In the context of this discussion, in contradistinction to the theory outlined above, Gassendi came close to suggesting that if nothing intervenes, a man will always seek pleasure and avoid pain, once the balance between pleasure and pain is overcome in one direction or another.[45] When Gassendi sounded this chord, as Gianni Paganini has suggested, he came close to Hobbes's mechanistic account of passion and action. While Paganini recognizes that Gassendi preserved a place for a governing and free intellect—and for a rational will which seeks long-term good according to the free calculation of the intellect—he also argues that such arguments are an attempt to preserve theological orthodoxy, added late in Gassendi's composition to disguise his materialistic, and extraordinarily Hobbesian, human physiological psychology.[46]

[43] Gianni Paganini, "Épicurisme et philosophie au XVIIème siecle," 28–30. The evolution of the concept of passion in the seventeenth century is analyzed by Albert O. Hirschman, *The Passions and the Interests*, 9–66. He argues that at this time passion was counterpoised to interest increasingly, with passion itself retaining the traditional negative connotations of irrational, unbridled behavior, while interest, and especially self-interest, was seen as a rational, utilitarian form of passion leading to results advantageous for the individual and society. Hirschman states, "A maxim such as 'Interest Will Not Lie'" was originally an exhortation to pursue *all* of one's aspirations in an orderly and calculating manner; it advocated the injection of an element of calculating efficiency, as well as prudence, into human behavior whatever might be the passion by which it is basically motivated. . . . the opposition between interests and passions could also mean or convey a different thought, much more startling in view of traditional values: namely, that one set of passions, hitherto known variously as greed, avarice, or love of lucre, could be usefully employed to oppose and bridle such other passions as ambition, lust for power, or sexual lust" (40). Gassendi certainly adhered to the first view, and sometimes to the second to the extent that the desire for pleasure, in whatever form, can have beneficial effects.
[44] Gassendi, "Ethics," in *SP, Opera*, 2:703; Hobbes, *Elements of Law*, 30. On Hobbes's theory of vital motion, pleasure and felicity, see Gauthier, *Logic of Leviathan*, 9–10, and Herbert, *Thomas Hobbes*, 67–72.
[45] Gassendi, "Ethics," in *SP, Opera*, 2:698–99.
[46] Paganini, "Hobbes, Gassendi, e la psicologia del meccanicismo," 354–410.

It is indeed true that parts of Gassendi's physiological account of appetite and passion in the "Physics" suggest a strong Hobbesian influence. But before the resemblance between Gassendi and Hobbes can be drawn, the terms of Gassendi's analysis have to be clarified.

Gassendi divided the soul into two different parts. The higher part, the *animus*, is the rational soul, which includes the faculties of the intellect and the rational will. The animus is incorporeal, infused into each person by God in an act of special creation, and possesses the ability to apprehend universals, as well as being self-referential.[47] The lower part is the *anima*, which is irrational, governing both the nutritive and vegetative aspects of life, and is common to both humans and animals. It is corporeal, and includes the imagination or phantasy, through which we have simple perceptions of individual objects of sense, and from which we can see similarities and aggregates of singulars, and even recognize universals, but without a self-referential knowledge of their universality, which characterizes the *animus* only. The imagination can feel, and to some extent know pleasure and pain, and is closely connected to the human appetite, which "is either the part or the faculty, by which the *anima* from the apprehension or cognition of good and evil, is moved and affected."[48]

Gassendi viewed appetite as a kind of irrational will, and its action is a form of motion in the body, whereby the subject is drawn toward the good and repelled by the bad: "The appetite can be moved in the breast, which is best described as a certain kind of diffusion on account of a good imagination, or a contraction on account of an evil imagination."[49] Such good and evil are seen purely in physical terms: The dilation of the *anima* causes pleasure while the constriction causes pain, both reflected in the systolic or diastolic motion of the heart itself.[50] Pleasure and pain are the fundamental passions of the appetite, where pleasure is seen as the restitution of the organism to its natural constitution, and pain as an interruption of that constitution—which spurs one to act to remove the pain.

As Gassendi worked out the details of his theory of appetite, it became

---

[47] Gassendi, "Physics," in *SP*, *Opera*, 2:398–99. Analyses of Gassendi's concept of the soul can be found in the following works: Osler, "Baptizing Epicurean Atomism," 163–84, and *Divine Will and the Mechanical Philosophy*, 59–75; L. Mandon, *Étude sur le Syntagma Philosophicum de Gassendi* (Montpelier, 1858; reprint, New York, 1964), 36–72; and G. S. Brett, *The Philosophy of Gassendi* (London, 1908), 98–183.

[48] Gassendi, "Physics," in *SP*, *Opera*, 2:469.

[49] Ibid., 2:472.

[50] Ibid., 2:472, 475–79.

barely distinguishable from the physical action of the heart itself, and heart and appetite became virtual synonyms. The causes of this motion of the heart are physical species impinging either immediately on the different parts of the body, and running through the nerves to the heart, or indirectly through an image composed in the human imagination from the reception of physical species in the brain. Accordingly, the imagination is both moved by and mover of the heart, which is "the principle of life" and "is the dominating machine, which as it lies between the body and the parts, maintains them and therefore perceives beforehand whatever touches of good and evil." Moreover, this continuous reciprocity between the heart and the brain results in the vital motion of the body becoming ever more powerful.[51]

Such a deterministic physiological description of the motion of the heart and pleasure and pain evokes Hobbes's similar explanation of human psychology in *The Elements of Law*.[52] For Hobbes, the continuation and augmentation of vital motion is the first object of human desire and results in the first right of nature: the right of self-preservation. Pleasure and pain are the incidental, but not unimportant, concomitants of the perpetual effort to maintain self-movement and life.

Paganini argues that Gassendi, when true to the egoistic psycho-physiology he outlined in the "Physics," also viewed self-preservation as the motivating and continual aim of human beings. He emphasizes those parts of Gassendi's text that give a mechanistic account of human sensation and feeling, and that imply that ultimately the appetite's effort to continue motion—to preserve itself—overwhelms any other part of the human psyche, sometimes even the intellect itself.[53]

If Paganini's account is correct, Gassendi's argument in favor of human freedom becomes somewhat problematic, to say the least. There are indeed places in the "Physics" which do suggest a kind of physiological determinism. After describing the vital motion of the heart and its reciprocal relationship with the imagination, Gassendi stated, "And from this it may be understood, how the appetite may be detached from the intellect or the reason or the will, and it may triumph as if it is alone." Moreover, the motion that is created in the body by the attraction to or repulsion from an object cannot be stopped, unless through the ebbing of time or by a stronger passion intervening.[54] The idea of

[51] Ibid.
[52] Thomas Hobbes, *Elements of Law*, 31.
[53] Paganini, "Psicologia del meccanicismo," 397.
[54] Gassendi, "Physics," 2: 474, 476.

continuous motion, even if vulnerable to time's effect, shows once again the importance of mechanistic metaphors of motion to Gassendi.

Nevertheless, Gassendi's account of the passions in the "Physics" is full of qualifying statements, which essentially undermine the idea of a deterministic physiology of motion. They also bring him back to the normative system of the "Ethics," which he repeatedly cites as a fuller explication of his discussion.[55] While some of these qualifiers may have been added when he rewrote this part of the "Physics" after 1644, and thus represent an attempt to satisfy orthodoxy, they cannot be dismissed as a departure from a fundamental Hobbesian materialism. Rather they reflect a more mature position, unifying all aspects of Gassendi's philosophic corpus.

First of all, the physiological pursuit of pleasure and the physiological flight from pain, as described in the "Physics," are almost always connected with the *anima* or irrational soul, which is common to both humans and animals. According to Gassendi, there are three passions associated with the *anima* or the appetite—pain, pleasure, and desire—"which are expressed and felt without opinion, choice, or judgment, even by brutes and children, which leads them forward into the light." The action of the *anima,* and the heart associated with it, happens willingly, but not rationally: "desire is instituted by Nature and is willingly (*sponte*) excited by nature, and the *anima* is excited, not by memory, or opinion or reason, but only by the presence of pain."[56]

By now the terms of this discussion are all too familiar. This is the most instinctive component or level of the pleasure-pain principle. Just as its counterpart in the "Ethics," it suggests that from the moment of birth all living creatures, out of a need and a desire instituted by some higher power—God, or in this case Nature (Gassendi also uses the phase Author of Nature in the "Physics")—seek to abolish pain and thereby gain pleasure by a "blind impulse".[57] This is done willingly, but not freely, and certainly agrees with the Hobbesian account of human psycho-physiology given above. Thus, when Gassendi, in the "Ethics," referred to pleasure as a continuous insatiability, the subject of his discussion was irrational or instinctive human action, not the action of the human being who is wise or even rational.

---

[55] See, for example, "Physics," in *SP, Opera,* 2:471 where Gassendi argued, "But what ought to be said concerning the imperium of the intellect and free judgment, and the dependence of the will on the intellect, and more generally concerning liberty, will be found in the 'Ethics.' "
[56] Ibid., 2:479.
[57] Ibid., 2:479.

Both Hobbes and Gassendi anchor human motivation in a need, but the teleological and metaphysical aspect—the action of Gassendi's *animus*—is absent from the Hobbesian account.[58] What Gassendi saw as an attribute of the *anima* or appetite, Hobbes viewed as the governing characteristic of the entire human organism.

Thus, nature, according to Gassendi, incites human beings to action, and the more necessary the action is for human preservation, the more pressing is the felt pain, and the more pleasurable its removal.[59] Self-preservation is the consequence of the search for pleasure, not its instigation as it is in Hobbes. In both the "Physics" and the "Ethics," Gassendi argued that the conservation of both individuals and the entire genus is due to the desire for pleasure and avoidance of pain. This view is stated most boldly in the "Ethics": "one desires the preservation of life, the health of the body and the faculties, not on account of themselves, only to the extent that life and health are pleasurable and enjoyable."[60]

Indeed, Gassendi collapsed pleasure, utility, and virtue or honesty together, making the desire for pleasure the unifying attribute of all human action: "What is useful clearly is not desired for its own sake, but on account of something else, and that either is pleasure, or recalls a man to pleasure."[61] In this case, even the man who is not wise can become virtuous through the search for pleasure.

If self-preservation rather than pleasure is the first thing humans desired, as Hobbes claimed, then Gassendi's system would be as egoistic as Hobbes's. But his insistence on the primacy of pleasure and pain allowed Gassendi to introduce a metaphysical and theological dimension to his account of human psychology: the design of the creator and the rationality of the creature.

In the "Physics," as in the "Ethics," the means pursued to restore the human being to his happiest state are the choices of the sovereign and free intellect: "From which it is understood, that the first motion (toward pleasure and away from pain) is not in our power, but what happens afterward is in our power, because our opinions are not simple

---

[58] Paganini, "Psicologia del meccanicismo," 403–4, recognizes these differences between Hobbes and Gassendi, but largely discounts them.

[59] Gassendi, "Physics," in *SP, Opera*, 2:478.

[60] Gassendi, "Ethics," in *SP, Opera*, 2:700; "Physics," in *SP, Opera*, 2:478–79.

[61] Gassendi, "Ethics," in *SP, Opera*, 2:702–3. Paganini, "Psicologia del meccanicismo," 351–445, disagrees with this reading of Gassendi, because he thinks that Gassendi viewed self-love and utility as the ultimate mainspring of action. Gassendi certainly valued an egoistic and utilitarian appetitive psychology, but traced the desire for self-preservation back to the desire for pleasure.

and naked, but due to the intervention of judgment and command."[62] While the motion of the appetite may momentarily overwhelm the intellect and the rational will, "then the light of reason spreads over and extinguishes it, and makes it weak and as nothing. So reason should look to the distance so that a barrier is put on the motion."[63] Human motion becomes not the arbiter of one's destiny, but the servant of the mind.

Here is the second level of Gassendi's appetitive psychology: The ability to plan how to achieve pleasure and avoid pain is produced by human rationality. While Gassendi's psychology is certainly imbued with and haunted by physiological attributes, in the end they give way before an intellect and a rational will independent of the constraining motion of the *anima* or the appetite.

Gassendi was careful, in both the "Ethics" and the "Physics," to distinguish between the necessity that characterizes the physical world, and animate beings without reason, and the liberty that belongs to the rational man alone. Agreeing with Aquinas, Gassendi argued that God has created both necessary and free causes, and the necessary causes act necessarily and the free causes act freely.[64] But while the physical universe is governed by general providence, expressed through motion, God governs man through his special providence and "allows us to do our own things, but we are not less in his care because of this. Because we are free by nature . . . God permits us to enjoy our liberty, and directs us at a distance toward the better of two ways."[65] Only humans are free from the chain of natural or physiological causality, freely making decisions as the vehicles but not the tools of God's providence.

Thus, in using motion as an analog for human and natural behavior, Gassendi demoted Hobbesian spontaneity to the status of quasi-liberty, and created a privileged place in the universe for humanity, by virtue of its unique ability to move not just in one direction but in either of two. Gassendi had responded to Hobbes by converting the kinetic metaphor into an explanation of human liberty rather than an endorsement of human determinism.

This move parallels Epicurus's conversion of Democritean natural necessity and fate by rearranging ubiquitously moving atoms into descending straight lines and then introducing the fortuitous movement of the

[62] Gassendi, "Physics," in *SP, Opera,* 2:471, 479.
[63] Ibid., 2:471, 479, 474.
[64] Gassendi, "Ethics," in *SP, Opera,* 2:841.
[65] Gassendi, "Physics," in *SP, Opera,* 2:330.

swerve—thus producing liberty for both nature and humankind. It would not be surprising if Gassendi viewed Hobbes as Democritus reincarnated, and challenged the ancient materialist with the modern one in mind. This comparison becomes even more plausible if we are aware of Hobbes's own acknowledged debt to Democritus: "Democritus taught me what was silly/ and how much more one man knows than the crowd."[66]

Gassendi and Democritean Determinism

In the last part of the "Ethics," there is a chapter entitled "In what way fate can be reconciled with fortune and liberty."[67] This section of Gassendi's text is extremely important in understanding Gassendi's theory of human liberty and its relation to motion. It also provides another way to see Gassendi's attitude toward Hobbesian materialism, when the French philosopher contrasts the views of Democritus and Epicurus.

In a close analysis of Democritus's system, Gassendi credited the ancient philosopher with a deterministic cosmology based on mechanical motion: The motion of the atoms, their percussion and repulsion, is the cause of all things, and things have to happen necessarily as they have happened because of this motion.[68] Gassendi asserts that the Democritean concept of freedom is *libentia* or voluntary motion in pursuit of the good, itself determined by the series of motions which constitute fate or necessity.[69]

To Democritus, Gassendi explained, all actions, including human actions, are determined by mechanistic motion. "Democritus taught that the cause of any kind of human action was caused by some other cause proceeding it, and this cause by another cause, and so on to infinity. Thus, such a series of causes was always in motion, so that such a series of actions could not but happen."[70] Gassendi might as well have been describing Hobbes's cosmology.

Gassendi rejected Democritean determinism because it "takes from God the administration of things," and is inconsistent with the Christian faith, and because "it is repugnant to the light of nature, by means of

---

[66] Thomas Hobbes, *Thomae Hobbesii Malmesburiensis Vita* (London, 1679), 4.
[67] This is the section of Gassendi's philosophy that had originally been part of his physics, as described in the 1631 letter to Peiresc. It was, then, in the second composition, interrupted midway by the four-year suspension of Gassendi's Epicurean studies, and finally moved into the "Ethics" after 1641. On this history, see the Appendix.
[68] Gassendi, "Ethics," in *SP, Opera*, 2:834.
[69] Ibid., 2:834.
[70] Ibid., 2:835.

which we experience ourselves to be free." By contrast, contended Gassendi, Epicurus "ought to be praised because he maintained an element of pure indeterminism in nature," even if he was wrong in attributing this kind of freedom to the arbitrary declination of the atoms.[71]

In the third part of the "Ethics," Gassendi discusses the Epicurean swerve at length. The means that Epicurus had used to save the universe from natural necessity, and humans from destiny, was the *clinamen* or declination of the atoms. Everything hung on a tiny swerve from the descending motion of atoms or of the atoms which constitute the soul, a swerve utterly fortuitous and unpredictable, justifying a cosmology of chance.[72]

The swerve had been considered an absurd, non-philosophical device by every non-Epicurean philosopher who had mentioned it from Epicurus's time to Gassendi's.[73] Yet, the neo-Epicurean priest asks, "How can this fiction [the swerve] be accommodated to liberty?"[74] Just as Epicurus had introduced a kind of motion—the swerve of the atom—to integrate randomness and indeterminism into both his ethics and his physics, Gassendi utilized metaphors of motion to solve the same dilemma. In defending his ancient mentor, and in addressing possible Democritean objections, undoubtedly Gassendi saw himself answering Hobbes as well.

Gassendi argued that the *clinamen* can be understood in terms of the three kinds of motion that characterize animate movement, and human movement in particular: natural, violent, and voluntary or free.[75] Although the terminology is Aristotelian, the interpretation is seventeenth-century mechanistic. In this ethical context, Gassendi identified natural motion as "that motion inherent in the primary atoms, which is called gravity, and weight, and by means of which the atom is said to be moved in a line or perpendicularly." Natural motion is, in other words, identical with the spontaneous motion Gassendi characterized as *libentia* in Book 2 of the "Ethics." Violent motion is the percussive movement resulting from the strikes and rebounds of the atoms. This leaves free or voluntary motion, for which Gassendi uses the Epicurean terminology at this point in the text: it is "the motion of the declination, to which no region has been determined, and no time has been fixed beforehand."[76]

[71] Ibid., 2:840, 838.
[72] The declination of the atoms is also discussed in the "Physics," in *SP, Opera*, 1:275–79.
[73] Mitsis, *Epicurus' Ethical Theory*, 153–60.
[74] Gassendi, "Ethics," in *SP, Opera*, 2:838. Gassendi repeats many of the ancient objections to the swerve in the "Physics," in *SP, Opera*, 1:275.
[75] Gassendi, "Physics," in *SP, Opera*, 1:275.
[76] Ibid. The definitions of natural motion, as an impressed force which makes a piece of matter move perpetually, spontaneously and uniformly in a straight line is given in much greater detail in *De motu impresso*, in *Opera*, 3:487–96.

At his point in the text Gassendi created an imaginary dialogue between Democritus and Epicurus; his use of the dialogue form links him to other early modern thinkers who saw the dialogue as a particularly useful dialectical or rhetorical tool to establish probable truth.[77] In this imaginary dialogue, Gassendi has Democritus saying that Epicurus's description of motion is no answer at all to the problem of determinism. Since the *clinamen*—assuming one accepts it—is inherent in the atoms, and just like natural motion is perpendicular, Gassendi's Democritus argues, "and those things which happen, have always the same necessity, that they were going to have, because of the variety of motions, strikes, rebounds, *clinamens*, etc., and are the consequence of a chain of events, and especially in what pertains to cognition and appetite, to which liberty ought to be referred."[78]

Democritus would contend that when the visible species of an apple are drawn into the eye, we must desire that particular apple, because of the chain of events—germination, gestation, maturation, etc.—which led up to the creation and recognition of that apple. Just like Hobbes, whose terminology Gassendi borrowed in this explanation, Democritus would argue, "from eternity until now causes cohered to other causes, so that the last of these things finally came together, by which it had been fixed, so that the mind could not but recognize and desire the apple. And whatever we say about causes, the same thing ought to be said about atoms."[79] The swerve, thus, becomes part of the natural chain of events which necessitates human action.

How could Epicurus answer this fundamental attack on the very basis of his concept of liberty, one which accepts the possibility of the swerve, but denies its significance? Gassendi answered for him. The modern philosopher argued that unlike other atoms, the atoms of the soul are free: "The soul is not so bound by the image of something, that it cannot turn away from it if another image impresses it more vehemently." The soul, Gassendi maintained,

> is constituted like the place where two roads meet, and it is placed as if in the middle of two ways, and it is indifferent to each part, because it is free. Because the soul, since it is so flexible and indifferent, may determine itself to one [road] rather than to another equally. This arises from the

[77] On the dialogue and its role in early modern dialectic and rhetoric, see C. J. R. Armstrong, "The Dialectical Road to Truth: the Dialogue," in *French Renaissance Studies, 1540–1570*, ed. Peter Sharratt (Edinburgh, 1976), 36–46.
[78] Gassendi, "Ethics," in *SP, Opera*, 2:838.
[79] Ibid.

impression of one being more vehement than another; and thus the choice follows the apprehension of this thing, as the image is perceived as either good or better. The soul, when it chooses something, or wishes it, is like the most noble machine, from whose motion . . . all the faculties are excited.[80]

These metaphors display the roots of this passage. The analogy between the soul's action and movement on either of two roads should be noted; it is similar to Gassendi's description of special providence given above, where "God permits us to enjoy our liberty, and directs us at a distance toward the better of two ways."[81] The metaphor for binary choice, to be able to choose either of two roads or ways, also is found in Molina, although it appears in other scholastic texts as well. Molina characterizes free choice as the ability "by means of which one bends oneself to either of two ways."[82] Gassendi seems to have combined the theories of both Epicurus and Molina, locating liberty in the indifference of the soul and its ability to move in either of two ways. Indeed, Molina had argued that the Protestants destroy the notion of true liberty by denying that the will cannot turn, *declinare*, in anything but one direction.[83]

Nevertheless, this motive explanation of liberty by Gassendi, whether it was inspired by Molina or not, sounds curiously mechanical. Like the image of the balance discussed in Chapter 3, it leaves one wondering to what extent choice is free or merely the result of an overwhelming perception. This problem is particularly pressing, because Gassendi claimed this is what Epicurus himself would have said, and the Epicurean soul is material, a substance composed of very fine atoms, which does not possess the metaphysical autonomy of Gassendi's *animus*.

Gassendi tries to avoid this problem by insisting that the "substance" (*contexturam*) of the soul, even in an Epicurean context, is different from that of the rest of matter. Other matter is rigid, but the soul "has a natural flexibility in every part, which is the root of liberty." This soul is self-directed, and is independent of external influences. In fact, in this discussion, Gassendi superimposed his concept of the *animus*, or incor-

---

[80] Ibid., 2:838–39.
[81] Gassendi, "Physics," in *SP, Opera*, 1:330.
[82] Compare Molina's language, "*liberum arbitrium, quo ea se in utramvis flectat*" (quoted in Pegis, "Molina and Human Liberty," 94n) with Gassendi's formulation: "*adeo ut, a priore deflectans, constituatur in bivio, & ad utramque partem indifferens sit; quod sane est liberum esse*" ("Physics," in *SP, Opera*, 1:330).
[83] Pegis, "Molina and Human Liberty," 95.

poreal soul, onto the material soul envisioned by Epicurus, although this is only implicit, not explicit, in the text. It is not a completely successful imposition, and consequently Gassendi's dependable terminology becomes mangled by the end of the chapter, when he conflated his usually extraordinarily careful usage of the terms free (*liber*) and voluntarily (*spontanei*):

> notwithstanding that the soul is constituted so that it may be moved by eternal causes, it still . . . has a certain kind of motion from itself, not from external causes, . . . which can be called spontaneous and voluntary [*spontanei voluntariique*], and on account of which it may obstruct the external motion of things, and thus it is not borne so to one, but that it may be deflected to another, and thus it is understood, that it is not tied to one by necessity, but it is constituted to both freely.[84]

This passage makes sense only when one realizes that Epicurean material soul, according to Gassendi's concept of the corporeal soul or *anima*, would have only voluntary motion, unlike Gassendi's incorporeal soul or *animus* which escapes from the web of perception and appetite and is free. The conflated soul Gassendi described here combines the attributes of both: its motion is both spontaneous and free, it is both moved by and independent of external motions.

Gassendi tried to reconcile the contradictory aspects of his version of the Epicurean soul by arguing that Epicurus would have maintained a third kind of motion in the soul, previously identified with the *clinamen*. This third motion is in actuality the result of the mixture of the other varied natural motions of the soul, and it is free.[85] Thus, the motion of the soul can be at once natural, voluntary, and free. All motions of the soul, although spontaneously necessitated by nature, combine to form a kind of free motion: The sum is more than the parts. Because of this third kind of free motion, our choices are free, particularly in regard to future events: Even if what has happened is necessary, what is going to happen is contingent.[86] Motion remains the explanandum of human

---

[84] Gassendi, "Ethics," in *SP, Opera*, 2:839–40. The language used in the Latin is interesting and should be noted: Quippe tametsi animus eiusmodi texturae sit, ut possit a causis externis moveri; est tamen etiam eiusmodi, ut modus quosdam a seipso, non a causis externis habeat, ut pote in quos sponte prorumpat, quique adeo *spontanei*, voluntariique dici possint, & propter quos obsistere rerum externarum motionibus valet, & non ita ad unam feratur, quin *deflecti* in alium; sicque intelligatur, non unius necessitate alligari, sed ad utramvis *liberi* constitui" (my emphasis).

[85] Ibid., 2:839.

[86] Ibid. Gassendi himself uses the terms "necessary" and "contingent" in this rather imprecise way.

action and freedom, but whether a mixed motion of the soul is any more plausible than Epicurus's original concept of the *clinamen* certainly remains a question.

Gassendi took all these metaphors of motion and used them according to his own understanding of freedom and necessity. Later in the same passage, Gassendi will redefine *declinare*, to swerve, as it is used in Lucretius, to mean both *flectere*, to bend, and *dirigere*, to direct, creating a motion both physical and volitional.[87] The Epicurean *clinamen* has been converted into the motion of the free soul, whether or not the soul in question is material or immaterial.

Flectere is also a rhetorical term; it is the duty of the orator to move and carry away (*movere et flectere*) his audience. In the ethical sense, the self-orator moves and carries away his free and indifferent soul through judging both sides of the question. Unlike the response to inflammatory rhetoric, however, this judgment is based on reason rather than emotion. In a further analysis of Lucretius, Gassendi asserted that while the soul may be impelled by an external force, or even more by the vehemence of its own passions, "the mind or reason can make a stand against them for the sake of its own liberty."[88]

The entire thrust of this convoluted argument is an attempt to foster a theory of freedom onto a materialistic philosophy. Gassendi desperately wanted the Epicurean soul to possess freedom, even if this soul was material, and so he invented a third kind of motion to replace the discredited notion of the swerve. His own theory of the *animus*, a metaphysical imposition on a material and mechanistic universe, is in itself more coherent. It allows a clean distinction between the *libertas* possessed by rational human beings, and the *libentia* characterizing the rest of the created world.

Gassendi was acutely aware of the implications of materialism and mechanism, whether in its ancient guise, or in its modern interpretation by Thomas Hobbes. Gassendi's theory of free motion, the ability to choose different routes to the final end of pleasure, separated his philosophy from that of Democritus and Hobbes. His way around the abrogation of freedom in the mechanical universe was through a novel utilization of the concept of motion, the other fundamental attribute of the new world-view.

[87] Ibid. "Quod loco, *declinare* est flectere, ac dirigere motus" (my emphasis).
[88] Ibid.

The Role of Freedom and Pleasure
in the State and Society

Gassendi's Political Philosophy and Its Context

Human beings pursue what is pleasurable and conducive to life, and flee from what is painful and detrimental to life. Gassendi and Hobbes agreed on this fundamental human imperative—although Gassendi emphasized pleasure as the primary end, while Hobbes thought that the desire for self-preservation initiated human motion. Whatever the teleological substratum of choice and avoidance, Gassendi and Hobbes were in concord that the motivation for forming the state was a utilitarian calculation of the way life could best be lived.

For both, individual self-interest was the starting point for discussing not only how human beings act as individuals, but also how they act as members of society and the state. Both Gassendi and Hobbes, starting from the importance each saw in the passions, developed concepts of prudence, deliberation and social contract to explain how human beings emerged from a state of nature to become members of a polity that guarantees life and circumscribes choices.

Gassendi was one of the first thinkers to realize the implications of Hobbes's political ideas, just as he understood Hobbes's psychological maxims. But instead of simply rejecting Hobbes's ideas about nature, man, politics, and God, Gassendi subtly adapted them to his own Catholic and philosophic sensibilities.[1] Gassendi articulated his own political

[1] Bloch has noted that Gassendi's political ideas in Bk. 2 of the "Ethics" seem to be strongly affected by his knowledge of the philosophy of Thomas Hobbes, particularly when Gassendi deals with the state of nature, social contract theory, and the emergence of political man (Bloch, *Philosophie de Gassendi*, xxii–xxiii).

philosophy at the same time he confronted Hobbes's radical political ideas.

The French philosopher acknowledged that Hobbes's analysis of political behavior had some validity, as Gassendi's prefatory letter to the 1647 edition of *De Cive* makes clear:

> It is assuredly a work outside the common and worthy of being touched by all those who have a desire for elevated things. If I put aside what regards the Catholic religion, about which we disagree, I know no writer who scrutinizes more profoundly than he the subject that he treats in *De Cive*. . . . I know no one who has shown himself in philosophy more free from prejudice; no one who penetrates more into the matters upon which he theorizes.[2]

The differences between the Frenchman and his English friend lie most in how they defined reason and sociability. In Gassendi's analysis of human development, he emphasized human rationality and freedom of choice rather than Hobbes's stimulus to action, which was fear.

Gassendi believed that human beings possess the natural ability to reason and to create society. But with what criteria do they decide to do so? His answer shows that the basic coherence of his system lies in his explanation that human beings form societies "in which it would be permitted to live more comfortably, and thus to live more pleasurably; and they were led to this by nature, by reason of which they flee evil and strive after the good."[3] Pleasure, as the ultimate *telos*, is both the motivation for and the ultimate aim of human action, which in this case results in a social contract constituting civil society. The "good" itself is realized pleasure, and society is the medium for such pleasure. Thus, nature, by means of human nature, endowed man with the natural criterion, which initially motivated him to pursue the things necessary to life and consequently to devise things to make life more pleasurable.

While Gassendi rarely referred to God explicitly in his discussion of political philosophy, it seems clear that in his view nature is simply the immanent aspect of God's providential action: The instinctive search for pleasure, endowed by God, acts as the stimulus for societal development. Human beings form social pacts with one another as the natural result of the divinely ordained—but not determined—search for pleasure.

For Hobbes the social contract is artificial; law is imposed by the sover-

---

[2] Quoted by Sortais, *Philosophie moderne*, 2:215.
[3] Gassendi, "Ethics," in *SP, Opera*, 2:795.

eign to curb man's natural passions. This cold-eyed evaluation of the origin of the state had vast ramifications for the rest of his political system. Hobbes intertwined the social contract, law, and the creation of a supreme and absolute authority so intricately that they can be separated only with the utmost difficulty. Human beings may have made the state, and created the sovereign authority, but the antithetical nature of the civil state to man's natural instincts means that this construction must be immutable—or crumble away completely.[4]

The naturalness of the pact that Gassendi envisioned is likewise crucial for his description of the civil state. In opposition to Hobbes, Gassendi adopted the view that the state, which reflects man's nature, is adaptable to changing circumstances—if the calculus of pleasure and pain dictates that change is necessary. Because the state exists to guarantee the pleasurable life, its citizens retain a power of consent.

It is important to understand that Gassendi was drawn to questions of political philosophy not only because of his relationship with Hobbes, but also for other reasons; most fundamentally, political philosophy was integral to the fabric of his moral philosophy. The three books of the "Ethics" consider, in order, happiness, virtue and fate, fortune and liberty. Gassendi's discussion of pleasure in the first book is intimately related to his theory of freedom in the third book. Not surprisingly, the second book, which contains Gassendi's political philosophy, is integrated into this structure.

In developing this schema in the "Ethics," particularly in the first two books, Gassendi followed the traditional division of the ethics course as it was taught in the French universities of the seventeenth century. According to L. W. B. Brockliss, in his history of higher education in early modern France, "The seventeenth- and eighteenth-century ethics course was divided into two parts, *ethica generalis* and *ethica particularis*. The first dealt with man as an ethical individual; the second with the individual as a member of the family and the State; hence it was divided into economics and politics."[5]

Ethica generalis was devoted to the elucidation of the highest good, and although the professors followed an Aristotelian line, Gassendi's discussion of ethical theory essentially paralleled the university course. And just like his university contemporaries, Gassendi then turned from the general to the particular: man as a social and political being.

---

[4] Hobbes's early political doctrines can be found in *Elements of Law* and *Philosophical Rudiments*, in *English Works of Thomas Hobbes*. *Philosophical Rudiments* is Hobbes's own translation of *De Cive* (1642), originally published in 1651.

[5] Brockliss, *French Higher Education*, 216–27.

But politics was not just part of a pedagogical program in the seventeenth century, characterized by modern historians as "an age of crisis."[6] Major political upheavals—the Thirty Years War, the English Civil War, the Fronde in France—ripped through the rising nation-states. Many countries were struggling with the emergence of a strong centralized authority and its composition and relationship to the traditional orders of society. Gassendi's awareness of this turmoil is shown in a 1645 letter to his patron, Louis of Valois, commenting on everything from the English Civil War to the distribution of supplies in Lorraine.[7]

Although the crisis was reflected in every aspect of society and culture, it left its deepest mark in political theory. Some thinkers endorsed the new absolutism, while others developed systems of popular sovereignty and constitutionalism. Both defenders of the traditional rights of the aristocracy and apologists for religious rebellion adopted theories of social contract. The transformed Machiavellian concept of "reason of state" became increasingly popular at this time.[8] Hugo Grotius speculated on natural law and the law of nations. Gassendi was familiar with these schools of political thought and adapted elements of some, just as he absorbed various Hobbesian arguments.

Gassendi's philosophic work on Epicurus in the early 1630s also encouraged this interest in politics and its philosophic justification. Defending Epicurus against the charge of disparaging rhetoric—the most political of the liberal arts—in his 1633 *Vita* of the Greek philosopher, Gassendi challenged Cicero's claim that "the philosophy of Epicurus is useless for the political man."[9] Gassendi directly addressed the question of the relationship between religion and politics when discussing Epicurus's participation in public religious ceremonies, in which the Greek philosopher did not believe:

He was present because the civil law and public tranquillity necessitated it: He condemned it because the soul gained no wisdom from it. . . .
Inside, he was by his own law; outside, by the laws which oblige human

[6] The best treatment of the "crisis of the seventeenth century" remains Rabb, *The Struggle for Stability in Early Modern Europe.*
[7] Gassendi to Valois, January 5, 1645, in "Letters," *Opera,* 6:214–15. Many of Gassendi's letters to his friends comment on current affairs.
[8] On reason of state, see William F. Church, *Richelieu and Reason of State* (Princeton, 1972), and Keohane, *Philosophy and the State,* 112–13, 241–42. Lionel Rothkrug, *Opposition to Louis XIV: The Political and Social Origins of the French Enlightenment* (Princeton, 1965), 82, states, "Words like expedience, necessity, self-interest, and the general welfare appear with increasing frequency in the early seventeenth century."
[9] Pierre Gassendi, *De Vita et Moribus Epicuri,* in *Opera,* 5:233–34.

society. Thus, at the same time he rendered what he owed to himself and
to others. And I maintain that nothing could be more laudable, either in
words or actions. . . . . It is part of wisdom, that philosophers feel with a
few, and as it is said, act with many.[10]

This stance certainly conflicted sharply with the ideals of Christian
piety and Renaissance ideas of active citizenship and public responsibility. Both emphasized the ethical character of the state, a normative view
which is absent here. Moreover, Gassendi's position reflects an almost
Hobbesian double standard of private morality and public conformity—
which somehow does not touch private integrity. But it demonstrates
that questions of the nature of law, of obligation, and of the place of the
individual within the state were important to Gassendi and integral to
his study of Epicurus.

Prudence and Passion

Gassendi's analysis of politics in Book 2 of the "Ethics" of the *Syntagma Philosophicum* is integrated within a general discussion of the virtues, beginning with a definition of prudence. Prudence is "a moral
virtue, which moderates all the actions of our life correctly, both discerning good from evil, and useful from harmful, it prescribes what it is
necessary to follow or avoid, and consequently it establishes men in a
good and happy way of living." It is part of the intellectual faculty, although it is so closely related to moral action and the will "that it is
intertwined and mingled with it and is customarily called 'the prince of
Morality.' "[11]

This definition is by now familiar: Gassendi's account of prudence is
another formula for the calculation of pleasure and pain. Prudence
teaches the "art of life"—the very aim of ethics itself—in both the social
and political spheres of human activity. Private prudence teaches an individual how to conduct his private and public life; political prudence
teaches how the citizens of a state can live harmoniously and happily.[12]

At the very base of this doctrine of prudence is Gassendi's unshakable
conviction of individual responsibility and freedom of choice, the ubiquitous characteristic of his entire ethical theory. Prudence dictates the
moral virtues, "which reasonably are not moral unless it is understood

[10] Ibid., 5:202.
[11] Gassendi, "Ethics," in *SP, Opera,* 2:743, 737.
[12] Ibid., 2:746–51.

that acts of this kind are done from voluntary choice." Prudence "is a habit of the mind, which is not certain, but conjectural; and in this it differs from science" (*scientia* as Aristotle defines it), because science has necessary things for its object, which cannot be otherwise. Prudence is directed toward contingent things, "which are or are not, thus they can be or be not." Prudence is a kind of art "in which the artificer cannot fail except by his own will" and it prescribes "the ends of virtue, when we pursue good things, and the opposite of these ends, when we pursue evil things." The general end of prudence is a happy and blessed life.[13]

Prudence is under our control since we construct our own moral lives. Moral action must be voluntary. Gassendi here used the term *ex electione voluntarieque*, "from voluntary choice," which is derived from *voluntas* or "will," but still conveys the meaning of a self-constituted or free choice. This contrasts with its near synonym *sponte*, which Gassendi usually used for a willing but not free choice. Prudential behavior is moral because it is free.

Gassendi's view of prudence contrasts sharply with Hobbes's definition. In *The Elements of Law*, Hobbes defined prudence simply as "nothing but to conjecture from experience."[14] The normative character of prudence is absent from Hobbes's account—although like Gassendi, Hobbes thought that prudential judgments are conjectural rather than certain. But in his discussion of prudence, Hobbes went further than Gassendi.

Since Hobbes dismissed the realist idea of extramental universals, he thought prudence—or reaching a conclusion based on past experiences—was extremely problematical. The meaning of justice, for example, may change with each particular circumstance. Thus, while past experiences are helpful in making choices, they do not result in a judgment with any supramental authority, except what is founded in individual opinion at the time of the judgment.[15]

Hobbes did not regard prudence as the God-endowed "prince of morality" because he downgraded the rationality of the deliberative process itself. Deliberation was for him a succession of appetites and fears that finally end in a non-voluntary act of will. Hobbes taught that human beings calculate during this deliberation, but such calculation is so con-

---

[13] Ibid., 2:734–44.
[14] Hobbes, *Elements of Law*, 18.
[15] Ibid., 18–19.

nected to the passions and the act of will that it loses its character as a free rational decision.[16]

Hobbes, in *De Cive*, argued that man in the state of nature is motivated primarily by his passions, and most of all by fear—although in his calmer moments, man also possesses "right reason" in the sense of a practical reasoning ability. Thus, "the original of all great and lasting societies consisted not in the mutual good men had towards each other, but in the mutual fear they had of each other."[17]

All men, Hobbes argued, want to preserve their own lives, but since they are all equally capable of killing each other in the state of nature, and because there are some men who from vainglory want to dominate, men are forced by their own fear to constitute civil society. Hobbes defined mutual fear in a manner consistent with his psychological theories: "I comprehend in the word fear, a certain foresight of future evil; neither do I conceive flight the sole property of fear, but to distrust, suspect, take heed, provide so that they may not fear, is also incident to the fearful."[18]

Hobbes then argued that fear produces the decision to create the state:

> for every man, by natural necessity desires that which is good for him: nor
> is there any that esteems a war of all against all, which necessarily adheres
> to such a state, to be good for him. And so it happens, that through fear
> of each other we think it is fair to rid ourselves of this condition, and to
> get some fellows; and if there needs must be war, it may yet not be against
> all men, nor without some helps.[19]

In psychological terms, Gassendi denied the Hobbesian arguments that humans are determined by their passions. He also denied the political consequences of the psychological necessitarianism: the necessary and immutable character of civil association. For Gassendi, passion does not proscribe the state, because prudence always allows human beings to calculate what is best for them—as individuals in the state of nature, and as members of the state.

---

[16] Ibid., 67–69.
[17] Hobbes, *Philosophical Rudiments*, 5–6, 16. There is a good deal of debate in the recent literature on Hobbes about whether he was a "psychological egoist." I agree with those scholars who argue that he is. On this question, see Jean Hampton, *Hobbes and the Social Contract Tradition*, 9–24.
[18] Hobbes, *Philosophical Rudiments*, 6n.
[19] Ibid., 12.

The State of Nature and Natural Right

Gassendi shared Hobbes's interest in the state of nature, but his approach to the question was initially historical. Gassendi began his discussion of political philosophy with a discussion of the state of nature as seen by the ancients, who portrayed it as either a golden or a bestial age. He did not believe that these views necessarily contradicted each other: There may have been a progressive degeneration from one to the other.

In fact, he found such a development posited in Book 5 of Lucretius's *De Rerum Natura*, the only extant description of Epicurean political theory. Book 5 clearly inspired Hobbes's description as well.[20] According to Gassendi's interpretation of the meaning of the text, Lucretius taught that man lived originally in a golden age, but because of the fear of violence and wild beasts, pity for the vulnerability of the weak, the inconveniences of the solitary life, and the lust of stronger men, he was impelled to enter society.[21]

Man then, according to Lucretius, created society and government out of the state of nature by means of a dual social contract, a first contract establishing society and then a second agreeing to obey legal codes. The aim of these contracts is to provide the peaceful environment vital to individual tranquillity and happiness. Gassendi commended the Lucretian analysis of why laws are obeyed: so that violence is contained and a peaceful life exists for the common good.[22]

But Gassendi was dissatisfied with the Epicurean discussion because it was sketchy on the nature of right and justice, both before and after the social contract, a problem Hobbes had also addressed.[23] Epicurus had described justice as a utilitarian contract in which men swore neither to harm nor be harmed by each other; it has no transcendent or absolute value or meaning.[24] After a long and erudite discussion, Gassendi re-

---

[20] Guyau, *Morale d'Épicure*, 198. Hobbes's contemporaries often accused him of being an Epicurean. See Richard S. Westfall, *Science and Religion in Seventeenth-Century England* (New Haven, 1958), 22, 108–9, and Richard Tuck, "The 'Modern' Theory of Natural Law," in *The Languages of Political Theory in Early-Modern Europe*, ed. Anthony Pagden (Cambridge, 1987), 107, who cites Pufendorf who believed that Hobbes was an Epicurean.

[21] Lucretius, *On the Nature of the Universe*, 147–77.

[22] Gassendi, "Ethics," in *SP, Opera*, 2:789. Lucretius's dual contract consists of a contract establishing society and a later agreement to obey legal codes (*On the Nature of the Universe*, 165–69).

[23] Gassendi, "Ethics," in *SP, Opera*, 2:787–91.

[24] Epicurus wrote: "Justice never is anything in itself, but in the dealings of men with one another in any place whatever and at any time it is a kind of compact not to harm or be harmed" (*Extant Remains*, 103). On Epicurus's political philosophy, see James H. Nichols, *Epicurean Political Philosophy: The De Rerum Natura of Lucretius* (Ithaca, 1972, 1976).

jected this concept and accepted the traditional legal definition of justice, *tribuendi cuique suum ius*: "to give to each one his own right."[25]

But, Gassendi admitted, "right" had been interpreted in different
ways by different people. In particular, there had been much contention
concerning whether someone has right by nature (the Stoic view) or by
utility (the Epicurean view).[26] Gassendi believed that the only way to
discover what human right is, and consequently, what justice is, is to
examine very closely man's beginnings in the state of nature and the
subsequent development of the political state.[27] Just as Hobbes had, Gassendi returned to the constituent member of society—the individual in
the state of nature—to determine the nature of natural right, political
association, and justice.

Ethics professors in the French universities were also concerned with
the state of nature. They equated it with the state of rational man before
the Fall, that is, the state of a classical philosopher without the gift of
grace. This idea was controversial. The Jansenists, notes Brockliss,
thought "the idea was a Molinist subterfuge to mitigate the effects of
the Fall; it was a theory used by 'laxist' theologians to suggest that God
only deprived Adam of his supernatural not his natural powers, the latter, especially his reason, remaining unmarred."[28]

If the Jansenist accusation holds, it would suggest that Gassendi was
inspired in his political philosophy as well as his moral psychology by
the sixteenth-century Spanish Jesuit; Gassendi's political theory credits
man with the full use of reason in the state of nature.

In his own description of the state of nature, Gassendi argued that an
individual can be viewed in two ways:

> first absolutely, or according to himself, and as he is a man; then secondly,
> or comparatively, as he is related to others, and is a certain part or desires
> to be part of society. And certainly in the first way, he is viewed as solitary,
> and in a pure state of nature; that is, such as man is made by nature with
> all his parts, from which he is constructed, and with all his faculties, by
> which he is instructed.[29]

In this first, solitary state, man is not self-sufficient, in that he does not
possess within himself all the things he needs to maintain life but must

[25] Gassendi, "Ethics," in *SP, Opera*, 2:786.
[26] Ibid., 2:786–87. This was a common topic in the seventeenth century. See Tuck, "The
'Modern' Theory of Natural Law," 105.
[27] Gassendi, "Ethics," in *SP, Opera*, 2:786–95.
[28] Brockliss, *French Higher Education*, 219–20.
[29] Gassendi, "Ethics," in *SP, Opera*, 2:794.

seek them externally. However, nature makes these necessities, food and shelter, easily obtainable, and endows man with the innate faculty of seeking for these things and transforming them into use. Gassendi concluded:

> Nature gave to man, so that he might exist, the faculty to maintain and to preserve himself. And Nature gave the ability to use all things which are necessary, conducive, and useful for his preservation. Furthermore, it is this faculty itself, which is the first right of nature; consequently, however often we use this faculty, we are judged to use a right of nature, and, in fact, the right of nature which is primary, or the most ancient gift of nature.[30]

Thus, man's first right is the ability to use anything that he considers necessary to preserve his own life. In the state of nature, moreover, "when one person desires and pursues something, there will be other who desire and pursue it equally; and hence will arise strife, rapine, and hatred."[31] The cause of contention in the state of nature is not that man is naturally violent or bestial, but rather that any man has a right to anything and that no one has a secure possession in what he uses. Although man appropriates goods and property in the state of nature, he does not hold them securely. Thus, while personal use of property exists in the state of nature, private ownership does not.

Up to this point, Gassendi's description of human beings in the state of nature is close to Hobbes's, if man is considered "absolutely, or according to himself, as he is a man."[32] That is, if man is considered apart from any social intercourse whatsoever. For both Hobbes and Gassendi, the first right human beings possess is self-preservation, and the result of everyone's effort to preserve himself is war.

Hobbes's definition of the character of the state of nature is well known: "it cannot be denied but that the natural state of men, before they entered into society, was a mere war, and that not simply, but a war of all men against all men." The root of this war of all against all is that "Nature hath given to every one a right to all" because everyone has the equal right to use anything or do anything to preserve himself."[33] These views have a clear tie to Gassendi's remarks about the state of nature in the "Ethics": "For in that bestial state, which is presumed free, it reason-

---

[30] Ibid., 2:794–95.
[31] Ibid.
[32] Ibid.
[33] Hobbes, *Philosophical Rudiments*, 9–11.

ably cost most dear, since as it was observed not long ago, there would be perpetual life and death combat, insofar as, everything belonging to everyone with equal right, no one could use anything for himself, but that another would seize it."[34]

Gassendi was invariably more wordy than Hobbes, but the message is the same. It is quite possible that this passage referred explicitly to Hobbes in the expression "since as it was observed not long ago."

But Gassendi believed that a state of war actually rarely existed in the state of nature, because a person not only exists as a solitary being, but also as a potential member of the social organism. In order to avoid constant war, people make pacts by which they exchange an uncertain right to everything for a certain right to something.[35] Thus, the fact that man can use his reason to avoid war, and consequently to make pacts to establish the state, is a second right of nature, and is as "natural" as the first right of nature.

"Therefore," Gassendi continued, so that man does not have to stay in this state, he "is made a sociable animal by nature." Nature "granted him the inclination to enter upon pacts, by means of which he might take council with one another and be turned into society rightly." Gassendi later made clear that natural right (*ius naturale*) can be taken in two ways: as man's faculty for maintaining life, common to all organic beings (*ius animale*, or animal right), and also as all his reasoning properties (*ius humanum*, or the right of man).[36] Both are equally natural and innate, but the latter enables man to realize that his interests would be served best by remitting to some extent his natural right in everything. It leads a man to make pacts with other men, who make similar remissions, leaving all with a defined and secure right in those possessions remaining. It is at this point that private property in the traditional sense, or "mine and thine" as Gassendi called it, actually comes into being.

In his description of the *ius humanum*, Gassendi enumerated its abilities: "Of planning, or investigating, of teaching, or learning the various arts and especially the use of fire, of pacifying among themselves and joining together in society, and living in it by certain laws. And the laws of this kind are varied, as it is necessary, either by the occasion, or on account of some better utility urging."[37]

People also realize by the *ius humanum* that all needs will be more

---

[34] Gassendi, "Ethics," in *SP, Opera*, 2:755.
[35] Ibid., 2:795.
[36] Ibid., 2:795, 798. This distinction is part of the common parlance of the schools. See Brockliss, *French Higher Education*, 292–93.
[37] Gassendi, "Ethics," in *SP, Opera*, 2:798.

easily fulfilled by the mutual assistance of others. Gassendi called this initial period of social reciprocity "a state of modified nature," and it paralleled his secondary definition of man as part of society.[38] It seems, for Gassendi, that this stage of human development served as both a more advanced state of nature and the beginning of human society itself. It is a transitional state that contains both elements within itself.

Another contract during this state of modified nature protects the weak against the attacks of the stronger by establishing law and justice. These contracts are natural and the state of affairs and laws established by them are consequently also natural because they emanate from the faculty of human reason.[39] The *ius humanum* is transformed from a guide for individual action into a social dynamic propelling man into society.

Thus, Gassendi's social pact is natural, the outgrowth of natural reason:

> Because life was uncomfortable and dangerous in that ferocious state or state without pacts, people formed an assemblage, so that they could live more comfortably and delightfully. They did this because of their own natures which led them to flee evil and seek good. . . . Thus, from nature, the state can be no other than society, in which pacts are begun and preserved reciprocally. For this reason people determined in common to undertake these things among themselves, so that laws or narrowed rights are retained. Since laws are nothing else but pacts.[40]

This pact is vastly different from the pact Hobbes envisioned:

> Last of all, the consent of those brutal creatures is natural; that of man by contract only, that is to say, artificial. It is therefore no matter of wonder, if somewhat more is needful for man to the end that they live in peace. Wherefore consent or contracted society, without some common power whereby particular men may be ruled through fear or punishment, doth

---

[38] Ibid., 2:795. This seems to duplicate Aristotle's "second nature," where custom arises from man's rational nature. See Brockliss, *French Higher Education*, 293, and Donald Kelley, "Civil Science in the Renaissance: The Problem of Interpretation," in *Languages of Political Theory*, 66.

[39] Gassendi, "Ethics," in *SP, Opera*, 2:755, 795. The idea that man is naturally sociable but that it requires an act of will to establish society is not original with Gassendi. J. W. Gough, in *The Social Contract: A Critical Study of Its Development* (Oxford, 1936, 1957), traces this *topos* from its origin in Aristotle, through medieval social-contract theories, until it became fairly commonplace in the seventeenth century.

[40] Gassendi, "Ethics," in *SP, Opera*, 2:795.

not suffice to make up that security which is requisite for the exercise of natural justice.[41]

Thus, for Hobbes the artificial construction of society by pact does not in itself provide a legitimate and obligatory set of laws—only the supreme authority can do that once the state is created.[42]

Gassendi's political philosophy, on the other hand, based legitimacy and obligation within the state on the voluntary actions of free agents creating a political society through social contracts, rather than the command of the supreme authority. Civil society, which is natural because it is the outcome of human nature, remains a construct of voluntary association emanating from the innate desire for pleasure. The purpose of such political bonds is to guarantee freedom and liberty to the individual. Gassendi wrote, "true and natural liberty is discovered rather in that society only, in which a man submits to the laws of society (this by his own approval or to his own advantage) and he does whatever is pleasing with what remains, and he possesses the right in his own goods, which no one can snatch away because of the public power which defends them."[43]

Gassendi has now determined what right is: Right is whatever remains in the power of the individual after he has established the pact. These original rights may be further limited because of utilitarian concerns, but although they have been limited, they remain "certain and free."[44]

Civil Society, the State, and the Right of Consent

For Gassendi, the social contract sets up a limited arena of political liberties or laws, enforced by the supreme authority. But because Gassendi believed that man should always strive for happiness—inside the state as well as outside it—the establishment of the social contract was not the end of political development.

For Hobbes, human nature is static; the individual is always motivated by the same passions, and the laws of nature and human nature always

[41] Hobbes, *Philosophical Rudiments*, 67–68.
[42] Probably no part of Hobbes's political philosophy has received as much scholarly attention as the discussion of obligation and particularly what obligates in the state of nature. A good bibliography of the literature on obligation is given in Alan Ryan, "Hobbes and Individualism," 90–99.
[43] Gassendi, "Ethics," in *SP, Opera*, 2:755.
[44] Ibid., 2:799.

reflect these psychological constants. The artificial construction of the social pact is the only dynamic moment in Hobbes's schema; afterwards, man is caught fast by his own nature and the state.

By contrast, Gassendi, while conceding a psychological constant in human behavior, believed that the prudential calculation of pleasure and pain led to constant revisions of human existence and therefore to human progress.

Gassendi elaborated these themes as he developed his political theory. He believed that although the original social contracts—to form society and to establish laws—removed many of the inconveniences of the state of nature, some remained. Accordingly, human beings—still guided by their reason to pursue what is best for themselves—make a third contract, to delegate authority to a government. Again borrowing from Lucretius, Gassendi explained, "Because it would be inconvenient for the whole multitude to come together to decide something, and individually (or even by tribe) to state an opinion, or to cast a vote; for this reason the multitude itself willingly (*sponte*) transfers the power either to a few people, or to some one person."[45] Government, then, is not divine—except incidentally, as a product of man's providentially inspired pursuit of pleasure. It is the result of volition, and it is natural because it is a product of natural reason.

J. W. Gough, in his history of political thought, calls this delegation of authority to government a "contract of government" or "contract of submission."[46] Bloch asserts that the dual or triple social contract—the contract of association and the contract of submission—found in Gassendi may be the earliest formulation of this complex kind of political theory articulated in the seventeenth century.[47] But while Gassendi's thinking does look forward to Locke and the liberal tradition of the eighteenth century, it also looks backward to the dual contract found in Lucretius.

Moreover, his work reflects social contract thinking from the middle ages, ideas further developed to justify rebellion and even tyrannicide by sixteenth-century Jesuit and Calvinist thinkers—who claimed that kings following the wrong religious formula were breaking social contracts with both God and the people. Humanist jurists of the late fifteenth

---

[45] Ibid., 2:755.
[46] Gough, *The Social Contract*, 1–7.
[47] Olivier René Bloch, "Gassendi and the Transition from the Middle Ages to the Classical Era," *Yale French Studies* 49 (1973): 52.

century and sixteenth century employed similar contractual arguments, contending that ancient French history showed an aristocracy delegating its authority to a monarch by means of a social contract.[48]

Bloch's assertion that the state is not "properly founded" until the third contract is also open to interpretation. Gassendi never directly addressed the question, but he implied that some kind of state exists as soon as the multitude forms a society, and particularly after the society begins to make laws. "The laws, which are decreed in order to produce a civil society," he wrote at the end of his discussion of natural law, "are produced for the common utility or the common good." The words "civil society" seem to indicate that some kind of state is produced immediately by the establishment of law, an event which Gassendi clearly placed before any delegation of authority to leaders. Furthermore, when Gassendi spoke of "the highest power," he associated that power with the multitude who make laws, rather than with the government, which is created by the third contract.[49] If the making of law—in contrast to the creation of an institutional framework—is the mark of statehood, Gassendi clearly implied that the state predates government.

In a state structure, Gassendi maintained, sovereignty cannot be divided after it is transferred. It must reside in either the monarch, in the optimates, or in the people. Although a state may have a semblance of mixed government, in actuality only one unit possesses the supreme power, and this fact determines the nature of the state.

This analysis of the indivisibility of sovereignty is similar to Jean Bodin's, but Bodin and Gassendi differ fundamentally on the question of whether the people retain the right of consent to law.[50] Bodin, who was the foremost proponent of absolutism in the sixteenth century and still extremely influential in the seventeenth, did not envision any form of sovereignty residing in the people or arising from individuals in a state of nature. Bodin's state was formed when a sovereign power held a virtually unlimited ability to compose the law, which the citizens of the state were compelled to obey without question.[51]

Gassendi was responding to exigencies different from Bodin's. The sixteenth-century theorist was concerned with defending the inviolability of the state from the threatening dissolution of religious civil war.

---

[48] Quentin Skinner, *The Foundations of Modern Political Thought, Vol. 2: The Age of Reformation* (Cambridge, 1978), 302–38; Keohane, *Philosophy and the State*, 316.

[49] Gassendi, "Ethics," in *SP, Opera*, 2:801, 755, 795.

[50] On Bodin's theory of the indivisibility of sovereignty, see Keohane, *Philosophy and the State*, 70–71, and Skinner, *Modern Political Theory*, 288–89.

[51] Pierre Mesnard, "Jean Bodin," in *Encyclopedia of Philosophy*, 1:325–28.

Absolute monarchy, a monarch *legibus solutus*, was the only response to the Calvinist and Jesuit justifications of tyrannicide and rebellion. Almost a hundred years later, new realities permitted Gassendi to utilize the "contract of submission" and to advocate a form of limited monarchy, drawing from but avoiding both the absolutism of Bodin and the radical resistance of the religious militants. The eclecticism of Gassendi's political thought is truly extraordinary.

Of the three traditional kinds of government, Gassendi favored monarchy because it provokes the fewest difficulties (one man can execute laws more efficiently than several), and those can be remedied by either succession or election. (Gassendi's casual reference to election shows his familiarity with Huguenot and constitutional arguments that monarchy was originally, and to some degree continuously, elective.)[52] Furthermore, he argued, empirical evidence shows that the rule of one is best: The home has one master, the army one general, the universe one ruler.[53] Gassendi consistently compared the state to the home.

But Gassendi designated boundaries of monarchical power. In his discussion of political prudence, he argued that the ruler's duties concerned particularly war and peace. In addition, "he should hold fixed in his soul the aim and end for the sake of which he rules, and to which he is subservient. This truly is the health, security, and utility of the people."[54] This claim duplicates the arguments of sixteenth-century Huguenot theorists, who proclaimed that magistrates were created for "the safety, the welfare and the conservation of the people" and who argued that kings should remember "it is due to the people, and for the sake of the people's welfare, that they exercise their power."[55]

Later, in his analysis "Of Justice, Right, and Laws," Gassendi explicitly claimed that the people always retain some power of consent after the contract of government has been made: "next some laws were laid down by the princes; but it should be understood, nevertheless, that the consent of the people intervened, either expressly . . . or tacitly, because the power had been given and had been received mutually."[56]

Gassendi followed this passage with many of the arguments traditionally used by those arguing for some form of popular sovereignty. For example, he cited the *lex regia*, a principle taken from Roman law, which was interpreted to mean that when the *imperium* is granted to a ruler, it

[52] Skinner, *Modern Political Theory*, 316–17.
[53] Gassendi, "Ethics," in *SP, Opera*, 2:756–58.
[54] Ibid., 2:758.
[55] Quoted in Skinner, *Modern Political Theory*, 327.
[56] Gassendi, "Ethics," in *SP, Opera*, 2:796.

is delegated rather that irretrievably transferred, and therefore sovereignty remains with the people. Gassendi also included a long discussion of the difference between a king—the shepherd of his people, who rules according to the law—and a tyrant—the wolf of his people, who cares only for himself.[57]

Gassendi believed that it is in the best interests of the king not to act like a tyrant. A king's chief aim, as for any man, should be tranquillity. For a king, as for any man, tranquillity is impossible without virtue, "because . . . the Prince is also a private man, for whom it is necessary always to possess a good character, and who will prove so much more suitable for ruling others, as much as he knows how to rule himself and order his own passions."[58]

Gassendi's good king will therefore conduct himself virtuously, for the good not only of his people, but of himself. The people will love and revere him, and he will live peacefully. But realizing that simple virtue will not always suffice in a world plagued by misguided subjects and external enemies, Gassendi provided detailed and intricate rules for running a country successfully. He advised the king to distribute justice "exquisitely," to tax justly and to inform the people why there are taxes, to maintain a strong army and to use spies, and to punish the leaders of sedition harshly, but to be lenient to the followers.[59] The government Gassendi described certainly is not constitutionalism, but neither is it absolutism. It has the flavor of Machiavelli and *raison d'etat*, yet another tradition Gassendi was happy to utilize in his own political philosophy.

In general, Gassendi was drawn to arguments against absolutism. Such arguments were traditionally associated with theories of social contract, and complemented his belief that government is the result of the voluntary desires of free individuals. The entire purpose of government is to secure the greatest happiness of the individual: The individual, therefore, will not give the government the irrevocable right to tyrannize him.[60]

Gassendi did not, however, draw any final implications from these arguments. He did not defend the right of the people to rebel; rather, he stated that it was in a person's best interest to obey the sovereign author-

[57] Ibid., 2:757, 796. On the *lex regia*, see Skinner, *Modern Political Theory*, 130–40, 331. The *lex regia* can also be used to justify absolutism, if consent is given irretrievably. In this discussion of consent, Gassendi's thought coheres closely to the traditional teaching of the universities. See Brockliss, *French Higher Education*, 255–56.
[58] Gassendi, "Ethics," in *SP, Opera*, 2:659.
[59] Ibid., 2:759–60.
[60] Ibid., 2:755.

ity. During his discussion of public calamities—war, tyranny, the subversion of the state—he argued, "Since we may not change fate, or if you please, the decrees of eternal providence, it is better to soften the harshness by our own consent, rather than to exasperate them more by fruitless opposition."[61]

Gassendi insisted that one is obligated to obey the customs of any society while living in it, because "while either nature, or law, or custom may make a thing proper, it is nature itself which orders it to be maintained, insofar as it may serve the common good, on whose preservation depends the preservation of each individual, which is natural for everyone."[62]

This view seems to contradict the idea of the free creation of the state and continued voluntary consent after the state has been created. It reflects an ambiguity in the terminology Gassendi employed in this political discussion. He fairly often used the Latin *sponte*, meaning "voluntarily," when he discussed the social contract, rather than *libere*, meaning "freely." This choice implies that the formation of the state is natural and inevitable, leaving little room for the kind of free association that he usually advocated. To the extent that the state is the result of our natures, in their inevitable pursuit of pleasure, it comes into being willingly, but perhaps not freely.

This fact may explain why we are obligated to obey and not resist political authority. In the long run, happiness is better served by obeying than rebelling. The ambiguity in Gassendi's analysis originates in his dual concept of human nature: Man necessarily pursues pleasure, but through his reason, naturally makes free choices on how that pleasure is to be achieved.

Gassendi's ambiguous analysis of freedom and necessity in the creation of the state may reflect other semantic problems as well. Patrick Riley has argued that social contract theory from the time of Hobbes was "voluntarist," that the contract establishing the political state is

---

[61] Ibid., 2:669–70.
[62] Ibid., 2:778. A. Adam, "Gassendi: L'influence posthume," in *Pierre Gassendi: Sa vie et son oeuvre*, 170, believes that the idea of a natural right founded upon the laws, traditions, and manners of human beings, "lorsqu'il fonde ainsi un véritable empiricisme historique" is in its origins a Gassendist doctrine. It seems more likely that Gassendi was familiar with Aristotelian and early modern discussions of custom, where custom was viewed as a "second nature." Most early modern philosophers and jurists differentiated between nature and custom, and therefore would not view custom as natural in the way Gassendi did. On the history of the concept of custom, see Donald R. Kelley, " 'Second Nature': The Idea of Custom in European Law, Society, and Culture," in *The Transmission of Culture in Early Modern Europe*, ed. Anthony Grafton and Ann Blair (Philadelphia, 1990), 131–61.

legitimate because founded on the individual wills of the constituent members, freely willing whatever form the political state takes. This notion of the free will of individuals can be traced back to medieval theology, but it takes a particularly political turn in the seventeenth century: "consent or agreement based on will, understood as a moral 'faculty,' came to occupy a place in the seventeenth to the early nineteenth century political philosophy which it had never occupied before (not at least in the political, as distinguished from the moral and legal, realms)."[63]

Riley also argues that the primary ambiguities found in the theories of Hobbes and other political philosophers arise because "the will" is so variously and confusedly understood in early modern times. It can be viewed as a simple physiological movement in response to external stimuli, in which case human behavior is determined, or as a moral faculty which has the power, based on knowledge, freely to strive for and choose a certain moral action. The will, understood in the second sense, then obligates because someone "freely chooses something . . . which is not causally necessary." A free action is moral because it is based on the free choice of an individual, based on reason, to do or refrain from doing something. Unlike a stone, argues Riley, which must fall downward, human actions are not necessitated—because the will is free.[64]

It is in just this sense that Gassendi understood human beings as the free makers and participants in political society, although for him the ambiguous connotations of the human will suggested a psychological theory that associated freedom with the intellect rather than the will. For the French philosopher, the actions of the will were always caused and therefore, to some degree, necessitated.[65] Thus, when Gassendi used language drawn from the developing voluntarist tradition, his political philosophy absorbed an element of ambiguity that made his theory less than consistent.

Justice, Utility, and the Laws of Nature

This seeming ambiguity—between the volitional and necessary origins of the state—is also reflected in Gassendi's concept of law. Law is a contract between people formed together in a particular society; Gassendi did not believe in a universal contract, a universal concept of justice. He

---

[63] Patrick Riley, "How Coherent Is the Social Contract Tradition?" *Journal of the History of Ideas* 34 (1973): 548.
[64] Ibid., 550–52.
[65] On causal necessity, see Chap. 4 above.

noted that in different circumstances, such as when climate and terrain differ, societies develop differently—creating a great diversity of customs and laws. The particularity of the pact also means that there is no natural law among nations—particularly since one of the characteristics of law is its ability to compel, impossible among peoples of diverse customs.[66]

But this state of affairs does not mean that law is completely positive or conventional in nature. While Gassendi, like Hobbes, believed that there are no universal principles with a reified existence, he did find a kind of universalism in human nature itself. Although the particular laws themselves will differ depending on how and where they are made, the process by which they are established is natural (the *ius humanum*), and therefore the laws are natural even if not universal. That is, the same law is both natural and the product of positive choice, just as the social contract is the product of both instinct and deliberation.[67]

Gassendi experienced some of the same difficulties in deciding whether there is indeed some universal "law of nature" (*lex naturae*), existing before the creation of the state. On the one hand, he realized that natural law can be equated with natural instinct, which "is like a certain kind of spontaneous dictate" that leads us to eat, drink, procreate, and so forth. Presumably, obedience to such a law is voluntary (spontaneous), but not free. But there is another definition: "Natural law can be said to be found in man alone, insofar as reason is directed toward the nature of things . . . and thus the law of nature in these matters is nothing else than the law of reason or reason itself."[68]

In discussing the law of nature, Gassendi returned to the omnipresent binary composition of his ethical system. Clearly, natural instinct, when described as a "spontaneous dictate" (*spontaneum dictamen*) of human nature is the type of human freedom described elsewhere as *libentia* or willingness, while the secondary rational nature of humans is the same thing as *libertas* or the true human freedom.[69] When human beings act on instinct, their actions are voluntary; when they act on the basis of rational choice, they are free. Both states characterize men before and after the pact. Natural law spans the apparent contradiction between consent and obedience.

Once Gassendi had established the parameters of natural law, he felt he could establish some basic principles, which—if we disregard our

---

[66] Gassendi, "Ethics," in *SP, Opera*, 2:799.
[67] Ibid., 2:797–801.
[68] Ibid., 2:800.
[69] In Gassendi's text, a willing or spontaneous action, *spontaneum*, is linked with "willingness," *libentia*. See "Ethics," in *SP, Opera*, 2:822–23.

"prejudices and preoccupations"—can be seen to characterize all humans. Essentially, in this discussion, he reiterated his view of the characteristics of human right and prudential action. First, "the most common and innate law in all men is that they pursue that which is good, advantageous, and gratifying, and they flee from what is evil, disadvantageous, and ungratifying." Not all men feel the same thing is a good, but all will seek what they perceive to be good. Second, "anyone loves himself more than the rest, or prefers good for himself, rather than another."[70] Here the egoism that found its original philosophic expression in ancient Epicureanism surfaced in the writings of the neo-Epicurean, where it underwrote an emerging individualistic moral code.

This conclusion has led Gianni Paganini to emphasize egoism and self-love in his analysis of Gassendi's political thought. He argues that this idea, adopted from Epicurus, was most difficult for Gassendi to reconcile with a Christianized Epicureanism. To Gassendi, argues Paganini, "self-love constitutes not only the motive of all ethical behavior, but also the cement of the political universe." Consequently, Gassendi's universe has lost any moral anchor and its members act only out of utilitarian expediency. In this argument, Gassendi duplicates Hobbes.[71]

This charge echoes a similar accusation directed against Epicurus himself, by both ancient and modern commentators. Epicurus had urged the wise man to withdraw from society in order to live in self-sufficient tranquillity, thinking only of himself. Cicero reacted to the implicit selfishness of this doctrine, by insisting that in Epicureanism, "Justice totters or rather I should say, lies already prostrate, so also with all those virtues which are discernible in social life and the fellowship of human society. For neither goodness nor generosity nor courtesy can exist" in such circumstances.[72] More modern critics have been equally scathing: Cyril Bailey accused Epicurus of "Egoistic Hedonism" and A. E. Taylor charged the philosopher with "moral invalidism."[73]

Other critics, however, from Seneca to more recent commentators such as Phillip Mitsis, David K. O'Connor, and P. A. Vander Waert, believe that Epicurean egoism can be accommodated to justice, fellowship, and even, in the case of Mitsis, altruism.[74] These critics, to varying de-

---

[70] Gassendi, "Ethics," in *SP, Opera*, 2:800.
[71] Paganini, "Epicurisme et Philosophie," 33, 31.
[72] Cicero, *On Ends*, 203.
[73] Bailey, *Greek Atomists*, 515; A. E. Taylor, *Epicurus* (London, 1911), 22.
[74] Mitsis, *Epicurus' Ethical Theory*, 98–128; P. A. Vander Waerdt, "The Justice of the Epicurean Wise Man," *Classical Quarterly* n.s. 37, no. 2 (1987): 402–22; and David K. O'Connor, "The Invulnerable Pleasures of Epicurean Friendship," *Greek, Roman, and Byzantine Studies* 30 (1989): 165–86.

grees, emphasize the importance of happiness, community, and friendship in Epicurean philosophy, which links virtue, pleasure, and friendship so closely that the terms are virtually interchangeable. In Epicureanism, there can be no conflict between utilitarian and "pure" motives. People do things, including refraining from injustice and participating in social relationships, because they are useful and bring pleasure, a good both for the actors and others.[75]

Whether this interpretation is valid for the original philosophy remains open to question, but clearly Gassendi himself argued for an integration of utilitarian egoism and altruistic action. Immediately after proclaiming his second law of nature or reason, Gassendi argued that since it is natural to love those close to oneself like offspring, loving oneself is even more natural. Likewise, it is natural to love fellow citizens more than foreigners. It is even possible to love a friend so much that one could be willing to die for him if it brought one happiness and glory. Whatever service one person does for another will bring him some personal good, if nothing else "the consciousness of being a benefactor, which is of incomparable worth."[76]

Thus, for Gassendi, individual utility blends seamlessly into sociability and love for others. It does not concern him that the original spur for such action is a kind of selfishness, because the result is an ethics of caring. One of the most fundamental axioms of the neo-Epicurean's thought is that virtue and utility are indistinguishable from pleasure, the impetus to all actions, "the first accommodation of nature."[77]

So, when Paganini argues that Gassendi's endorsement of self-interest and utility links him closely to Hobbes, he emphasizes one element of Gassendi's thought at the expense of broader themes in the Frenchman's philosophy. Paganini rightly points out that Gassendi, in a discussion of Epicurus's *Principal Sayings* that was part of the *Animadversiones in Decimum Diogenis Laertii* (1649) sounded very Hobbesian in his discussion of Epicurean concepts of justice and injustice, which are founded completely on individual utility.[78] Gassendi goes so far as to equate man in the state of nature with a wolf, just as Hobbes did.

But Paganini acknowledges that Gassendi also accepted the idea that the rule of reason exists in the state of nature, allowing human beings to act for their common benefit. So, argues Paganini, Gassendi "oscillates

---

[75] This kind of interpretation can also be found in less recent critics. See Guyau, *Morale d'Épicure*, 139, and Festugière, *Epicurus and His Gods*, 62.

[76] Gassendi, "Ethics," in *SP, Opera*, 2:801.

[77] Ibid., 2:700.

[78] Paganini, "Epicurisme et philosophie," 11–12.

between positive conventionalism and the traditional paradigm of rationality." However, Paganini argues that when Gassendi is true to his mechanistic psychology and utilitarian individualism, he falls squarely in the positivistic camp.[79]

But even in Gassendi's discussion of Epicurean concepts of justice, and immediately following the analogy he drew between some humans and wolfish animality, Gassendi clarified his interpretation by arguing that such animal behavior is aberrant—just as physical deformity is the exception rather than the norm of human appearance. Most people are guided by rationality, which leads human beings to practice the golden rule and to be good, kind, and gentle.[80] Thus, confronted with the teachings of both Epicurus and Hobbes, Gassendi maintained the basic rationality and sociability of human beings throughout his ethical writings.

Such rationality starts with care for oneself. So Gassendi's third law of nature in the "Ethics" states, "each one wishes to prolong life and the integrity and free use of the members and senses and all the faculties."[81] While self-preservation is the first right of animate beings, it counts only as the third law of nature. While right characterizes all creatures, law pertains only to human beings.

Lastly, Gassendi argued, "human beings are sociable and they live in society. . . . The reason why men are desirous of society, as we said before, is their mutual need which is devised by nature." Thus, society is constructed from human freedom and rationality, but at the same time is a product of a "nature" that manipulates human instinct to accomplish the creation of society. The Latin here is interesting too—Gassendi used "*machinata*" for devised, suggesting an almost mechanical origin of this naturally created social organism.[82] For this early proponent of the mechanical philosophy, there is not yet the rigid distinction between nature and artifact that will characterize the formation of the state for Hobbes.

After discussing the laws of nature, Gassendi turned for a second time to the nature of positive law within the state. The laws of civil society, or the state, are created by human beings after they have composed themselves into a society. Laws reflect the common utility of the people composing the state, each recognizing that the laws must be maintained for the common good, which includes each individual's good. Once again,

[79] Ibid., 17–18.
[80] Pierre Gassendi, *Diogenis Laertii Liber X, cum nova Interpretione & Notis*, in *Opera*, 5:158–59.
[81] Gassendi, "Ethics," in *SP*, *Opera*, 2:800.
[82] Ibid., 2:800–801.

expediency and utility are linked indissolubly with fellowship and altruism, with reason as the binding force. The ultimate validation of positive law is human prudence, which also obligates one to obey the law after it has been established.[83]

Even without positive law, rational men recognize the obligation to obey the golden rule, by imagining themselves in the place of other men. Such sympathetic projection is connected to the human conscience, "which is the best and most excellent councillor" a man can have. Thus, if all men were wise, "public justice would be unnecessary and useless."[84]

Both Gassendi and Hobbes realized that if all men followed the dictates of prudence or right reason, the state itself would be superfluous. But Gassendi was more positive about man's eventual rise to wisdom than Hobbes was, and this optimism may underlie his vigorous espousal of a theory emphasizing the consent of the citizens as basic to the functioning of the state and the legitimacy of the positive law.[85] Nevertheless, given the nature of most men, Gassendi agreed with Hobbes that there must be some kind of coercive power behind the positive law. Human beings do not always act with prudence.

For Gassendi, the malleability of prudential behavior is grounded in the provisional nature of ethics itself. Hobbes believed he had founded a science of politics, a science more evident than physics itself, since it was based on a deductive knowledge of human behavior.[86] Gassendi's political philosophy rested on the probable and contingent, and therefore allowed more contingency in both political behavior and the study of politics.

As a political philosopher, Gassendi reflected a diverse spectrum of political theory, taking what he wanted from many prior formulations. In addition to Epicurean political philosophy, Gassendi used the ideas of proponents of both constitutionalism and absolutism. He also borrowed some notions from what Anthony Pagden calls the tradition of "political Aristotelianism"—a tradition of political thinking, reinvigorated by Thomas Aquinas, which sought the moral and universal origin of all forms of positive law, and grounded the state in natural morality and the law of nature. The adherents of this tradition, also called "iusnaturalism," felt they were constructing a "science" of politics, an *episteme*.

---

[83] Ibid., 2:797–99.
[84] Ibid., 2:802. On this, see Paganini, "Epicurisme et philosophie," 37–38.
[85] Gassendi, "Ethics," in *SP, Opera*, 2:799.
[86] On the notion of politics as science, see Tom Sorell, "The Science in Hobbes's Politics," in *Perspectives on Hobbes*, 7.

Grotius and Samuel von Pufendorf are the most famous seventeenth-century adherents of this school of political philosophy. And like Gassendi, these natural rights philosophers connected right (*honestum*) and utility (*utile*) with natural law and the preservation of the state.[87] They saw no contradiction between utilitarian and social concerns.

Gassendi corresponded with Grotius, who was closely tied to Gassendi's patron, Peiresc.[88] According to Richard Tuck, Grotius was responding to the skeptical crisis of the seventeenth century, with its implicit moral relativism, by advancing a political philosophy that demonstrated that "there were at least two universal moral beliefs (the right of self-preservation and the ban on wanton injury), and that these minimalist ethics could be used as the basis for a universal moral science."[89] For Grotius, the principles of natural law are rooted in human reason and are consequently immutable and eternal.

Gassendi was close to this tradition when he posited a universal desire of self-preservation founded on the desire for pleasure, which is both instinctive and rational. For Gassendi, a psychological constant becomes a moral imperative, although the object of that constant is relative and transitory. But Gassendi did not reify natural law to the extent that Grotius had, because Gassendi's orientation was always to the individual who constituted society, rather than to any metaphysical principle detached from individuals.[90] The French philosopher also, of course, parted company with the natural law philosophers on the question of whether one could construct a "science" of politics, just as he rejected Hobbes's similar claim for his philosophy.

Gassendi's political philosophy is distinct in the way it combines elements from previous and contemporary political philosophies to support a new understanding of the role of the state and the individual within it. The pursuit of pleasure underlies the human constitution, and the emergence of societal custom and habit.

Thus, for Gassendi, the state itself is the product of both instinct and free choice. Civil society is both natural and a construct. It is the result of human passion—the desire for pleasure and avoidance of pain—but a passion circumscribed by reason or prudence and directed by a provi-

[87] Anthony Pagden, "Introduction," in *The Languages of Political Theory in Early-Modern Europe*, 1–17.
[88] Gassendi to Grotius, April 2, 1632, "Letters," *Opera*, 6:47. The tone of this letter is formal rather than intimate and it does not concern questions of political philosophy.
[89] Tuck, " 'Modern' Theory of Natural Law," 115. Gassendi's relationship with Grotius could use more study.
[90] Paganini, "Epicurisme et philosophie," 33–34.

dential force, which finds the objects of its desires and aversions now in one thing and now in another.

In the next chapter, I demonstrate what some historians have claimed: that Gassendi is a precursor of political liberalism, and that his political and ethical thought strongly influenced John Locke. Gassendi did link ideas about liberty and the social contract formulated in earlier times to a sophisticated understanding and reformulation of Hobbesian ideas about the creation and nature of the state. Most fundamentally, Gassendi understood that an ethics based on freedom and pleasure had to accommodate a political philosophy that included both.

But in advocating these ideas, Gassendi avoided their most radical implications—the right of the individual to rebel against an authority who destroyed rights of life, liberty, and property. Temperamentally, Gassendi was one with Epicurus, who thought the wise man could best find tranquillity by withdrawing from participation in the state. Gassendi constructed a bold, influential political philosophy based on his view of human nature—but his own nature limited how far he would take it.

CHAPTER EIGHT

Gassendi and Locke

The Fate of Gassendism

Gassendi's near oblivion in the twentieth century would have surprised the savants of the seventeenth. Though modern readers find his Latin impenetrable and his style distasteful, in his own time and for more than a century afterward Gassendi was viewed as the great—and by some, victorious—opponent of Descartes, as the presenter of a viable alternative to Cartesian rationalism.[1] Gassendi's Christianized Epicureanism—with its shadings of hedonism, individualism, and freedom—found a receptive contemporary audience, particularly in England, and especially in John Locke.

Leibniz's pronouncement on the relationship between Gassendi and Locke is well known. He commented that Locke "is pretty much in agreement with M. Gassendi's system, which is fundamentally that of Democritus: he supports vacuum and atoms, he believes that matter could think, that there are no innate ideas, that our mind is a *tabula rasa*, and that we do not think all the time; and he seems to agree with most of M. Gassendi's objections against Descartes."[2] Although this assessment seems a fairly straightforward one by someone who might be considered authoritative, Locke scholars have received it with varying degrees of skepticism. Many either do not note or are not concerned

---

[1] The most recent discussion of the continued prominence of Gassendi in the late seventeenth century, and the progressive debate between Cartesians and admirers of Gassendi, can be found in Lennon, *Gods and Giants*.

[2] Quoted in Lennon, *Gods and Giants*, 149.

with Locke's relationship to Gassendi, while others admit the influence
but downplay its significance.

James Tully suggests that Locke was indebted to Gassendi for his epistemology, hedonism, and voluntarism, but these remarks are made in
passing without drawing a definitive conclusion.[3] M. A. Ayers argues that
Locke "agreed with" Gassendi in his doctrine of indicative signs and
that Locke's doctrine of substance has "an obvious precedent" in Gassendi. Moreover, Locke's early epistemology "whether or not in imita-
tion of Gassendi" was similar to that of the French philosopher. It is
only in his later work that Locke moved away from a Gassendist position.[4] Thus far the case is made tentatively, without drawing a conclusion.

Coming at the material from the Gassendist side, Emily and Fred
Michael conclude that Locke drew much of his theory of ideas, as well
as his ideas about space, time, and infinity, from Gassendi, but nevertheless was not Gassendi's disciple—although they consider Gassendi, not
Locke, the founder of modern empiricism.[5]

Likewise, in the case of ethics, Thomas Lennon—after vigorously defending Gassendi's influence on Locke in epistemology and ontology—
suggests that although their "psychological hedonism" is similar, "The
result is that while Locke's reading of Gassendi may have provided a
support and even an inspiration for his ethical views, it cannot properly
be described as a source of them." But in a note commenting on E. A.
Driscoll's contention that Gassendi was indeed the source of Locke's
hedonism, Lennon adds, "I should like Driscoll to be shown right and
myself wrong on this point."[6]

---

[3] James Tully, *An Approach to Political Philosophy: Locke in Contexts* (Cambridge, 1993), 194,
197–98, 201–2. Tully is hampered by dependence on the secondary literature, particularly
Gabriel Bonno, *Les relations intellectuelles de Locke avec la France* (Berkeley, 1955), and Edward A. Driscoll, "The Influence of Gassendi on Locke's Hedonism," *International Philosophic Quarterly* 12 (1972): 87–110.
[4] M. R. Ayers, "The Foundations of Knowledge and the Logic of Substance: The Structure
of Locke's General Philosophy," in *Locke's Philosophy: Content and Context*, ed. G. A. J. Rogers (Oxford, 1994), 54, 60.
[5] Fred S. Michael and Emily Michael, "The Theory of Ideas in Gassendi and Locke,"
Journal of the History of Ideas 51 (1990), 398. The Michaels are taking issue with Richard
W. F. Kroll, "The Question of Locke's Relation to Gassendi," *Journal of the History of Ideas*
45 (1984): 339–60, about the significance of "morphological" or similar ideas in Locke
and Gassendi. Kroll, while admitting that Locke was certainly influenced by Gassendi, is
less inclined to see an immediate influence, and more ready to accept the importance of
intermediaries between Gassendi and Locke as well as the general climate of opinions
(380).
[6] Lennon, *Gods and Giants*, 153, 153n. Other works which analyze Gassendi's influence or
lack of influence on Locke include the following: Antoine Adam, "L'influence de Gas-

Driscoll's arguments about Locke and Gassendi seem the most persuasive; he identifies similarities in Gassendi and Locke's theories of pleasure and pain, providence and freedom. But his discussion is short, and depends largely on François Bernier's *Abregé* of Gassendi's *Syntagma Philosophicum*, a popular French adaptation which appeared in 1678.[7] While Locke may have received his first exposure to Gassendi's ideas indirectly through Bernier or other sources indicated below, the many correspondences between the ethical and epistemological thought of the two philosophers indicate that Locke had a thorough knowledge of Gassendi's work itself.

A close reading of both philosophers argues for an enormous debt. Scholars, perhaps out of respect for Locke's eminence in current philosophy and political science, have missed the significance of the debt, and the extent to which Locke is a Gassendist.[8]

A rollcall of similar passages in the work of the two philosophers, impressive though it is, understates the connection. Some themes in Locke that are viewed as obscure and debatable by modern scholars become understandable when seen against the Gassendist background. In fact, especially in Locke's theory of the faculties and psychological "uneasiness," obscurity marks Locke's account in part because he deviated from the doctrines of Gassendi.

Locke's closeness to Gassendi fits into the general popularity of Epicureanism in the second half of the seventeenth century. The Baconian tradition, with its repudiation of Aristotelian natural philosophy, made English thinkers sympathetic to the mechanistic philosophy, with its close ties to atomism. English exiles during the Civil War period, particularly the circle associated with the duke of Newcastle, William Cavendish, and his wife Margaret, had patronized Thomas Hobbes, and associated

sendi sur le mouvement des idees à la fin du XVII siècle," *Actes du Congrès du Tricentenaire de Pierre Gassendi* (Paris, 1955); Bonno, *Relations intellectuelles*; Raymond Polin, *La politique morale de John Locke* (Paris, 1960); Richard I. Aaron, *John Locke* (Oxford, 1963); Driscoll, *Influence of Gassendi*; David Fate Norton, "The Myth of 'British Empiricism,' " *History of European Ideas* 1 (1981): 331–44; Kroll, "The Question of Locke's Relation to Gassendi," 339–59; Joy, *Gassendi the Atomist*, 198–203.
[7] Driscoll, "Influence of Gassendi," 87–110. François Bernier, *Abregé de la Philosophie de M. Gassendi*, 8 vols. (Lyon, 1678, 1684).
[8] J. R. Milton, "Locke at Oxford," in *Locke's Philosophy: Context and Content*, 27, and "Locke's Life and Times," in *The Cambridge Companion to Locke*, ed. Vere Chappell (Cambridge, 1994), 12–13, argues that there is little evidence that Locke knew or cared about Gassendi. His conclusion seems to rest mainly on Locke's personal papers, and not on a reading of the text of Locke's works, which I believe is more revealing. I await with interest a more detailed presentation of his arguments in "Locke and Gassendi: A Reappraisal," in *Studies in Seventeenth-Century Philosophy*, ed. M. A. Stewart (Oxford, forthcoming).

with Gassendi and Descartes. They became the conduit for atomistic ideas to cross the English Channel when they returned with the Restoration.[9] The doctrine that pleasure is the highest good—whether correctly understood or not—may also have appealed to the Restoration public. Richard Kroll goes so far as to argue that Epicureanism supplied a "newer culture to displace an older one" to the English neoclassicists of the late seventeenth century, seeking for models to justify a less traditional world-view.[10] Thirteen editions, translations, and interpretations of Lucretius's *De Rerum Natura* were published, and numerous mentions of Epicureanism appeared in English works.[11]

At the same time that Epicurus and Lucretius were received so warmly, several works of Gassendi were translated into English, including *The Life of Peiresc* (1657), *The Vanity of Judiciary Astrology* (1659), the *De Vita et Moribus Epicuri* and the *Philosophiae Epicuri Syntagma* in Thomas Stanley's *History of Philosophy* (1687), and finally, in 1699, parts of Bernier's *Abregé* which were a paraphrase of the "Ethics" of Gassendi.[12] The impression that Gassendi made in England was so significant that Sorbière, one of Gassendi's disciples—perhaps not an altogether reliable witness—claimed that the Royal Society was divided into a Gassendist and a Cartesian camp.[13]

Gassendi in England

It would be difficult to imagine a more receptive climate for Gassendi's influence than England in the late seventeenth century. Turning away from the turmoil of civil war and religious change, thinkers of the Restoration period embraced the newly emerging mechanistic worldview and the probabilistic epistemology which supported it. The men who gathered to conduct experiments and witness each other's work at the Royal Society were fascinated with atomism; but Epicureanism

---

[9] Robert H. Kargon, *Atomism in England from Hariot to Newton* (Oxford, 1966), 68–77.

[10] Richard W. F. Kroll, *Material Word*, 85–86. On the effect of Epicureanism in England, see also Thomas Mayo, *Epicurus in England (1650–1725)* (Dallas, Tex., 1934); Kargon, *Atomism in England.*

[11] Mayo, *Epicurus in England*, xi.

[12] Gassendus, Pierre, *The Mirrour of True Nobility and Gentility. Being the Life of the Renowned Nicolaus Lord of Peiresck; The Vanity of Judiciary Astrology;* Thomas Stanley, *The History of Philosophy: Containing the Lives, Opinions, Actions, and Discourses of the Philosophers of Every Sect,* 2d ed., 3 vols. (London, 1687); and François Bernier, *Three Discourses of Happiness, Virtue, and Liberty, collected from the works of the Learn'd Gassendi* (London, 1699). Also see, Don C. Allen, "The Rehabilitation of Epicurus and His Theory of Pleasure in the Early Renaissance," *Studies in Philology* 41 (1944): 3.

[13] Sorbière, *Voyage to England*, 38.

provided the philosophic home quarters for atheism, which made the virtuosi more than uncomfortable. Its materialism seemed to be re-emerging in the thought of Thomas Hobbes, who was perhaps even more threatening than Epicurus himself. The restoration rakes seemed to embrace the moral laxity and decadence popularly associated with the ancient philosophy.[14] Some way had to be found to permit the science of Epicureanism without succumbing to its purported moral and religious excesses. It was Gassendi who demonstrated how the previously heterodox doctrine could be rehabilitated for the Christian conscience.[15]

The virtuosi praised the wisdom of God as revealed in his creation. Like Gassendi, they viewed the study of the natural world as an almost religious enterprise. Natural philosophers, natural theologians, Latitudinarians, and Anglicans (several thinkers spanned more than one category) all believed that God was revealed in the cosmos he created and his law could be apprehended by reason with "moral certainty."[16] Some of these men, such as John Wilkins (1614–1672), a founding member of the Royal Society, and John Tillotson, a close friend of Locke, adopted an epistemological probabilism to underscore their rejection of reverence for authority and to distance themselves from complete skepticism. They too, as had Gassendi, proclaimed the importance of the freedom to philosophize, and felt demonstrative certainty would limit human freedom by compelling human belief.[17] To people with these attitudes, Gassendi, if they had read him, must have seemed like a compatriot, even though he was a Catholic priest from a different land. How closely they read Gassendi remains open to speculation, except in the case of Robert Boyle, who readily admitted his debt to Gassendi and commended his physics. Boyle's corpuscular philosophy drew on both Gassendi and Descartes, and validated corpuscularism in the English scientific community in the late seventeenth century.[18] Another example

---

[14] Westfall, *Science and Religion*, 107–11; Shapiro, *Probability and Certainty*, 85–86.

[15] J. J. MacIntosh, "Robert Boyle on Epicurean Atheism and Atomism," in *Atoms, Pneuma, and Tranquillity*, 198, while investigating whether Robert Boyle was an atomist, asks, "Hadn't Gassendi made it clear to all that atomism was the thinking experimentalist's hypothesis of choice?"

[16] Shapiro, *Probability and Certainty*, 74–118.

[17] Ibid., 74–75, 86–87. On Wilkins, see also Barbara J. Shapiro, *John Wilkins, 1614–1672: Intellectual Biography* (Berkeley, 1969); and Barbara J. Shapiro, "Latitudinarianism and Science in Seventeenth-Century England," and S. F. Mason, "Science and Religion in Seventeenth-Century England," both in *The Intellectual Revolution of the Seventeenth Century*, Past and Present Series, ed. Charles Webster (London, 1974).

[18] Marie Boas Hall, *Robert Boyle on Natural Philosophy: An Essay with Selections from His Writings* (Bloomington, Ind., 1965), 281–82, and Robert H. Kargon, "Walter Charleton, Rob-

of pronounced Gassendist is Walter Charleton (1619–1707), who not only read the French philosopher, but also translated his work and incorporated his ideas into his own treatises.

Charleton was an Anglican and a staunch royalist. According to John Aubrey, Charleton was a good friend of Thomas Hobbes, and his active participation in the Royal Society must have served to acquaint him with Robert Boyle and perhaps with Locke.[19] He published four books which show his interest in Epicureanism, containing as they do almost the entire corpus of Epicurean physical and ethical beliefs. Several scholars have realized that his *Physiologia Epicuro-Gassendo-Charletoniana* (1654) is for the most part a translation of the physical part of Gassendi's *Animadversiones*, but it has not been noticed that *The Darkness of Atheism* (1652) is also largely a selective translation from Gassendi's *Animadversiones*, published in 1648 and containing (in a somewhat fragmented form) Gassendi's entire system.[20] Charleton's dependence on Gassendi is so intimate that the same arguments, phraseology, and metaphors appear in the works of both.

Since Charleton was a physician, his interest in the scientific aspects of Epicureanism is not surprising. His fascination with ethical theory as well demonstrates how intertwined Epicurean atomism and morality were to seventeenth-century thinkers. Charleton was careful not to become associated with materialism and atheism. Because Gassendi had faced the same problem, Charleton could happily adopt the Frenchman's philosophy as his own.[21]

Charleton attacked Epicurean materialism as nonrational, and insisted instead on both the special and general providence of God. He realized, however, perhaps more clearly than Gassendi, the implications of an overwhelming providence for human liberty. Charleton empha-

---

ert Boyle, and the Acceptance of Epicurean Atomism in England," *Isis* 55 (1964): 184–92. Also on Boyle's knowledge of Gassendi, see MacIntosh, "Boyle on Epicurean Atomism," and Margaret J. Osler, "The Intellectual Sources of Robert Boyle's Philosophy of Nature: Gassendi's Voluntarism and Boyle's Physico-Theological Project," in *Philosophy, Science, and Religion, 1640–1700*, ed. Richard Ashcraft, Richard Kroll, and Perez Zagorin (Cambridge, 1991), 178–98.

[19] Lindsey Sharp, "Walter Charleton's Early Life, 1620–1659, and the Relationship to Natural Philosophy in Seventeenth-Century England," *Annals of Science* 30 (1973): 311–40; Westfall, *Science and Religion*, 17.

[20] Walter Charleton, *The Darkness of Atheism Dispelled by the Light of Nature: A Physico-Theological Treatise* (London, 1652); and *Physiologia Epicuro-Gassendo-Charletoniana, or a Fabrick of Science Natural Upon the Hypothesis of Atoms, Founded by Epicurus, Repaired by Petrus Gassendus, Augmented by Walter Charleton* (London, 1654; reprint, New York, 1966).

[21] On Charleton and Gassendi, see Margaret J. Osler, "Descartes and Charleton on Nature and God," *Journal of the History of Ideas* 40 (1979): 445–56.

sized the voluntaristic themes in Gassendi's theology, arguing for God's absolute power in establishing the chain of causes and effects in the natural world, which then can be changed only by God's direct action. Elaborating on this theme, he concluded provisionally, "That Man is the object of God's special Providence, and by consequence, that all occurrences of his life are punctually predetermined, ordered, and brought to pass by fortune."[22]

Charleton was as unhappy with this conclusion as Gassendi had been. He was a high church Anglican, and rejected Calvinism as fervently as Gassendi had rejected Oratorianism and Jansenism. To both, a human being must be responsible for his own acts, or else the whole fabric of Christian morality comes apart. To avoid falling into the trap of absolute fatality, or complete predestination, while at the same time avoiding the chance of the Epicureans, Charleton adopts "a middle way"— Gassendi's Molinist-colored doctrine of freedom.[23] At the very beginning of this discussion, Charleton summarized his theory:

> God hath set on our right real and true Good, on our left only specious and apparent: the election of either is dependent on our Will, our Will is guided by our Judgement, and our Judgement is the determination or resolve of our Intellect (for without dispute, though common physiology had founded this Liberty on the indifferency of the Will; yet is it radicated in the indifferency of the Intellect, or Cognoscent Faculty, primarily, and the Will only secondarily, insomuch as that ever follows the mauduction of the Intellect) but yet that he might in a manner direct us in our choice, he hath annexed Happiness as reward to invite us to one, and Misery as a punishment to deter us from the other: and therefore 'tis manifest that God wills the felicity of all men, more than they themselves can desire it.[24]

Freedom of the will is possible because of a prior freedom of the intellect, which is indifferent and is able to suspend its judgments, a point Charleton elaborated at great length. God's providence consists in endowing us with the capacity to pursue happiness and avoid misery. Error consists in our mistaking evil for good, and the judgment of the intellect is founded on the "simple apprehensions" of sense perception. Man is always striving for the good, but it is only possible for the Elect in heaven to obtain.[25]

[22] Charleton, *Darkness of Atheism*, 136, 170.
[23] Ibid., 215, 218, 211–19.
[24] Ibid., 182–83.
[25] Ibid., 263–69.

Charleton, like Gassendi, believed that freedom determined by causal factors is merely "libency," or spontaneity, "no more than a certain blind impulse of nature grounded upon no praecedent ratiocination," like the actions of brutes and children, or the laws of natural phenomena.[26] Thus, humans possess freedom (*libertas*) because of both the abilities and the weaknesses of their faculties, and this freedom is inescapable while one is human.

Clearly Charleton recapitulated parts of Gassendi's ethical system and made it available to the English reading public. Locke could have known Gassendi's ideas from either Charleton or Boyle, or as Richard Kroll argues, through Thomas Stanley's *History of Philosophy*, which contained a translation of Gassendi's *Syntagma Philosophiae Epicuri*, an appendix and summary of Gassendi's *Animadversiones*.[27]

According to Driscoll, from the time of Locke's first meeting with Boyle in the 1660s, there appeared references in his notebooks to the works of Gassendi: these include quotations from the *Life of Peiresc* and quotations from the "Physics" of the *Syntagma Philosophicum*. The quotations from the *Life of Peiresc* occur in the 1664–1666 notebooks and concern Gassendi's analysis of the accomplishments of famous scholars. A 1660–1661 notebook contains the material from the "Physics," which is drawn from a section of the *Syntagma* about experiments for the existence of the void.[28] This notebook also includes transcriptions of the praises of Gassendi by Boyle and other writers. Locke may also have purchased the *Opera Omnia* for himself later in his life, during his time of exile in Holland between 1683 and 1689.[29] Taken together, these references to Gassendi and his works testify to Locke's long and sympathetic acquaintance with the doctrines of the French neo-Epicurean.

Gassendi and Locke's early writings

Similarities in background and temperament may in part explain the sympathy of the English thinker for his French predecessor. Both had

[26] Ibid., 264.
[27] Kroll, "Locke's Relation to Gassendi," 339–59. Kroll does not sufficiently distinguish between the *Syntagma Philosophiae Epicuri*, in *Opera*, 3:1–94, and the *Syntagma Philosophicum*, which leads to some confusion in his argument. Fred and Emily Michael, "Theory of Ideas," note that Locke could have learned the Epicurean Canonic included in this work from a number of Gassendi's other works, including the *Syntagma Philosophicum* (383).
[28] Driscoll, "Influence of Gassendi," 90, believes this notebook was written in 1667, but Milton, "Locke in Oxford," in *Locke's Philosophy*, 39, dates it to 1660–61.
[29] Driscoll, "Influence of Gassendi," 89–90.

survived a scholastic education and university career which they, for the most part, repudiated. Both were tolerant in matters of religion, and unhappy with the divisions caused by sectarian quarrels. Both had noble patrons; Louis of Valois for Gassendi and the earl of Shaftesbury for Locke. Both found much to trouble them in the rationalist doctrines of Descartes, which they viewed as creating a new dogmatism in philosophy.[30]

But the comparison has limits, which may account for some of the subtle differences between their ethical philosophies. One of Gassendi's aims was to articulate a philosophy that could allow the wise man to achieve tranquillity even while he was—usually unwillingly—caught up in the active world of affairs. Locke, on the other hand, was developing an ethics, and a concomitant ontology and epistemology, with a more pronounced redemptive aim: the education and molding of an enlightened, progressive, and tolerant individual who would happily participate in the life of his times.[31]

Gassendi lived in an absolute state, which encouraged political abstention as far as the demands of society allowed, and fostered the cultivation of the distanced life. Locke lived during a time of moral and political turmoil, when a new constitution and a new kind of citizenship were being developed in England. Locke, himself, was an actor in the drama of his days, even having to flee in 1683 from England when Shaftesbury and the Whigs failed to exclude or remove James II from succession to the crown.[32] Consequently, Locke's hedonism is less concerned with an internalized state of tranquillity and more centered on the active life, and his political philosophy is a support for forms of political rebellion, something Gassendi would never have condoned.

Long before these events, however, Locke was exposed to Gassendist ideas. While Locke pursued his early medical and scientific studies in Oxford, Boyle may have introduced him to Gassendi. In 1676, Locke went to France for his health, and he came into contact with many of the most prominent Gassendists, including François Bernier. When Locke returned to England, he carried a copy of Bernier's *Abregé* of Gassendi's

---

[30] Lennon, *Gods and Giants*, 172–73, argues that Locke's anti-dogmatic stance was directed as much toward Cartesian rationalism as toward religious enthusiasm. His point, which is very well taken, is that any dogmatic attitude engenders a militaristic self-righteousness which endangers morality and politics.
[31] Tully, *Locke in Contexts*, 218, emphasizes the prescriptive nature of Locke's moral philosophy.
[32] A good, short summary of Locke's life can be found in Milton, "Locke's Life and Times," 5–25.

Syntagma Philosophicum, the most extensive edition of which had appeared in 1678.[33] Even though Bernier's account diverged in some ways from Gassendi's philosophy, a person could still receive a comprehensive introduction to Gassendism by reading it.[34] Locke's journals indicate that Locke and Bernier spent a good deal of time together, but there is no reference to discussions on anything but travel and strange customs.[35] This omission, combined with Locke's frequently denial of any direct philosophic influences, might support the view that Locke was not at all influenced by Gassendi, and that the similarities between their work reflect nothing more than their common philosophic milieu.[36] But many modern scholars have noted that Locke never credited philosophic mentors when he was contemplating ideas in his journals, and any specific citations are confined to the sources for particular facts.[37] Locke's lack of citations, therefore, hardly outweighs the reality that at exactly the same time Locke had access to Gassendist writings, and was in daily contact with Bernier, passages start to appear in his journal dealing with will, power, pleasure, and pain in a remarkably Gassendist style.[38]

Moreover, what Locke did say about his conversations with Bernier is revealing. Bernier, in addition to his interest in Gassendism, was a famous travel writer who had traveled extensively in the East. His *Histoire de la dernière révolution des États du Grand Mogol* appeared in 1670–1671, just five years before he and Locke met, and other travel works appeared throughout the decade. Bernier shared his expert knowledge of strange lands and peoples with Locke, who wrote about one of their conversations: "Monsieur Bernier told me that the heathens of Hindoostan pretend to great antiquity; that they have books and histories in their language; that their nodus in their numbers is ten, as ours, and their circuit of days seven."[39] Other conversations included discussions of different moral and religious customs.[40]

[33] Driscoll, "Influence of Gassendi," 89–94.

[34] Sylvia Murr, "Bernier et le gassendisme," in *Bernier et les Gassendistes*, ed. Sylvia Murr, *Corpus: revue de philosophie* 20–21 (1992): 115–35.

[35] Bonno, *Relations intellectuelles*, 39–41.

[36] Driscoll, "Influence of Gassendi," 88.

[37] For example, see Bonno, *Relations intellectuelles*, 87, and the introduction to John Locke, *Two Treatises of Government: A Critical Edition with an Introduction and Apparatus Criticus*, ed. Peter Laslett (Cambridge, 1967), 130.

[38] Aaron, *John Locke*, 53; Driscoll, "Influence of Gassendi," 88.

[39] Peter, Lord King, *The Life and Letters of John Locke with extracts from His Journals and Common-Place Books* (1884; reprint, New York, 1972), 73.

[40] Lennon, *Gods and Giants*, 158–59. Lennon also notes that Locke possessed all of the works of Bernier, but in different editions from those originally published.

As Paul Hazard has established, travel literature and the accounts it had of foreign cultures were not intellectually neutral. The fascination with the other led Europeans to doubt the infallibility and truth of their own cultural forms and beliefs.[41] Bernier brought the knowledge he had gained of other cultures to his reading of Gassendi, inserting comments on other places into his *Abregé* whenever they seemed appropriate to embellish the text and make it seem more "modern," which was one of his aims.[42] For example, after translating most of Gassendi's discussion of Epicurus's espousal of the frugal life, Bernier commented, "I think I ought not here to omit, what I know concerning the manner of the Eastern Indians Living, if it were only to shew that all these fine things we have spoken of, are not only bare Philosophical Speculations."[43]

At the same time Bernier was publishing various editions of the *Abregé* in the 1670s, he was also at the forefront of a defense of Gassendi against Descartes. The quarrel between Descartes and Gassendi transcended their deaths and was at the forefront of French intellectual life in the second half of the seventeenth century.[44] Much of this debate revolved around the status of innate ideas; later in the century Locke would join the chorus of those who denied the possibility of their existence. But Gassendi's rejection of innate ideas had a moral and social component. His doctrine of pleasure and pain established an internal, instinctive normative psychology, without advocating innate moral norms. Hence, he believed there were no laws of nature which transcended cultural borders, but only certain human inclinations which made us pursue what was individually or culturally seen as pleasurable.[45] Such a view might have inspired or at least confirmed the acceptance of cultural relativity found in Bernier. Thus, when Bernier discussed different foreign customs with Locke, the implications are that the conversation was more than a travelogue. It may have contributed to Locke's growing empiricist epistemology and his emerging hedonism.

In France, Locke adopted the cardinal Epicurean principle that pleasure is the greatest good and pain the greatest evil. He was greatly concerned with "happiness" during this period, and in 1677, he wrote,

[41] Paul Hazard, *The European Mind [1680–1715]*, trans. J. Lewis May (French edition, Paris, 1935; English edition, New York, 1952), 10–12.
[42] On Bernier's modernity, see Jean Mesnard, "La modernité de Bernier," in *Bernier et les Gassendistes*, 105–13.
[43] Bernier, *Three Discourses*, 171.
[44] Lennon, *Gods and Giants*, 34–51; Murr, "Bernier et le gassendisme," 128–29.
[45] Gassendi, "Ethics," in *SP, Opera*, 2:799–801.

The business of men being to be happy in this world by the enjoyment of the things of nature subservient to life ease and pleasure and by the comfortable hope of an other world when this is ended: and in the other world by the accumulation of higher degrees in an everlasting security, we need noe other knowledge for the attainment of those ends but of the history and observation of the effects and operations of naturall bodies within our power, and of our dutys in the management of our owne actions as they depend on our wills i. e. as far as they are in our power.[46]

Throughout his work, from these early statements to the final composition of *An Essay concerning Human Understanding,* Locke saw the study of nature and the study of ethics as complementary enterprises. In Book 4 of the *Essay,* after stating that "Morality is the proper Science and Business of Mankind in general; (who are both concerned and fitted to search out their *Summum Bonum),*" Locke added, "I would not therefore be thought to dis-esteem, or dissuade the Study of Nature."[47]

Both ethics and scientific and epistemological investigations interested Gassendi and Locke. In the case of both thinkers some scholars have concentrated on their scientific and epistemological ideas and have discounted their ethical and religious ideas, which in fact may have held primacy in their thinking.[48] It is the hedonistic strand that unites Locke's earlier and later ethical thought, just as it was a constant in Gassendi's philosophy.

Locke's interest in hedonism may have been encouraged by a discussion of hedonistic and utilitarian ethics pursued by proponents of natural religion in the 1660s and 1670s. John Wilkins and John Tillotson had argued that individuals made moral decisions by calculating what would bring them the greatest pleasure, both while on earth and in the celestial hereafter. These divines belonged to a tradition of Anglican casuistry, which made moral decision the result of "a reasoned calculation of probabilities based on the best and most complete information and evidence available." Wilkins argued, moreover, that one should sus-

---

[46] John Locke, *An Early Draft of Locke's Essay,* ed. R. I. Aaron and Joscelyn Gibb (Oxford, 1936), 88. This will be cited as Aaron and Gibb.

[47] John Locke, *An Essay concerning Human Understanding,* ed. Peter H. Nidditch (Oxford, 1975, 1979), 4.12.11 & 12 (646–47). A similar statement can be found in an unpublished paper of Locke's called "Of Ethics in general": "morality be the great business and concernment of mankind, and so deserves our most attentive application and study" (King, *Life and Letters,* 308). The Nidditch edition of the *Essay* will be cited by book, chapter, and paragraph with the page numbers following in parentheses.

[48] This argument about Locke is made by Nidditch in his Introduction to the *Essay* (xix), and John Colman, *John Locke's Moral Philosophy* (Edinburgh, 1983), 1.

pend one's belief in obscure matters and debate pro and con when making a decision.[49] The resonances to Gassendi's ethics are clear; whether they developed independently of knowledge of his moral philosophy is not. Whatever may be the case, this theological discussion may have caught Locke's attention and directed him to examine a hedonism he had also encountered in Gassendi.[50]

In a journal entry dated July 13, 1676, Locke credited pleasure and pain as two of the "four simple ideas we have of the minde." We possess perception and will ("wherein the mind doth after consideration . . . begin continue or change some action which it findes in its power to do") and pleasure or delight and pain or uneasiness. In the next entry, Locke argued that the reason we act morally is because of the possibility of eternal bliss or damnation: "It would make a man very wary how he embraces an opinion where there is such unequal odds and where the consequences are of such moment and soe infinitely different." This passage suggests that moral behavior is contingent on a calculation of what will lead to heavenly pleasure.[51]

Locke was fascinated with the doctrines of pleasure and pain not just from an epistemological standpoint—as the necessary accompaniment of perception and action—but also as a moral and theological constant. He embraced a theologically oriented hedonism that varies little from Gassendi's, except perhaps in his theory of will, which at this point is closer to Descartes's. This development was completed by fall, 1678, when Locke wrote in his journal:

> That the happiness of man consists in pleasure whether of body or mind, according to everyone's relish. The *summum malum* is pain, or dolor of body and mind; that this is so, I appeal not only to the experience of all mankind, and the thoughts of all mankind, and the thoughts of every man's breast, but to the best rule of this—the Scripture, which tells that at the right-hand of God, the place of bliss, are pleasures forevermore; and that which men are condemned for, is not for seeking momentary pleasures, but for preferring the momentary pleasures of this life to those joys which shall have no end.[52]

[49] Shapiro, *Probability and Certainty*, 87–88, 104–5. See Chap. 1 for the beginnings of this kind of hedonistic ethics in the Renaissance and sixteenth century.

[50] I thank the anonymous reviewer of my manuscript for Cornell University Press for this suggestion. It is well worth pursuing.

[51] Aaron and Gibb, 81–82.

[52] Quoted in Driscoll, "Influence of Gassendi," 100, where he compares it with a parallel passage in Bernier. Locke's doctrine of pleasure in his journal also is similar to that of Lorenzo Valla, who in *De vero bono* also articulated a theological hedonism or Christian Epicureanism. See Trinkaus, *In Our Image*, 1:103–70 and Chap. 1 above.

The similarity between Gassendi's and Locke's doctrines is striking. Locke emphasized the importance of pleasure as a motivation for human action, within the context of divine bliss. This fascination with pleasure and pain continued after Locke returned to England in the 1680s, when his ethics became ever more hedonistic and Gassendist. This is particularly so of two manuscript pieces quoted by Lord King in his biography of Locke, "Thus I think" and "Of Ethics in general."[53]

In "Thus I think" Locke stated again that, "It is a man's proper business to seek happiness and avoid misery. . . . But here I must mistake not; for if I prefer a short pleasure to a lasting one, it is plain I cross my own happiness." This is a clear statement of the calculus of pleasure and pain. The pleasures of this life consist in health, reputation, knowledge, and doing good—in short, in a moderate and virtuous life—but most especially, "The expectation of eternal and incomprehensible happiness in another world is that also which carries a constant pleasure with it."[54] The teleological emphasis of Locke's hedonism is perhaps even more evident than in Gassendi's ethics. Obviously, striving for the eternal good is the ultimate motivation of action for both, but since Gassendi thought the realization of such happiness abrogated human liberty, he emphasized this motif far less than Locke did.

In "Of Ethics in general," Locke expanded on the moral and theological character of pleasure and pain. "Happiness and misery are the two great springs of human action," Locke wrote, although the nature of what brings happiness or pain is relative to the circumstances one finds oneself in, "that which is good for one man is bad for another." Gassendi also endorsed a concept of moral relativity, but both he and Locke stepped back from complete moral anarchy. Both agreed that as a general rule an action is moral or not according to the judgment of the society in which one lives.[55] But a moral constant is established by the predisposition to good and an aversion to evil, and this is related to pleasure and pain: "Now, though it be not so apprehended generally, yet it is from this tendency to produce to us pleasure and pain, that moral good or evil has its name, as well as natural . . . there is nothing morally good which does not produce pleasure to a man, nor nothing morally evil that does not bring pain to him."[56]

Pleasure and pain become the criterion for good and evil, just as they

[53] King, *Life and Letters*, 306–22.
[54] Ibid., 306–7.
[55] Ibid., 311, 309.
[56] Ibid., 311.

are in Gassendi. According to Locke, natural good and evil is the result of something naturally producing pleasure and pain in us. This corresponds to Gassendi's assertion that all natural actions—eating, drinking, procreating—are pursued to the extent that they produce pleasure and diminish pain. On this level, the desire for pleasure and the aversion to pain seem to be instinctive. But just as Gassendi did, Locke employed another level in his hedonistic ethics: moral good and evil result when a rational agent freely chooses an action which will result in pleasure or pain. According to Locke, "Moral actions are only those that depend upon the choice of an understanding and free agent." The connection of pleasure and pain, good and evil, and rationality and freedom echoed Gassendi—although once again, Locke emphasized the ultimate moral standard created by God when he instituted reward and punishment for morally good and evil acts.[57]

Gassendi and Locke's *Essay concerning Human Understanding*

Not surprisingly, when Locke continued this same discussion in *An Essay concerning Human Understanding*, the chapter "Of modes of pleasure and pain" precedes the chapter, "Of power," which is concerned with the question of human liberty. Earlier in the text Locke once again espouses the pleasure-pain principle and puts it within a providential framework:

> Nature, I confess, has put into Man a desire of Happiness and an aversion to Misery: These indeed are innate practical Principles which (as practical Principles ought) do continue constantly to operate and influence all our Actions, without ceasing: These may be observ'd in all Persons and all Ages, steady and universal; but there are Inclinations of the Appetite to good, not Impressions of truth on the Understanding.[58]

Locke followed Gassendi in defining the pleasure-pain principle as instinctive in every person—in the sense that the desire for pleasure and avoidance of pain is a psychological constant, not an innate moral

---

[57] Ibid., 310. Tully, *Locke in Contexts*, emphasizes what he calls the "penal" rather than hedonistic element in Locke's morality. Pleasure and pain, or happiness and misery, are the devices both human legislators and God use (or should use in the human case) to shape conduct. Tully mentions that Locke may have gotten this idea from Gassendi (200–203).

[58] Locke, *Essay*, 1.3.3 (Nidditch, 67).

disposition.[59] Locke further agreed that once these desires affect us, they motivate our actions. This dynamic element of pleasure and pain duplicates Gassendi's argument and seems to affirm Locke's debt to him. Later in the *Essay*, Locke asks whether such inclinations are free or determined, and whether someone who willingly pursues a pleasure or avoids a pain is acting freely.

Locke broadened his analysis of the relationship between God, happiness, and the development of human society in the same chapter: "For God, having, by an inseparable connexion, joined Virtue and publick Happiness together; and made the Practice thereof necessary to the preservation of Society, and visibly beneficial to all, with whom the Virtuous Man has to do; it is no wonder that every one should, not only allow, but recommend and magnifie those Rules to others, from whose observance of them, he is sure to reap Advantage to himself."[60]

Here the public good of the state is guaranteed by the virtuous behavior of everyone in it, individuals who value virtuous behavior as vital to themselves. The connection of happiness and utility and providence is one of the Epicurean motifs Gassendi most emphasized, and it seemed to be equally evident for Locke. Both philosophers share a commitment to a utilitarian ethics grounded in God's providential plan. In this context, the search for pleasure and the avoidance of pain becomes a principle of obligation, because our own natures obligate us to obey laws in both the spiritual and civil realms.[61]

Locke continued his discussion of pleasure and pain in Book 2, chapter 20, "Of modes of pleasure and pain." Here he again defined the pleasure principle, and showed how it relates to various passions. In this chapter, he affirmed strongly that the experience of pleasure and pain, although dependent to some extent on the body, is most intimately con-

[59] Tully, *Locke in Contexts*, 183, argues that Locke denied that there were any innate dispositions toward good and evil. All human action is the result of external stimuli, upon which a neutral mind works. I would agree that Locke held that there are no innate principles of morality which guide the mind, but he did believe that there are powerful predispositions toward pleasure and away from pain, predispositions which act as a psychological constant. Some commentators, however, have pointed out that Locke sometimes seems more inclined to give virtue and vice an objective value of their own. See, for example, Hans Aarsleff, "The State of Nature and the Nature of Man," in *John Locke: Problems and Perspectives*, ed. John W. Yolton (Cambridge, 1969), 111.

[60] Locke, *Essay*, 1.3.6 (Nidditch, 69).

[61] Raymond Polin, "Locke's Conception of Freedom," in *John Locke: Problems and Perspectives*, 1–18, argues that Locke's theory of freedom is based on man's possession of reason: "Reason, like liberty, appears in him in the form of an obligation, in the form of a law: to be obliged to be free in conformity with the law of man is to be obliged to be reasonable, to act freely in a reasonable manner." (8).

nected with the mind. Although Locke never recited the traditional Epicurean formula of tranquillity in the soul and absence of pain in the body, it is plain that to him these are the fundamentals of happiness: "By Pleasure and Pain, I must be understood to mean of Body or Mind, as they are commonly distinguished; though in truth, they be only different Constitutions of the Mind, sometimes occasioned by disorder in the Body, sometimes by Thoughts of the mind."[62]

Pleasure and pain determine what is considered good and what is considered evil. Good increases pleasure and diminishes pain, while evil does the opposite. If someone finds himself without something which might bring pleasure, he feels uneasiness, and then desire for the absent good. Uneasiness and desire result in human action: "the chief if not only spur to humane Industry and Action is uneasiness."[63]

Thus, Locke again emphasized the motivational propensities of pleasure and pain, but he further distinguished the very simple modes of pleasure and pain, such as hunger and thirst, from the more nuanced modes: the various passions, the results of sensation and reflection.[64] This is Gassendi's distinction between levels of the pleasure-pain principle: The simplest desire for pleasure and aversion to pain is instinctive, while the more complex forms involve long-term calculations.

In chapter 21, "Of Power," Locke elaborated his concepts of pleasure and pain, and connected them with his theory of the mind and his concept of human liberty. Again like Gassendi, Locke considered these inseparable elements in understanding actions.

According to Locke, power itself is either active or passive: active when an agent can change simple ideas, passive when simple ideas can be changed in the agent.[65] The meaning of power is seen most clearly from observing the operations of the mind. These operations are commonly called Will and Understanding: "This Power which the mind has, thus to order the consideration of any Idea, or the forbearing to consider it; or to prefer the motion of any part of the body to its rest . . . , is that which we call the Will. . . . The power of Perception is that which we call

---

[62] Locke, *Essay*, 2.20.2 (Nidditch, 229).
[63] Ibid., 2.20.6 (Nidditch, 230).
[64] Ibid., 2.20.18 (Nidditch, 233).
[65] Ibid., 2.21.1 & 2 (Nidditch, 234–35). Joy argues in *Gassendi the Atomist*, 220–23, that Gassendi and Locke had very different epistemologies, and especially that Locke's concept of "idea" was very different from Gassendi's theory of "image," or what the senses present to judgment. Hence, for this reason and others, she feels that Locke was not greatly influenced by Gassendi. There are certainly differences in the content of Locke's epistemology from Gassendi's, but in terms of the relationship of an empirical epistemology to ethics they remain very similar.

the Understanding."[66] Once an individual realizes what is in his power, he quickly develops a concept of liberty and necessity: "Every one, I think, finds in himself a Power to begin or forbear, continue or put an end to several Actions in himself. From the consideration of the extent of this power of the mind over the actions of the Man, which everyone finds in himself, arise the Ideas of Liberty and Necessity."[67]

So far, all of this sounds very much like Gassendi, and like many other seventeenth-century philosophers. Both Locke and Gassendi repeated the traditional motif, recognized by almost all involved in this debate, that part of man's liberty is to be free from restraint or compulsion and thus to choose or reject as he pleases. Locke wrote, "For wherever restraint comes to check that Power, or compulsion takes away the Indifferency of Ability on either side to act, or to forebear acting, there liberty and our Notion of it presently ceases."[68] This is Locke's first mention of "indifference," a concept integral to Gassendi's theory of liberty, and to which Locke will return later.

At this point, Locke went out of his way to emphasize that the will and the understanding, traditionally treated as faculties of the mind— almost, in fact, as independent agents—are actually only "powers" of the mind. It is the whole mind—the person—who acts, not his faculties as if with a life of their own.[69]

Locke was clearly annoyed with the debate about the relative powers of the intellect and the will. It does not go too far to see in this impatience a response to the conflict about the mind's faculties that animated Gassendi's "Objection" to Descartes's *Meditations*, particularly Meditation Four. Gassendi himself had ridiculed the faculty theory of the mind, but nevertheless made good use of it.[70]

Both Locke and Gassendi seem uncomfortable with the traditional association of liberty with the will. Gassendi's response to this debate was essentially to transfer all the powers of the will to the intellect, with broad implications for his ethical theory. Locke responded, on the other hand, with the argument that the faculties are powers and not agents, so it is ridiculous to treat them as agents. And so, Locke concluded, "To return then to the Enquiry about Liberty, I think the Question is not proper, whether the Will be free, but whether a Man be free."[71]

[66] Locke, *Essay*, 2.21.5 (Nidditch, 236).
[67] Ibid., 2.21.7 (Nidditch, 237).
[68] Ibid., 2.21.10 (Nidditch, 238).
[69] Ibid., 2.21.15 (Nidditch, 240).
[70] This is even clearer in Locke, *Essay*, 2.21.14, 2.21.18, and 2.21.20 (Nidditch, 240–43). Locke knew the *Meditations* and therefore had access to Gassendi's "Objection."
[71] Locke, *Essay*, 2.21.21 (Nidditch, 244).

The answer to this question is fundamental to any ethical system. Locke's analysis of the problem was much more subtle than Gassendi's, yet in many ways, especially in his later reformulations, he almost replicated the French philosopher. In order to come up with his final theory of freedom, however, he had to repudiate his original understanding of the question.[72]

In the first edition of the *Essay*, Locke argued that the will—here he reverted to the traditional usage—must be determined in one way or another, to choose one thing or another, and that the determining factor is the pleasure or pain received from an action: "For the cause of every less degree of Pain, as well as every greater degree of Pleasure, has the nature of Good, and vice versa, and is that which determines our Choice and challenges our Preference. Good then, the greater Good, is that alone which determines the will." Locke contended that determination by the greater good is liberty: "This is not an imperfection in Man, it is the highest perfection of intellectual Natures . . . 'tis the end and use of our Liberty: and the farther we are removed from such determination to Good, the nearer we are to Misery and Slavery."[73]

This statement is very close to the Cartesian view of causal determination by the good discussed in Chapter 4. It is not surprising that this conclusion is followed by a reference to those most free of all creatures, the angels, who perpetually are freely but determinately caught in the rapt contemplation of God.[74]

Gassendi also endorsed the idea that determination by vision of God, with the consequent lack of indifference, is the highest good. But he denied this was possible for humans and he argued, moreover, such determination would preclude human freedom. Humans, maintained Gassendi, cannot be determined by the greater good, because they have only probable, not certain knowledge. Epistemological uncertainty undermines causal necessity, but is the enabling condition of human freedom.[75]

To a certain extent, Locke maintained this epistemological argument.

[72] In my analysis, I take it as given that Locke is a libertarian, not a determinist, as some scholars have maintained. For a thorough examination of the historiography of this question, see Peter A. Schouls, *Reasoned Freedom: John Locke and the Enlightenment* (Ithaca, 1992), 117–26. Schouls's analysis of Locke's doctrine of freedom is very interesting, and much of it agrees with my own views, particularly in the conclusion that "it is Locke's position that agents are free if their unobstructed action is guided by reason" (134–35).

[73] Locke, *Essay*, 2.21.29 and 2.21.30 first edition (Nidditch, 252–53n).

[74] Ibid.

[75] For a more detailed discussion of Gassendi and Descartes on the liberty of indifference, see Chap. 4 above.

In the 1690 edition of the *Essay*, he stated, "So that, that which determines the choice of the Will, and obtains the preference, is still Good, the greater Good: but it is also the Good that appears; that which carries with it the Expectation of Addition to our Happiness, by the increase of our Pleasures, either in Degrees, Sorts, or Duration, or by the preventing, lessening, or shortening of pain."[76]

It is the *appearance* of the greater good that determines action. For Gassendi, this qualification fulfilled the demands of a libertarian ethical theory, but only because it is the intellect that is determined by the appearances of things, not the will. And the judgment of the intellect is epistemologically uncertain, as well as indifferent. It can pause and reflect before it decides on an action that the will then implements.

Since Locke retained the traditional usage in this early edition of the *Essay*, one which makes free action a product of the will, his answer comes short of providing an adequate concept of freedom from causal determination. The will still has to follow whatever is perceived as the greater good, apparent or not, without reference to a hesitating intellect.

Clearly Locke perceived this problem himself because in the fourth edition of the *Essay* (1700), he repudiated his earlier contention that the greater good determines the will, or that lack of indifference is a good.[77] In chapter 21, he first emphasized that an action can be voluntary and yet not be free. A free action has to be in the power of the agent, and even if one acts willingly but under some form of causal compulsion, one is not free:

All the Actions, that we have any Idea of, reducing themselves, as has been said, to these two, viz. Thinking and Motion, so far as a Man has a power to think, or not to think; to move or not to move, according to the preference or direction of his own mind, so far is a Man Free. Where-ever any performance or forbearance are not equally in a man's power; where-ever doing or not doing, will not equally follow upon the preference of his mind directing it, there he is not Free, though perhaps the Action may be voluntary.[78]

A person is not free when he is under some compulsion—as when falling from a collapsed bridge—but neither is he free when willingly

---

[76] Locke, *Essay*, 2.21.38, first edition (Nidditch, 270–71n).
[77] Vere Chappell, "Locke on Freedom of the Will," in *Locke's Philosophy*, 101–21, traces the various changes and inconsistencies in Locke's doctrine of free will.
[78] Locke, *Essay*, 2.21.8 (Nidditch, 237).

doing something that he is compelled to do. Locke distinguished between volition and freedom: "Liberty is not an Idea belonging to Volition, or preferring; but to the Person having the Power of doing or
forbearing to do, according as the Mind shall chuse and direct." Freedom is not an attribute of the will, which is simply a principle of execut-
ing action, but an aspect of the mind or the man himself, who decides
to do or not to do something.[79]

This discussion so nearly duplicates Gassendi's analysis of voluntary
freedom (*libentia*), and freedom (*libertas*), in the "Ethics," that it is difficult to believe that Locke did not have it in mind when he wrote it. To
Gassendi, if choice is determined by any causal factors, it will be voluntary and not free unless some other conditions intervene.

When Locke reformulated his ethical doctrines in later editions of the
Essay, he returned to a concept he had alluded to briefly in the 1690
edition of the *Essay*: the idea of "uneasiness." By the fourth edition
(1700), he accepted that the will continues to be determined by the
desire for happiness, but instead of the desire for happiness translating
into a search for the greatest good, it results rather in an effort to remove any present uneasiness, which is the consciousness of an absent
pleasure: "Good and Evil, present and absent, 'tis true, work upon the
mind. But that which immediately determines the Will, from time to
time, to every voluntary Action, is the uneasiness of desire, fixed on
some absent good: either negative, as indolency to one in pain; or positive, as enjoyment of pleasure."[80]

Since Locke assumed our greatest motivation is the removal of a present uneasiness—even if we intellectually realize the greatest good is future heavenly bliss—we will not strive for it unless there is some present
uneasiness that makes us feel, really feel, the absence of that very future
good. Otherwise we will remain content as we are: "the greater good,
though apprehended and acknowledged to be so, does not determine
the will, until our desire raised proportionately to it makes us uneasy in
want of it. . . . as long as he is content . . . , and finds no uneasiness in
it, he moves not."[81]

Locke argued that uneasiness itself—the consciousness that there is
some absent good which results in desire—can provide a limited escape
from determinism by the greatest good, because an absent good may
not produce a feeling of uneasiness vehement enough to overcome the

[79] Ibid., 2.21.10 and 2.21.15 (Nidditch, 238, 241).
[80] Ibid., 2.21.33 (Nidditch, 252).
[81] Ibid., 2.21.35 (Nidditch, 253).

content one is presently enjoying. Present pleasures and pains, if without obstruction, are always more compelling than future pleasures and pains. But while uneasiness might provide an escape from determination by the greatest good, it seems merely to substitute determination by the most pressing pleasure or pain, with pain itself the most determining of all forces.[82]

Locke did assert, as Gassendi did, that God still uses the desire for pleasure and the aversion to pain as part of his providential plan for humanity: "And thus we see our All-wise Maker, suitable to our constitutions and frame, and knowing what it is that determines the Will, has put into Man the uneasiness of hunger and thirst, and other natural desires, that return at their Seasons, to move and determine their Wills, for the preservation of themselves, and the continuation of their Species."[83]

This should be compared with Gassendi's very similar statement:

> It is suitable that we regard with wonder that cunning of the most wise Artificer of nature; for as every action was going to be wearisome in itself, even those that would be natural . . . , he therefore seasoned every action with a certain allurement of pleasure; and the more necessary the particular action was to be, either for the preservation of the entire race or for the preservation of each individual being, the greater he willed the pleasure to be.[84]

Both Locke and Gassendi, when discussing divine providence, posit a continuum between instinctive desires and other forms of human action, whether caused by either "uneasiness" and desire in Locke, or by the "certain allurement of pleasure" in Gassendi.

In fact, at times in the *Syntagma*, Gassendi came very close to the formulation of uneasiness that Locke adopted. The Frenchman certainly admitted that pain, and the inquietude caused by a feeling of lacking some good, is an effective spur to action: "certainly we need first and then we desire, and we satisfy the desire, then we are affected with pleasure. . . . Pleasure, therefore, is only in the exemption from need itself . . . certainly the imagination, rising to a new level, realizes that it has been missing something, and from a new opinion of need . . . a new desire is excited, and then a new pleasure is forged by once more satisfy-

[82] Ibid., 2.21.43 and 2.21.44 (Nidditch, 259–61).
[83] Ibid., 2.21.34 (Nidditch, 252).
[84] Gassendi, "Ethics," in *SP, Opera*, 2:701. Both Gassendi and Locke could have been paraphrasing Aristotle in these statements.

ing it."[85] Gassendi emphasized the felt need or desire of an absent good, which Locke calls uneasiness, as much as the pleasure in obtaining the good itself.

Both of these feelings—uneasiness and the recognition of missing pleasure—motivate human action, but are those actions free or simply voluntary? Both philosophers ultimately developed theories of ethical behavior that introduced a more pronounced libertarianism into their discussion. By the fourth edition of the *Essay*, Locke elaborated a concept of suspension of the judgment very close to Gassendi's concept of the liberty of indifference. After arguing that we are almost always determined by the greatest uneasiness, Locke added,

> but not always. For the mind having in most cases, as is evident in Experience, a power to suspend the execution and satisfaction of any of its desires, and so all, one after another, is at liberty to consider the objects of them, examine them on all sides, and weigh them with others. . . . This seems to me the source of all liberty; in this seems to consist that, which is (as I think improperly) call'd Free-will.[86]

Gassendi spent thousands of words in the *Syntagma* and *Disquisitio Metaphysica* proving that a man is free because his understanding controls his will, and that the understanding, although it must always pursue what is perceived as pleasurable and good and avoid what is perceived of as painful and evil, still has the power to suspend judgment while evaluating what the good is. It has the power to weigh the pros and cons—the same metaphor Locke used—before allowing the will to act.[87] Locke wrote, "And therefore every Man is put under a necessity by his constitution as an intelligent Being, to be determined in willing by his own Thought and Judgment, what is best for him to do: else he would be under the determination of some other than himself, which is want of liberty."[88] To Locke as to Gassendi, the judgment or intellect determines the actions of the will, and therefore freedom finds its roots in man's ability to determine himself, based on his own perceptions.

Locke then considers the question of whether we are determined by judgments of good and evil, which ultimately terminate the indifference of the mind. Like Gassendi, he believed that indifference is the ability to do one thing or do another, and as such is the first condition of

[85] Ibid., 2:703.
[86] Locke, *Essay*, 2.21.47 (Nidditch, 263).
[87] Gassendi, "Ethics," in *SP, Opera*, 2:822–25.
[88] Locke, *Essay*, 2.21.48 (Nidditch, 264).

freedom, but it is a condition ultimately abrogated in rational and free decision. He argued that human beings are absolutely free and indifferent when it came to performing an action like lifting up a hand, but such indifference would be a handicap if it meant the indifference to raise the hand to protect one from a blow.[89]

Gassendi did not see the abrogation of indifference as a problem that needed to be dealt with at length. For him, it was self-evident that rational decision, after weighing the pros and cons, was absolutely free—even if the result of calculated judgment always had to be the pursuit of the greater good. Locke was much more sensitive to the charge that even reasoned judgment is in a sense determined by causal factors.

Gassendi's doctrine of indifference and freedom is based on the distinction between will and intellect, a distinction that Locke disliked. For the French philosopher, indifference can characterize the intellect, but the will remains a "blind" and determined faculty. Locke, on the other hand, was not sure where indifference lay, whether with the understanding (Locke often calls the intellect the understanding), the will, or the man. Since Locke had to deal with the mind or the man who acts, he had to somehow make indifference a characteristic of judgment, at the same time he had to associate it with the will.

The ambiguities in Locke's position become visible when he summarized his argument at the end of "Of Power." He argued "Liberty is a power to act or not to act according as the Mind directs." Clear enough, but Locke then complicated the argument by arguing that it is the will which directs the "operative faculties to motion or rest," and "That which in the train of our voluntary actions determines the Will to any change of operation, is some present uneasiness, which is, or at least is always accompanied with that of desire." This statement can be read to mean that the will is actually determined in its *voluntary* actions necessarily, either by the uneasiness caused by the felt absence of some good, or more pressingly, as Locke goes on to say, by the desire to flee pain. Such an account seems to make decision willing but not free. But then Locke switched faculties again, and argued that while the desire for happiness is constant and invariable, "the satisfaction of any particular Desire can be suspended from determining the will to any subservient action, till we have maturely examin'd, whether the particular apparent good, which we desire, makes a part of our real Happiness." Locke concluded that it is the judgment we make after this examination which determines our actions and makes us free: a man "could not be free if his will was

[89] Ibid., 2.21.48 (Nidditch, 264).

determined by any thing, but his own desire guided by his own Judgment."[90]

This is very close to Gassendi's view of freedom, where the intellect is indifferent until it analyzes whether some apparent good is really a good. For Gassendi, after that judgment is made by the intellect, the will immediately follows and the act is performed. Locke agreed: "the determination of the Will immediately follows the Judgment of the Understanding."

But, Locke asked, if this is the case, where does indifference lie? Does it come before the judgment of the understanding or between the judgment and its execution by the will? Locke believed that indifference antecedent to the Understanding places "liberty in a state of darkness." Instead of the absolutely prior indeterminacy, he argued that indifference exists after the judgment of the understanding and after the determination of the will, in the "operative powers" "which remaining equally able to operate, or to forebear operating after as before the decree of the will." Locke understood this kind of indifference as a kind of physical state, where the hand, for instance, is able to move whenever there is absence of restraint or compulsion. Yet this clarifies little, because Locke conceded "that is an indifferency not of the Man, (for after he has once judg'd which is best, viz. to do, or forbear, he is no longer indifferent)." Thus, Locke's entire doctrine of indifference and the faculties is obscure, and it is not surprising that he concluded, "I am not nice about Phrases."[91]

But whenever Locke used the term "judgment," without associating it with one aspect of the mind or another, his doctrine becomes more similar to Gassendi's. Locke argued that suspension of judgment and deliberation is "the great privilege of intellectual beings" who are given this capacity by God. Such an intellectual being sounds like Gassendi's wise man, but all men, argued Locke, have the capacity from God to suspend their judgments—a capacity which it is their obligation to use to inhibit immediate desires and passions in order to consider what will bring them true happiness. Ultimately, humans can inculcate a habit of suspension of judgment and learn to focus on the long-term pleasures, just as in Gassendi's system they can learn to be wise.[92]

Nevertheless, many human beings bring misery on themselves, rather than the pleasure they desire, because "Things come to be represented

[90] Ibid., 2.21.71 (Nidditch, 282–83).
[91] Ibid.
[92] Ibid., 2.21.69 (Nidditch, 280–81).

to our desires, under deceitful appearances: and that is by the Judgment pronouncing wrongly concerning them." To Gassendi, too, this is a cause of error. When we judge of present pleasure or pain, we are never wrong—Gassendi and Locke share this belief in the immediate veracity of perception based on sensation—but when we judge of future pleasure and pain, we often make a misjudgment. According to Locke, "The cause of our judging amiss, when we compare our Present Pleasure and Pain with future, seems to me to be the weak and narrow Constitution of our Minds." Error and sin are the consequence of not reflecting deeply enough, and of making decisions without thinking of their long-term consequences. When someone does not take the time to reflect deeply enough, the resulting wrong judgment and the actions concomitant upon it will bring "sickness and death," for which a person is only "answerable to himself."[93]

Gassendi wrote much the same thing. He argued that men often do not realize the consequences of their actions, since there are no immediate punishments for them. Nevertheless, because this ignorance is self-induced, it cannot be excused, "It is in the power of a man not to sin by the close application of the mind to what he is doing."[94] If this lack of forethought continues, it can become habitual. Locke also emphasized the power of bad habit in preventing rational decision, and like Gassendi did not excuse the individual because of this. Both agreed that one can, through reflection on the greatest good, habituate oneself to virtue.[95] To both, a person's ultimate fate rested on veracity and perspicacity of judgment.

To fully understand Locke's analysis of judgment, it is necessary to look at other parts of the *Essay*. Locke's doctrine of probable knowledge is close to Gassendi's and like Gassendi, he connected probable decisions to morality. Locke felt that most human knowledge lacked certainty, because we can never know essences: "Our Knowledge . . . being very narrow, and we are not happy enough to find certain Truth in everything we consider." This lack of certainty characterizes knowledge of natural things, as well as knowledge of practical things, although some truths can be demonstrated in both morality and mathematics.[96]

However, according to Locke, if a human being waited for demonstrable knowledge of essences in practical matters, if he did not eat until he

[93] Ibid., 2.21.61, 2.21.64, and 2.21.56 (Nidditch, 274, 276, 271).
[94] Gassendi, "Ethics," in *SP, Opera,* 2:825–26.
[95] Locke, *Essay,* 2.21.69 (Nidditch, 280); Gassendi, "Ethics," in *SP, Opera,* 2:738–41.
[96] Locke, *Essay,* 4.15.2 and 4.12.8–10 (Nidditch, 654–55, 643–45).

had certain knowledge, he would perish. Practical decisions must be expedient, and consequently human beings must rely on their judgments of probabilities when making a decision about whether something will preserve them. This kind of knowledge "is sufficient to direct us in the obtaining of Good and avoiding of Evil." Once the mind judges the various degrees of probability of whether something will lead to good or evil, to pleasure or pain, "then the greater probability, I think, will determine the Assent."⁹⁷

When Locke saw judgment as evaluating various degrees of probability, he echoed Gassendi and the whole skeptical and rhetorical tradition, and introduced Gassendi's mix of epistemological uncertainty into moral decision. By 1690 in England, however, probabilism was a stance commonly held by many thinkers, including the natural philosophers of the Royal Society and proponents of natural religion, many of whom Locke knew and admired.⁹⁸ This group, which included Walter Charleton, may have themselves been influenced by Gassendi's epistemology. Whether Locke adapted their views, or Gassendi's, or simply developed his own, he still holds a doctrine very close to the French philosopher.

Gassendi and Locke's *Two Treatises of Government*

Locke's political writings also show some similarity to Gassendi's political doctrines, although in these there is more likelihood that Locke was responding to his general intellectual milieu. Locke was reacting to specific historical events in politics, as well as to an entire British tradition of political theory. His ideas are also indebted to Grotius and the natural law philosophers.⁹⁹ Still, a Gassendist perspective can be found in the concept of freedom, property, and consent.

In the *Two Treatises of Government*, Locke followed the tradition of seventeenth-century political theory by postulating a state of nature, which apparently is a limiting case of actual society.¹⁰⁰ In this state of nature a person is free and equal, each person with a right to everything needed to preserve himself. According to John Dunn, this original communism is not a condition where everything belongs to everyone, but

---

⁹⁷ Ibid., 4.14.1, 4.21.8, and 4.20.16 (Nidditch, 652, 634–35, 718).
⁹⁸ Shapiro, *Probability and Certainty*, 74–118.
⁹⁹ On the events and the political doctrines that affected Locke, see Laslett's Introduction to Locke, *Two Treatises of Government;* J. B. Schneewind, "Locke's Moral Philosophy," in *Cambridge Companion to Locke*, 208–22. This topic is treated extensively in the Locke scholarship.
¹⁰⁰ C. B. Macpherson, *The Political Theory of Possessive Individualism: Hobbes to Locke* (Oxford, 1962), 197.

rather "the world is presented as belonging to nobody, but available for the appropriation of all."[101] In this state of nature, agreed Gassendi, Hobbes, and Locke, individuals use what they need in order to live. For Hobbes, this rivalry leads inevitably to a war of all against all. Both Gassendi and Locke were more optimistic, crediting man with a natural reason, endowed by God, that can help men avoid this state of universal rapine. Locke argued, "The State of Nature has a Law of Nature to govern it, which obliges everyone: And Reason, which is that Law, teaches all Mankind, who will but consult it, that being all equal and independent, no one ought to harm another in his Life, Health, Liberty, or Possessions."[102]

In a similar vein, Gassendi wrote, "Natural Law can be said to be in man alone; insofar as reason is directed toward the nature of things . . . reason's dictate is the same thing as the dictate of nature."[103] Thus, both Gassendi and Locke make reason the base of obligation in the state of nature.

They agreed that reason will lead man to the golden rule, out of naturally utilitarian goals to protect himself and his property. The motivation for acting is the desire for self-preservation and happiness. Gassendi and Locke agreed that the happiest state possible for man on this earth is found within the civil state, where one can pursue desires freely, make choices, or take actions with the security of some guaranteeing authority. The state does not destroy freedom; it perpetuates it. Thus Gassendi wrote that while natural rights are limited by the laws of the state, nevertheless they are "certain and free," and likewise Locke argued that "the end of law is not to abolish or restrain, but to preserve and enlarge Freedom."[104]

Both Gassendi and Locke see the holding of property as the most crucial element in the securing of happiness. In the state of nature we can take what we need to live—Locke's theory of labor is much more sophisticated than Gassendi's—but there is no security in this kind of life, and consequently no happiness. Gassendi wrote, "although from the first law of nature (the law of self-preservation), this is not yours more than mine; nevertheless, by this way everything would be for everybody . . . there would be perpetual strife . . . ; for that reason it seems from the beginning the matter was according to nature, that anyone

---

[101] John Dunn, *The Political Thought of John Locke: An Historical Account of the Argument of the Two Treatises of Government* (Cambridge, 1969), 67.
[102] Locke, *Two Treatises*, 2.2.6 (Laslett, 289).
[103] Gassendi, "Ethics," in *SP, Opera*, 2:800.
[104] Locke, *Two Treatises*, 2.6.57 (Laslett, 324).

who possessed anything for his own property, another would not be permitted to usurp it."[105]

This seems to put the possession of property prior to the creation of the civil state, just as it is in Locke.[106] And just as Locke presupposed that the state was to some extent created for the protection of individual property rights, so does Gassendi. Locke's doctrine is well known; Gassendi wrote on the subject: "Hence, it means that true and natural liberty is discovered rather in that society where a man submits to the laws of society (this is by his own approval, or for his own advantage), and he does whatever is pleasing to him with what remains, and he possesses the right in his own goods, which no one else can snatch away on account of the public power good which defends them."[107]

A closer prefiguring of Lockean political liberalism is hard to imagine. Political society exists to protect the property of individuals, by their own consent. Consent itself, which is the result of utilitarian interest, establishes law, but allows human beings to do whatever brings them pleasure in areas which the law does not touch. Locke also believed that government and law are founded on the consent of individuals, and that "Freedom of Men under Government, is, to have a standing Rule to live by . . . ; A liberty to follow my own Will in all things, where the Rule prescribes not; and not to be subject to the inconstant, uncertain, unknown, Arbitrary Will of another Man."[108]

Locke thought that his doctrine of consent justified rebellion when the arbitrary actions of the governor threatened the purposes for which the state was constructed: the freedom and well-being of the citizens. Gassendi, on the other hand, felt that while consent created the state, political order within the state, even under the rule of a tyrant, justified obedience, because this would maximize the chances of human happiness. Gassendi's thought reflected the climate of French absolutism, while Locke lived in the period of growing Parliamentary power.

Nevertheless, Locke's entire theory of social contract is very like Gassendi's. He also supposed a three-tier contract whereby man first comes into society, then gives the society the right to make laws, and finally sets up a sovereign power to execute the laws.[109] Moreover, for Gassendi and Locke, the state is a construct, and this construct is natural, a product

---

[105] Gassendi, "Ethics," in *SP, Opera,* 2:751.
[106] Locke, *Two Treatises,* 2.5.25–51 (Laslett, 303–20).
[107] Gassendi, "Ethics," in *SP, Opera,* 2:755.
[108] Locke, *Two Treatises,* 2.4.22 (Laslett, 302).
[109] Ibid., 2.7.89 (Laslett, 343). On the theory of social contract in Gassendi, see Chap. 7 above.

of the desire for pleasure that God implants in man. Locke wrote, "God having made man such a creature, that, in his own Judgment, it was not good for him to be alone, put him under strong obligations of Necessity, Convenience, and Inclination to drive him into Society, as well as fitted him with Understanding and Language to continue and enjoy it."[110]

Society is the result of the divinely inspired pursuit of advantages for human beings. This statement reflects the idea of willing necessity that is found in the *Essay* and in Gassendi's "Ethics." Our initial judgment, whether the result of instinct or reflection, propels us into society. God also gave us understanding or intellect—what Gassendi called the *ius humanum*—to continue to search for what will bring us enjoyment or pleasure. Rational action, for both Locke and Gassendi, is the source of human freedom and what distinguishes man from all other animate beings.[111]

Thus, whether Locke simply adopted, or elaborated, or merely confronted Gassendi's ideas about freedom and necessity, pleasure and pain, and will and intellect, it seems clear that he was influenced by the French philosopher. To the extent that the belief in the rationality, liberty, and happiness of the individual is a cornerstone of the liberal tradition, we can see Gassendi, through his influence on Locke, as one of the progenitors of modern democratic thought.

It is perhaps ironic that a Catholic priest living under the absolutism of Louis XIII and Richelieu should figure in such an evolution, but it would not have surprised Gassendi. He had made the initial radical move of taking the heterodox thought of Epicurus and transforming it into an ethic for a good Christian. It was just the first in a series of bold advances that produced a thought congenial to a radical republican across the English Channel, who was trying to create an epistemology and a morality to substantiate human freedom and happiness.

---

[110] Locke, *Two Treatises*, 2.7.77 (Laslett, 336–37).
[111] Ibid., 2.6.61–3 (Laslett, 326–27); Gassendi, "Ethics," in *SP, Opera,* 2:798.

CHAPTER NINE

Gassendi and the Enlightenment

Piece by piece, area by area, Gassendi built a consistent philosophic system. But his determination to distinguish between
ethics and natural philosophy has caused some commentators to
miss its cohesion.

Gassendi's assumptions about the different natures of the physical
universe and humanity—the first created and maintained according to
mechanistic laws of motion, the second free—caused an apparent rift
between morality and physics. Unlike his mentor, Epicurus, who could
attribute the same element of chance to both the cosmos and the soul,
Gassendi could not assume that the fortuitous action of the atoms would
support an explanation of liberty: that would undermine the belief in
God's providential ordering of the world and created being. To maintain the Epicurean emphasis on freedom, Gassendi had to find some
other method for understanding human liberty.

Gassendi knew that mechanical cosmologies, like that of the ancient
atomist Democritus, often led to an endorsement of natural necessity
and determinism. Epicureanism itself was a repudiation of these deterministic conclusions, and a vindication of human (and natural) freedom. Gassendi was forced by his project of revitalizing Epicurus, and
by his own scientific interests, to consider the moral implications of a
mechanistic universe.

Gassendi closely tied his ethical doctrine to his epistemology, which
argued that our knowledge of the world is probabilistic. He insisted that
we cannot know the essence of things, only their external appearances,
and while we know these appearances as they appear to our sense per-

ceptions, that knowledge can never rise to certainty. Since the act of judgment itself is fallible in its operations, we can always mistake the apparent good for the real good. In physics and ethics, our knowledge is equally probabilistic.

In both ethics and natural philosophy, probabilism is integral to the structure of Gassendi's argument in the *Syntagma Philosophicum*. He attempted to persuade the reader that an Epicurean interpretation of natural philosophy and ethics is the most probable, that is, the closest to truth. Since he was attempting to persuade, not to prove, in the fashioning of his philosophy he used the methodology of the rhetorician rather than the logician. Early seventeenth-century rhetoric, redefined in the sixteenth century by Peter Ramus, sought to preempt the monopoly of Aristotelian logic as the correct method of establishing the truth, or the most likely conjecture. By the time Gassendi wrote the *Syntagma*, rhetoric had incorporated strategies from Academic skepticism, in particular the use of *ad utramque partem* reasoning—reasoned debate on both sides of a question—to find the most probable conclusion.

Both rhetoric and Academic skepticism were intertwined with ethical assumptions. Rhetoric aimed at persuading to action. Academic skepticism, like Epicureanism, sought a way for an individual to live tranquilly in a world full of inconsistency and trouble. Combining these approaches, Gassendi felt, could lead the individual to wisdom—or at least to as much wisdom as was humanly possible.

Human beings could not become absolutely wise, not only because of the fallibility of their judgments and the impossibility of perceiving essences, but also because absolute knowledge would be absolutely compelling. Compulsion of any kind, either by certainty of the good or by coercion, was anathema to Gassendi's sense of freedom.

Gassendi felt that except for human beings, every created being or thing—from rocks to angels—was determined by its own particular nature or end. Thus, a stone cannot deviate from a determined path; it must move inertially unless it is affected by some other force. One could say that the good for a rock is to keep moving in a straight path just as it is the good for an angel to love God. Gassendi calls such action voluntary—*libentia*—since it is done with the full consent of the being involved, but not fully free—*libertas*—since the rock cannot deviate from the path, nor the angel from the love of God.

In one sense, human beings possess the same kind of motion as other created beings and objects. God created in humans the constant desire for pleasure, which acts on us as a continual motion does on a rock. Everything a human does, he does out of a desire for pleasure. But unlike that rock, God gave humans a second kind of motion—the ability to choose to go in one direction or another after deliberation. The moment of deliberation in the intellect is free and uncaused; we possess a liberty of indifference, an ability to suspend action, until we move ourselves in one way or the other.

Thus, God allows human beings to be free and to make their own judgments about what will ultimately bring the most pleasure and the least amount of pain. Gassendi adopted the Epicurean principle that pleasure is the highest good, and integrated it into a Christian cosmos, where the search for pleasure and the possession of freedom are the providentially endowed defining characteristics of a rational human being. Such a human being, if he is wise, will act morally as well, because he realizes that virtue is the best means to pleasure.

The advocacy of human freedom remained a constant in Gassendi's ethical thought, spanning individual and social behavior. Gassendi considered astrology to be one of the most pernicious threats to a belief in human freedom, and he argued strenuously against it throughout his career. He felt astrology depicted a universe governed by necessary laws, and that the astrologers taught that the stars caused sublunary effects inevitably and invariably. Astrology's denial of freedom made it antithetical to ethics itself. To accept astrology was to abrogate rational choice and to lose any chance for wisdom and happiness.

Astrologers also claimed that their discipline was a demonstrable science. Gassendi attacked the epistemological claims of astrology as false, and denied that it deserved the status of either art or science. No human knowledge could be more than probable, and astrology at best was mere guesswork. The cornerstone of Gassendi's critique of astrology was the same probabilistic epistemology supporting and structuring his ethics.

Gassendi's advocacy of human freedom also brought him into conflict with Descartes, with whom he disagreed on many other issues as well. In terms of human liberty, Gassendi assumed that Cartesian clear and evident ideas would result in the causal determination of human beings by their knowledge of the good and the true. Such determination would abrogate a doctrine Gassendi had adopted: the liberty of indifference, the ability to choose one thing or another or its opposite, articulated by the sixteenth-century Spanish Jesuit Luis de Molina and his followers.

Gassendi was sympathetic to the Molinist theological position— although instead of locating the liberty of indifference in the will as Molina had, he associated it with the intellect. In discussing human faculties, Gassendi followed Aquinas, who had emphasized the power of the intellect. Thus, his ethical theory eventually combined elements drawn from two Christian theologians—Molina and Aquinas—with the surprising addition of Epicurus' theories about pleasure.

Gassendi's attack on Descartes thus drew him into the theological debates of his times; their argument ultimately revolved around the problem of error and sin. Gassendi wanted to know why God did not create human beings who would always know the good and thus do the good. He was not satisfied with Descartes's explanation of error, which made the will independent of the judgment of the intellect.

For Gassendi, the intellect was the faculty that made all decisions, which the will simply put into operation. Gassendi believed that error is an unavoidable aspect of judgment, and hence human beings are doomed to err—and sin—while they live their lives on earth. Such error only ceases when humans are caught up in the beatific vision of God, but at that moment, human freedom in its broadest sense also ceases—because then one must necessarily love God. True freedom, therefore, hangs on the human propensity to err.

Natural necessity was as anathema to Gassendi as causal necessity. Just as Epicurus had repudiated the deterministic world-view of Democritus, Gassendi rejected the implicit necessitarianism he perceived in both the natural and psychological theories of Thomas Hobbes. Hobbes and Gassendi had a mutually productive relationship, and both shared a propensity to use metaphors of motion to clarify their understanding of the relationship of human and natural action. But Gassendi parted company with the English materialist on the subject of human freedom. Gassendi's distinction between true freedom and voluntary or willing freedom clearly reflected his disagreement with Hobbes about the nature of freedom. Gassendi's doctrine of voluntary freedom is very close to Hobbes's notion of human freedom, and in making it a subsidiary form of freedom, Gassendi denied Hobbesian libertarianism.

In an argument cast against the ancient materialist Democritus—who anticipated Hobbesian natural necessity—Gassendi elaborated on his arguments for human freedom, emphasizing not only the fallibility of sense impressions, but also an element of flexibility in the soul itself. While Gassendi did not accept the Epicurean *clinamen* or swerve—a tiny, fortuitous motion of the atoms that allowed for indeterminacy in both the universe and the soul—he substituted an uncaused capacity to pause and evaluate into the faculties of the soul, which preserves the soul's indifference and freedom as the prerequisite to choice.

Gassendi's ethical thought was applied consistently to his political doctrines, which were also a response to Hobbes. The calculus of pleasure and pain becomes an impetus for the establishment of society, law, and government. Human reason and a utilitarian calculus of what will bring the most pleasure obligates the rational man to obey the laws of nature. In the political state, individuals still maintain the right to consent to whatever may affect their pleasure or happiness, and continue to be obligated by the rational calculation of what will be good for them. Such calculation, since it is inextricably intertwined with virtue and pleasure, ultimately is subsumed in an almost altruistic ethic of caring.

Thus, Gassendi, in the *Syntagma Philosophicum*, articulated a coherent ethical theory integral to his entire philosophy. Morality was as basic as natural philosophy to Gassendi's rehabilitation of Epicureanism. His ethical system became an important influence on philosophical thought in the later half of the seventeenth century, particularly after François Bernier, a disciple of Gassendi, published his *Abregé* of Gassendi's *Syntagma*. While the followers of Gassendi and Descartes continued to debate their masters' principles in late seventeenth-century France, Gassendi's ideas on pleasure and pain, freedom and probabilistic epistemology were particularly influential in England. Walter Charleton produced a paraphrase of Gassendi's "Ethics" as part of his *Darkness of Atheism* and John Locke incorporated Epicurean and Gassendist ideas into his own moral philosophy.

The question of Locke's precise debt to Gassendi has been debated hotly in recent times. It seems clear that Locke, particularly in his early thought, was strongly influenced by Gassendi, and that the Gassendist reformulation of the Epicurean concept of pleasure and pain, with its connection to divine providence, is a prominent theme in *An Essay concerning Human Understanding*. Both Locke and Gassendi believed that human beings must be free to make their own choices and reap their own rewards and punishments. Without this we would live in a moral vacuum, and moral philosophy would be nothing but a joke.

To the extent that the belief in the liberty of the individual is a cornerstone of the liberal tradition, Gassendi, through his influence on Locke, was one of the progenitors of modern democratic thought. To the extent that Gassendi reflected the libertarian and probabilistic ideas of the humanists who preceded him, he served as a link between the Renaissance and the Enlightenment. Devotion to the freedom of the individual, and the emphasis on pleasure as the greatest good, were not the creation of the philosophes or the eighteenth-century utilitarians; directly or indirectly, both were spurred by the revived and Christianized Epicurean morality of Pierre Gassendi.

The precise debt the eighteenth century owes to Gassendi is difficult to determine and a detailed account is beyond the scope of this book. Sylvia Murr argues that while Gassendi's "ideas have fertilized and enlivened European thought" and were adopted in epistemology, physics, and ethics, "this was done without it being acknowledged and perhaps even without it even being known."[1] In part this was due to Gassendi's modesty in presenting his philosophy, what Lennon calls Gassendi's nondogmatic nondogmatism, but it is also rooted in the several different avenues by which the philosopher's ideas could have reached the philosophes of the Enlightenment.[2] Many, including Voltaire, D'Holbach, and Diderot, read Gassendi's *Opera*, but others knew Gassendi only through Bernier's *Abregé* or the writings of other late seventeenth-century Gassendists. In ethics, this would have been true particularly of the work of the philosophical hedonist Charles de Saint-Denys, Seigneur de St. Evremont, who readily acknowledged his debt to Gassendi in preaching a morality of moderate pleasure.[3]

But hedonism was not an exclusively Gassendist moral philosophy. The eighteenth century knew and admired Locke. Here was a conduit for Gassendi's ethical ideas without a direct acknowledgement. But hedonism not only characterized the philosophies of Locke and Gassendi, it was also part of the program of ancient Epicureanism. Epicurus was much admired in the eighteenth century, by an intelligentsia intoxicated with the idea that happiness or pleasure is the highest good. This love of pleasure, which included sensual pleasure at least in a moderate form, had infused the writings of the epicurean poets of the late seventeenth century, the plays of Molière and the speculations of Cyrano de Bergerac. The lives of the libertines from Gassendi's own time on into the Age of Reason gave pleasure a particular prominence, although not always in ways faithful to the thought of Epicurus or Gassendi.[4] A philosophe did not have to know Gassendi to know hedonism.

A rising cacophony of earlier hedonist notes overwhelmed the Gassendist tones. Nevertheless, there are some themes of the Enlightenment that resonate so deeply with the thought of the neo-Epicurean that they can be seen as places where his impact continued, even if it was diffused by other influences.

---

[1] Murr, "Introduction," in *Bernier et les Gassendistes*, 7.
[2] Lennon, *Gods and Giants*, 23.
[3] Wade, *The Intellectual Origins of the French Enlightenment*, 45, 229; Lester G. Crocker, *Nature and Culture: Ethical Thought in the French Enlightenment* (Baltimore, 1963), 231–32, 268; and Robert Mauzi, *L'Idée du bonheur dans la littérature et la pensée françaises au XVIIIe siècle* (Paris, 1969), 22.
[4] Spink, *French Free-Thought*, 133–68.

The eighteenth century sought to find a new basis for morality, something which was grounded in nature and open to reason.[5] Many concluded that the pursuit of pleasure was the mainspring of human life—each individual possesses self-love and seeks to obtain as much pleasure as possible in his effort to be happy. Utilitarian thinkers argued that anything that aids in the increase of pleasure is a good, and anything that decreases pleasure is an evil. Right and wrong take their normative value from these psychological facts.[6] Thus, philosophes as diverse as the materialist Baron d'Holbach (1723–1789), the scientist Pierre-Louis Moreau de Maupertius (1698–1759), and Voltaire, the archphilosophe, could argue that happiness or pleasure is the highest value in life and an individual can use his reason to calculate what will bring him the greatest amount of pleasure.[7]

The idea that pleasure is the impetus for human action and the calculus of pleasure and pain are notions common to both Gassendi and Epicurus. Since the thinkers of the eighteenth century, by and large, repudiated the idea of divine providence, this kind of hedonism invoked the ancient philosopher rather than his modern interpreter. But when the philosophes attempted to soften the ethical implications of their position, once again Gassendi seems to have been on the scene. In order to avoid a universe where every individual pursued his own pleasure without thought or care for anyone else than himself, some philosophes adhered to the idea of enlightened self-interest—that a calculation of personal pleasure and pain includes the realization that one has to care for others and live by societal rules. Enlightened self-interest is very similar to Gassendi's *ius humanum* or calculation of what will be beneficial to the individual in the long run. It incorporates the idea that a person may have to suffer pain for an ultimate good, and that human reason decides what sacrifice is necessary for the person's greater good. Other philosophes went a step further in an effort to avoid the negative implications of egoistic hedonism: they equated virtue to happiness and preached that the virtuous act itself is happiness.[8] The merging together of happiness, virtue, and utility was a principle most dear to Gassendi, who at least anticipated if he did not define the Enlightenment attempt at creating a morality of pleasure.

[5] Crocker, *Nature and Culture*, xii–xiii.
[6] Ibid., 221–46; Mauzi, *Idée du bonheur*, 636–41.
[7] Mauzi, *Idée du bonheur*, 636; Crocker, *Nature and Culture*, 273; and Ronald I. Boss, "The Development of Social Religion: A Contradiction of French Free-Thought," *International Philosophic Quarterly* 12 (1972): 587.
[8] Crocker, *Nature and Culture*, 266–67.

The element missing from the ethical philosophy of the Age of Enlightenment is the notion of a divinely inspired pursuit of pleasure. Without God, the pursuit of pleasure for some thinkers becomes part of the necessary functioning of the physical world. Pleasure is a "universal mover" and "a necessary principle."[9] Not surprisingly, the materialists of the eighteenth century, adopting the mechanistic world-view, attempted to eliminate the difference between the human and natural world. All was embraced within an endless chain of cause and effect, of matter in motion. There was no problem about substantiating freedom in a mechanistic universe, since it did not exist. The motion of the universe was unitary: humanity and nature following their paths without deviation or hesitation.[10]

Thus, it seems that while Gassendi might have contributed to the hedonistic tradition, the other, more crucial and original part of his moral philosophy faded with the triumph of nature over God in the next century. To the Enlightenment, there was no special place for man in the scheme of creation, if there was a creation or a creator at all. But there are indications that aspects of the divine still colored ethical thought.

The philosophes assumed that human beings pursue pleasure necessarily out of self-love. But implicit in their argument is a moral dimension beyond egoistic hedonism. Pleasure serves a social function. The utilitarians argued that individual pleasure must be subsumed into the greatest good of the greatest number, in order to maintain the best chance of each individual enjoying pleasure. The materialist D'Holbach argued that it is the continuous search for more pleasure, and unhappiness with what one has, which ultimately leads to societal progress as a byproduct.[11] It seems that the dynamic element of the search for pleasure, which Gassendi had argued was part of God's plan, became immanent in the natural universe of the philosophes. Attributes of creation which had been associated with the divine lost their transcendent warrant and devolved into the work of nature. This metamorphoses is perhaps analogous to the way God's attributes were absorbed into the Newtonian concepts of absolute time and space.[12] It became even more evident with those philosophes who objectified nature as an external ordering force in the universe. Human existence retained its purpose, but it was a purpose inherent in human nature and the nature of the universe: progress toward a happier and consequently better world.

[9] Mauzi, *Idée du bonheur,* 386–87.
[10] Wade, *Intellectual Origins,* 22; Mauzi, *Idée du bonheur,* 642–43.
[11] Crocker, *Nature and Culture,* 246.
[12] Burtt, *Metaphysical Foundations,* 244–64.

The materialists and the determinists also did not have the only word on the subject of human freedom. The philosophes were divided on this issue. Some argued that ultimately it could not be proven whether humans are free or not, but noted that everyone nevertheless acts as if he were free. In fact, the actual program of the philosophes, Peter Gay argues, was based on the premise of the freedom "of moral man to make his way in the world."[13]

Such an espousal of freedom is clear in the *Encyclopédie* article on "*Liberté.*" The article begins by arguing that "Liberty resides in the power that an intelligent being possesses to do what he wishes, conformable to his own determination." The author of this piece then attempted to destroy the argument for natural determinism associated with Hobbes and Spinoza, and proclaimed, "Nature has made us in a way so that we are carried toward the good and have a horror of the evil in general; but when it is a matter of detail, our liberty has a vast field, and can decide if something is a good by looking at it from different sides, according to the circumstances surrounding it." In other words, nature gives us certain propensities toward good and evil, but we decide on particular courses of actions after weighing the worth of something pro and con.[14] This account differs from Gassendi's notion of freedom and the good only to the extent that nature is substituted for God, and liberty—instead of being associated with the faculty of intellect—is an autonomous agent. Even that distinction becomes less clear as the argument is continued. We are told, "Free substance determines itself from itself, and this follows the incentive of the good which is perceived by the understanding which inclines without necessitating." Moreover, the soul itself possesses the liberty of indifference, which allows us to hesitate before choosing a good. This indifference is grounded on epistemological error, a state of ignorance endowed by God:

> the liberty of equilibrium is less a prerogative in which we must glory, it is rather an imperfection in our nature and our knowledge, which grows or diminishes by reason of the reciprocal growth of our enlightenment. God, foreseeing that our soul, because of its imperfection, will often be irreso-

---

[13] Peter Gay, *The Enlightenment: An Interpretation. The Rise of Modern Paganism* (New York, 1966), 3. On freedom, see also Henry Vyverberg, *Human Nature, Cultural Diversity, and the French Enlightenment* (New York, 1989), 30, and Wade, *Intellectual Origins*, 21.

[14] "*Liberté,*" in *Encyclopédie ou Dictionnaire Raisonné des Sciences, de Arts et des Métiers, par une Société de Gens de Lettres* (Neufchastel, 1765; facsimile reprint, Stuttgart-Bad Cannstatt, 1966), 9:462–71.

lute and suspended between two options, has given to it the power to leave this suspension, by a determination of which the principle is itself.[15]

The doctrine of freedom presented in this article, which ends by associating it with the teachings of the Roman Catholic Church, recalls Gassendi's concept of freedom in almost every particular. It emphasized both the power and limitation of reason, which is free because God has made human beings prone to error. Enlightenment itself becomes the human capacity for choice, succeeding hesitation and suspension in the soul. To those thinkers of the Age of Reason who retained their belief in a divine being, Gassendi's philosophy offered a way to reconcile a natural morality with a transcendent and providential theology.[16]

Thus, Enlightenment notions about pleasure and freedom resembled aspects of Gassendi's moral philosophy. Issues that had concerned him, particularly the role of freedom in a mechanical universe, remained alive in the discourse of the eighteenth century—although at that time the implications of mechanical and psychological determinism were accepted more readily, rather than being widely resisted. For some, eradicating the divine from the universe was liberating even if it left only pleasure to determine individual action. But for others, the pursuit of pleasure does not necessarily mean the exclusion of human freedom, whether it originates in God, nature, or man.

A century and a half after Gassendi's death, Thomas Jefferson, another voice for freedom, explained to John Quincy Adams that "the Epicurean philosophy came nearest to the truth, in his opinion, of any system of ancient philosophy, but that it had been misunderstood and misrepresented. He wished the work of Gassendi concerning it had been translated. . . . I mentioned Lucretius. He said that was only a part—only the natural philosophy. But the moral philosophy was only to be found in Gassendi."[17]

[15] Ibid., 471.
[16] Wade, *Intellectual Origins*, 414, also reaches a similar conclusion about Gassendi.
[17] John Quincy Adams, *Memoirs*, 1:472, quoted in James MacGregor Burns, *The Vineyard of Liberty* (New York, 1981), 650.

The Dating of the "Ethics" of
the Syntagma Philosophicum

There is a good deal of controversy about when the "Ethics" was written. I believe, from internal and external evidence, that Gassendi may have formulated the basics of his thought before 1641, but his ideas did not reach full maturity until his contact with Hobbes and Descartes, which came after that date.

There is no extant manuscript of the "Ethics," which is somewhat surprising since manuscript versions of almost all of the rest of the *Syntagma* exist. Pintard thinks that Gassendi wrote the "Ethics" by 1634, and did little or no modification of it for the rest of his life.[1] Bernard Rochot agrees with this interpretation, but does not accept Pintard's claim that this shows that Gassendi had little interest in this part of his work.[2] Bloch disputes this claim; he feels, instead, that the "Ethics" was written at the earliest in 1642, but more likely after 1645.[3]

Gassendi mentioned Epicurean ethics early in his carer. His outline of projected chapters for the *Exercitationes* includes one on moral philosophy: "it teaches Epicurus's doctrine of pleasure by showing in what way the greatest good consists of pleasure and how the reward of human deeds and virtues is based on this principle."[4] While this chapter was never written, it shows that he was already interested in the moral teachings of the philosopher of the Garden.

Gassendi's first Epicurean work was his *Apology* for Epicurus, which

---

[1] Pintard, *La Mothe le Vayer,* 35–45.
[2] Bernard Rochot, "Gassendi, vie et caractère," 46.
[3] Bloch, *Philosophie de Gassendi,* 64n.
[4] Gassendi, "Exercises against the Aristotelians," in *Selected Works,* 25.

was completed in 1629. An expanded version of this work, *De vita et moribus Epicuri*, was finished by 1634, but only published in 1647.[5] It contained a defense of Epicurus's personal morality and a summary of his teachings, including a discussion of fate and free will and a defense of the Epicurean pleasure principle.[6]

In the 1630s, according to a letter Gassendi sent to Peiresc, he was working on a detailed discussion and Christian rehabilitation of the entire Epicurean corpus. In 1631 he wrote to his patron that Mersenne and some others "swear with great zeal that they wish to see what I do notebook by notebook" and that he would be glad to send Peiresc any of the chapters he had already finished. He then included a list of chapter headings, which are relevant to the problem of the dating of the "Ethics." They consist of the following:

L'*apologie* pour la vie d'Epicure contient ces chapitres icy:

1. De serie vitae Epicuri.
2. De praecipuis authoribus a quibus quaesita Epicuro infamia.
3. De objecta Epicuro impietate ac malitia.
4. De objecta ingratitudine vanitate maledicentia.
5. De objecta gula.
6. De objecta venere.
7. De objecto odio liberalium disciplinarum.

La *doctrine* ou *philosophie* est divisée en trois parties dont:
La canonique expliquée en un seul livre contient ces chapitres:

1. De variis dijudicandae veritatis criteriis.
2. De canonibus vocum.
3. De canonibus sensuum.
4. De canonibus anticipationum.
5. De canonibus passionum.

La *physique* est expliquée en quartre livres dont le premier, qui est De natura, contient ces chapitres:

1. De natura rerum, seu de universo.
2. De natura corporea, seu de atomis, an sint.
3. De tribus atomorum proprietatibus magnitudine, figura, gravitate, ubi et de motu.
4. De natura incorporea, hoc est inani, seu loco.
5. De natura concreta, quaenam principia, seu quae elementa et quas caussas habeat.

---

[5] Rochot, *Travaux de Gassendi*, 128–43, gives a complete history of the *De vita et moribus Epicuri*.

[6] Gassendi, *De vita et moribus Epicuri in libri octo*, in *Opera*, 5:196.

6. De ortu et interitu, seu generatione et corruptione naturae concretae.

7. De mutationibus qualitatibusque naturae concretae.

8. De imagine naturae concretae, quam etiam speciem visibilem, et intentionalem vocant.

9. De existentia naturae divinae.

10. De forma naturae divinae, an humanae similis sit.

11. De immortalitate et foelicitate ejusdem naturae divinae.

12. De existentia naturae daemoniae.

Le deuxiesme De mundo ceux-cy:

1. De structura et forma mundi.

2. De origine mundi.

3. De caussa productrice mundi.

4. De serie ac modo quo productus mundus atque adeo primi homines.

5. De providentia, seu gubernatione mundi.

6. De fortuna et fato in mundo.

7. De interitu mundi.

8. De innumerabilibus mundis.

Le troisiesme dans lequel je suis, intitulé De sublimibus, ceux-cy:

1. De coeli siderumque substantia.

2. De variatate, positione et intervallis siderum.

3. De magnitudine et figura siderum.

4. De motu corporum coelestium.

5. De tempore, quod nonnulli volunt coelestis motus esse consequens.

6. De luce deque variis adspectibus siderum.

7. De eclipsibus, deque varietate ortuum et occasuum.

8. De proprietatibus siderum, quod ad effectus naturales spectat.

9. De effectibus arbitrariis et fortuitis quos presciri posse astrologi profitentur.

10. De impressionibus igneis.

11. De impressionibus aereis.

12. De impressionibus aqueis.

Le quatriesme suivra apres, De humilibus, avec ces chapitres:

1. De globo ipso telluris.

2. De rebus inanimis.

3. De anima deque corpore et membris animalium.

4. De generatione, nutritione et incremento animalium.

5. De sensibus animalium, ac primum de Visu.

6. De coeteris quattor sensibus Auditu, Olfactu, Gustatu, Tactu.

7. De mente, seu animo, ejusque sede et actione.

8. De Appetitu, motu, vigilia, somno, insomniis ac praesensionibus animalium.

9. De sanitate, morbo, statu, senio, vita et morte animalium.
10. De animorum immortalitate.

Je laisse la partie morale pour autre fois.[7]

Pintard believes that this catalogue of the chapters of Gassendi's work reflects an actual first composition, written between 1629 and 1634. According to Pintard, the "Ethics," which in 1631 Gassendi leaves "for another time," was actually written in 1633, and thereafter was altered very little until its publication in the *Syntagma* in 1658. He bases this claim on a letter Peiresc wrote to William Schickard in 1634, which is quoted by Joseph Bougerel in his *Vie de Gassendi*. According to Pintard, Peiresc mentioned the eight books of Gassendi's *Apology*, but also "62 livres 'de la philosophie du mesme,' le tout 'achevé et prêt a voir le jour.' "[8]

Pintard argues that the number of sixty-two "livres" reflects the forty-seven "chapitres" enumerated in the 1631 letter, with an addition of fifteen other chapters, which comprise the "Ethics." Since the edition of the "Ethics" which appears in the *Syntagma* consists of sixteen chapters rather than fifteen, Pintard capitalizes on the fact that one of the chapters that was originally in the "Physics" of the first composition (Part 2, chapter 6: "De fortuna et fato in Mundo") appears in the "Ethics" in the *Syntagma* (Book 3, chapter 2: "Quid fortuna et fato"). Pintard does not pinpoint when this transfer took place.

Bernard Rochot accepts, in the main, Pintard's analysis of the 1634 letter of Peiresc to Schickard: "la correspondance des chiffres nous paraît concluante, comme à M. Pintard, et convient aussi souligner que la constance de developpement de la Morale s'oppose aux variations de la Physique." The only argument Rochot makes with Pintard concerns the fate of chapter 6, that elusive link between the earlier "Physics" and the later "Ethics." He has read the relevant part of the "Ethics" and he realizes, "le chapitre suivant (3.3: "Quomodo Fatum cum Fortuna ac libertate conciliari possit") porte sur sujet qui suit et complete celui dont nous parlons, qui a sa place aussi bien *in mundo*, comme dit notre plan, que dans la vie morale." And so, Rochot suggests that instead of Chapter 6 being moved from the "Physics" to the "Ethics," it was divided into two, with one part remaining in the "Physics" and the other part in the "Ethics." The number sixty-two might be arrived at, in this

---

[7] Gassendi to Peiresc, April 28, 1631, in Peiresc, *Lettres de Peiresc*, 4:250–52. Osler, *Divine Will and the Mechanical Philosophy*, 78–79, also includes the text of this important letter.
[8] Pintard, *La Mothe le Vayer*, 35.

case, if one hypothesized that "le première chapitre donne en 1658 [of the "Ethics"] n'existait pas in 1634, car il a le caractère d'une introduction générale et ne se rattaché pas directement a la pensée d'Épicure comme devait le faire le travail de 1634."[9] Thus, Rochot concedes implicitly that the "Ethics" underwent some change, if only in size, between 1634 and 1658.

It is Bloch, however, who had provided the definitive proof that the "Ethics" were not composed in their essential form by 1634. He has showed that all of Part 3 of the "Ethics," except for four pages, were written after 1641. In order to understand his reasoning, it is necessary to note that Gassendi began a second composition of his Epicurean writings, *De vita et doctrina Epicuri*, which occupied him from 1633–1645. The manuscripts of this project are extant, except for the part concerning ethics, if it was part of this composition. Almost all of them have been definitively dated by Pintard. The second draft comprises mss. 707, 708, 709, and 710 at Tours, with 709 and 710 actually earlier in composition than 707 and 708. Ms. 706, which forms the first part of the *Syntagma*, was composed at the end of Gassendi's life.[10]

Bloch has shown that Book 3 of the "Ethics" ("De libertate, Fortuna, Fato, ac Divinatione") is essentially a new composition of two passages found in the "Physics" of the second composition, which were themselves drafted in 1637, 1641, and 1642. This dating demonstrates that Gassendi's ethical writings were not formalized in 1633. Specifically, Bloch has found the following: "SP (*Syntagma Philosophicum*) II 827–847 reprend, dans un autre et dans une rédaction souvent très differente et plus étoffee les chapitres 5 a 8 du Livre XVI (Tours 709f 255r-267v, datant de 1637 pour les quatre premières pages et de 1641 pour les autres); SP II 848–853 et 856–860 reprend, avec les memes caractéristiques, le chapitre 7 du Livre XXI (ASHB 1239f 564r-575r, datant de 1642)."[11]

Chapter 16, which is part of Tours 709, is one of the key elements in understanding the "Ethics." This chapter, "De caussis fortuna et fato," should deal with the same material examined in Book 6, "De fortuna et fato in Mundo," of the first composition, which Pintard suggest was transferred to the "Ethics" to become Book 3, chapter 2: "Quid Fortuna et Fato." It is the chapter that Rochot thought perhaps was divided between the "Physics" and the "Ethics." Yet, in 1641, the bulk of this

---

[9] Rochot, *Travaux de Gassendi*, 50–51.
[10] Pintard, *La Mothe le Vayer*, 32–44.
[11] Bloch, *Philosophie de Gassendi*, xxiii n19.

chapter remained in the "Physics" and it is only later that Gassendi transferred it to the "Ethics." Bloch believes this could only have happened between 1645, the end of the composition of the "Physics" of the *De vita et doctrina Epicuri*, and 1649, when this material was published in the *Animadversiones* in the same form found in the "Ethics."

Bloch has demonstrated, in addition, that the bulk of chapter 4 of Part 3 of the "Ethics" ("Quid sentiendum de Divinatione, seu praesensione rerum futurarum mere fortuitam") is based on chapter 7 of Book 21 (ASHB 1239f 564r-575r) of the *De vita et doctrina Epicuri*, written in 1642.[12] Pintard thought that Book 21 was lost, because Gassendi had been able "insérer sans aucune retouche, or presque, dans ses *Animadversiones*; sans doute, peut-on les identifier avec les six chapitres massifs que l'ouvrage contient sur ce subjet, pp. 1251–1295 et 708–750."[13] (Pintard suggests that this is the fate of the manuscript of the "Ethics" as well as Book 21. Actually, this manuscript exists in Florence, at the Bibiliotheque Laurentienne, and its subject is God's providence ("De Deo Authore et Rectore Mundi"), as Pintard suspected, but it also contributed to the "Ethics." It should be noted that Part 3, chapter 4 of the "Ethics" probably also reflects Book 9: "De effectibus arbitraris et fortuitis quos presciri posse astrologi profitentur," of the third part of the first composition, which in 1642 was still part of the "Physics."[14] One might ask, then, how does Pintard's analysis of the sixty-two books mentioned by Peiresc, stand up to not one, but two books of the sixteen he credits the "Ethics" with, remaining in the "Physics" until 1641 and 1642?

It is interesting to note that Gassendi broke off his work on Epicureanism in 1637 in the middle of chapter 14 of the second composition, "De caussis, fortuna et fato." This is the chapter that reprises chapter 6 of the first composition of Gassendi's Epicurean writings. The philosopher did not return to this work for five years, during which he was preoccupied with writing Peiresc's biography and doing scientific work. Gassendi wrote to Valois in 1641, "By reason of this and that care, I was interrupted for too many years. I approach these matters again as if it was the first time. A few things remain from the tract concerning chance, fortune and fate; I add to it already. Immediately, I will begin to write on birth and death."[15]

[12] Ibid.
[13] Pintard, *La Mothe le Vayer*, 38n.
[14] Bloch, *Philosophie de Gassendi*, xxiii.
[15] Gassendi to Valois, October 3, 1641, "Letters," *Opera*, 6:116.

Pintard has examined the manuscript of chapter 16, which is part of Tours 708. He suggests it reveals the enormous difficulty Gassendi felt in returning to his work: there is "un changement de papier et d'encre, une multitude de renvois, de retouches, d'annotations, révélent l'intervalle des temps, et les difficultés d'une remise en marche."[16] This analysis suggests that the subject of fate and providence was not easy for Gassendi, who I believe, soon after he began writing again, transferred this section of his work from this section dealing with physics to that devoted to ethics. His thought was apparently in process, perhaps because of his encounters with Descartes and Hobbes in 1641.

Bloch has also shown that chapter 1 of Book 3 of the "Ethics," ("Quid Libertas, seu liberum Arbitrium"), "reprise en substance, et pour une part littéralement" several pages of the *Instantia* written against Descartes in 1641 (*Instantia,* 367–371) and reproduces "du rest purement et simplement un passage de *Animadversiones* de 1649, pour lesquelles il doit avoir été redigé spécialement, ou tout au moins, sans doute, postérieurement à la *Disquisitio.*"[17] Thus, almost all of Book 3 of the "Ethics" were written or rewritten after 1641.

This leaves Books 1 and 2 of the "Ethics." Were they included in the later composition, as Bloch believes, or were they drafted once and for all in 1634? Bloch has pointed out that much of Book 2 reflects a profound knowledge of Hobbesian philosophy, a conclusion in which I concur.[18] Gassendi did not meet the English philosopher until 1641 upon his return to Paris after several years absence, and he had access to the manuscript of *De Cive* only at that time. So yet another part of the "Ethics" was composed in the 1640s.

As for Book 1 ("De felicitate"), it is possible that it was first written as early as 1634, because Gassendi formulated his defense of Epicurean pleasure very early. But, as I have tried to prove, all of the "Ethics" is a unity, with many elements of Books 2 and 3 anticipated in Book 1. Book 1 also incorporates many of the main themes of Gassendi's ethical theory, arguments which were not fully developed until after 1641. Therefore, it appears that Book 1 of the "Ethics," like the rest, was written, or at least rewritten, after 1641.

---

[16] Pintard, *La Mothe le Vayer,* 38.
[17] Ibid., 64.
[18] Ibid., xxiii.

Works Cited

Aaron, Richard I. *John Locke.* 3d ed. Oxford: Oxford University Press, 1971.

Aarsleff, Hans. "The State of Nature and the Nature of Man." In *John Locke: Problems and Perspectives.* Ed. John W. Yolton. Cambridge: Cambridge University Press, 1969.

Adam, Antoine. "Gassendi: L'influence posthume." In *Gassendi: Sa vie et son oeuvre.* Paris: Éditions Albin Michel, 1955.

——. "L'influence de Gassendi sur les mouvement des idées à la fin du XVII siècle." In *Actes du Congrès du Tricentenaire de Pierre Gassendi.* Paris: Centre Nationale de la Recherche Scientifique, 1955.

Agrippa, Henry Cornelius. *Of the Vanitie and Uncertaintie of Artes and Sciences.* Trans. James Sanford (1569, 1575). Ed. Catherine M. Dunn. Northridge: California State University, 1974.

Allen, Don Cameron. "The Rehabilitation of Epicurus and His Theory of Pleasure in the Early Renaissance." *Studies in Philology* 41 (1944): 1–15.

——. *The Star-Crossed Renaissance.* New York: Octagon Press, 1956.

Aquinas, St. Thomas. *St. Thomas on Politics and Ethics.* Ed. and trans. P. E. Sigmund. London: W. W. Norton, 1988.

——. *Summa Theologica.* Trans. Fathers of the English Dominican Province. New York: Benziger Brothers, 1948; reprint, Westminster, Mass.: Christian Classics, 1981.

Aristotle. *Nicomachean Ethics.* Trans. Martin Ostwald. Indianapolis: Liberal Arts Press, 1962.

Armstrong, C. J. R. "The Dialectical Road to Truth: The Dialogue." In *French Renaissance Studies, 1540–70.* Ed. Peter Sharratt. Edinburgh: Edinburgh University Press, 1976.

Ayers, M. R. "The Foundations of Knowledge and the Logic of Substance: The Structure of Locke's General Philosophy." In *Locke's Philosophy: Content and Context.* Ed. G. A. J. Rogers. Oxford: Clarendon Press, 1994.

Bailey, Cyril B. *The Greek Atomists and Epicurus*. Oxford: Clarendon Press, 1928.

Baumgold, Deborah. *Hobbes's Political Theory*. Cambridge: Cambridge University Press, 1988.

Beik, William. *Absolutism and Society in Seventeenth-Century France*. Cambridge: Cambridge University Press, 1985.

Bernier, François, *Abregé de la philosophie de M. Gassendi*. 8 vols. Lyons: Claude de la Roche, 1678, 1684.

———. *Three Discourses of Happiness, Virtue, and Liberty, collected from the Works of the Learn'd Gassendi*. London: Awnshawm & John Churchil, 1699.

Berr, Henri. *Du scepticisme de Gassendi*. Trans. Bernard Rochot. Paris: Albin Michel, 1960; first published in Latin, 1898.

Biagioli, Mario. *Galileo Courtier: The Practice of Science in the Culture of Absolutism*. Chicago: University of Chicago Press, 1993.

———. "Galileo the Emblem Maker." *History of Science* 28 (1990): 230–58.

———. "Galileo's System of Patronage." *History of Science* 28 (1990): 1–62.

Bloch, Olivier René. "Gassendi and the Transition from the Middle Ages to the Classical Era." *Yale French Studies* 49 (1973): 43–55.

———. "Gassendi critique de Descartes." *Revue philosophique de la France et l'étranger* 91 (1966): 217–36.

———. *La philosophie de Gassendi: Nominalisme, matérialisme, et métaphysique*. The Hague: Martinus Nijhoff, 1971.

Bonno, Gabriel. *Les relations intellectuelles de Locke avec la France*. Berkeley: University of California Press, 1955.

Boonin-Vail, David. *Thomas Hobbes and the Science of Moral Virtue*. Cambridge: Cambridge University Press, 1994.

Boss, Ronald I. "The Development of Social Religion: A Contradiction of French Free-Thought." *International Philosophic Quarterly* 12 (1972): 555–89.

Bougerel, Joseph. *Vie de Pierre Gassendi, Prévôt de l'Église de Digne et Professeur de Mathématiques au Collège Royal*. Paris, 1737, reprint, Geneva: Slatkine, 1970.

Bourke, Vernon J. "Thomas Aquinas, St." In *The Encyclopedia of Philosophy*. Ed. Paul Edwards. 8 vols. New York: Macmillan and the Free Press, 1967, 1972. 8:105–14.

Brandt, Frithiof. *Thomas Hobbes' Mechanical Conception of Nature*. Copenhagen: Levin and Munksgaard, 1927.

Brett, G. S. *The Philosophy of Gassendi*. London: Macmillan, 1908.

Brockliss, L. W. B. *French Higher Education in the Seventeenth and Eighteenth Centuries: A Cultural History*. Oxford: Clarendon Press, 1987.

Brown, Harcourt. *Scientific Organizations in Seventeenth-Century France (1620–1680)*. Baltimore: Williams and Williams, 1934.

Brundell, Barry. *Pierre Gassendi: From Aristotelianism to a New Natural Philosophy*. Dordrecht: Reidel, 1987.

Burke, Peter. *The Italian Renaissance: Culture and Society in Italy*. Cambridge: Cambridge University Press, 1986.

———. *Venice and Amsterdam: A Study of Seventeenth-Century Elites*. London: Temple Smith, 1974.

Burns, James MacGregor. *The Vineyards of Liberty*. New York: Knopf, 1981.

Burns, Norman T. *Christian Mortalism from Tyndale to Milton*. Cambridge: Harvard University Press, 1972.

Burtt, Edwin A. *The Metaphysical Foundations of Modern Science.* New York: Doubleday, 1954; first published London, 1932.

Cahné, Pierre-Alain. *Un autre Descartes: Le philosophe et son langage.* Paris: J. Vrin, 1980.

Carr, Thomas M. *Descartes and the Resilience of Rhetoric: Varieties of Cartesian Rhetorical Theory.* Carbondale: Southern Illinois Press, 1990.

Cassirer, Ernst. *The Individual and the Cosmos in Renaissance Philosophy.* Trans. Mario Domandi. New York: Harper & Row, 1963.

Chappell, Vere. "Locke on the Freedom of the Will." In *Locke's Philosophy: Content and Context.* Oxford: Clarendon Press, 1994.

Charleton, Walter. *The Darkness of Atheism Dispelled by the Light of Nature: A physicotheologicall treatise.* London: William Lee, 1652.

——. *Physiologia Epicuro-Gassendo-Charletoniana, or a Fabrick of Science Natural Upon the Hypothesis of Atoms, Founded by Epicurus, Repaired by Petrus Gassendus, Augmented by Walter Charleton.* London, 1654; reprint, New York: Johnson Reprint, 1966.

Church, William F. *Richelieu and Reason of State.* Princeton: Princeton University Press, 1972.

Cicero, Marcus Tullius. *On Ends [De Finibus].* In A. A. Long and D. N. Sedley, eds. *Hellenistic Philosophy.* 2 vols. Cambridge: Cambridge University Press, 1987.

——. *Tusculan Disputations.* Trans. J. E. King. Cambridge: Harvard University Press, 1945.

Colman, John. *John Locke's Moral Philosophy.* Edinburgh: Edinburgh University Press, 1983.

Copenhaver, Brian P. "Astrology and Magic." In *The Cambridge History of Renaissance Philosophy.* Ed. Charles B. Schmitt and Quentin Skinner. Cambridge: Cambridge University Press, 1988.

Copenhaver, Brian P., and Charles B. Schmitt. *Renaissance Philosophy.* Oxford: Oxford University Press, 1992.

Crocker, Lester G. *Nature and Culture: Ethical Thought in the French Enlightenment.* Baltimore: Johns Hopkins University Press, 1963.

Crombie, Alistair C. "Science and the Arts in the Renaissance: The Search for Truth and Certainty, Old and New." In *Science and the Arts in the Renaissance.* Ed. John W. Shirley and F. David Hoeniger. London: Associated University Press, 1985.

Curley, E. M. "Descartes, Spinoza, and the Ethics of Disbelief." In *Spinoza: Essays in Interpretation.* La Salle, Ill.: Open Court, 1975.

Curry, Patrick. *Prophecy and Power: Astrology in Early Modern England.* Princeton: Princeton University Press, 1989.

——. "Saving Astrology in Restoration England." In *Astrology, Science, and Society: Historical Essays.* Ed. Patrick Curry. Woodbridge, Suffolk: Boydell Press, 1987.

Dante Aligheri, *The Inferno.* Trans. John Chiari. Princeton: Princeton University Press, 1954.

Darnton, Robert. *The Great Cat Massacre and Other Episodes in French Cultural History.* New York: Random House, 1985.

Davis, H. Francis; Aidan Williams; Ivo Thomas; and Joseph Crehan, eds. *A Catholic Dictionary of Theology.* 3 vols. to date. London: Thomas Nelson, 1962–.

Dear, Peter. *Mersenne and the Learning of the Schools.* Ithaca: Cornell University Press, 1988.

Descartes, René. "Author's Replies to the Fifth Set of Objections." In *The Philosophical Writings of Descartes.* Trans. John Cottingham, Robert Stoothoff, and Dugald Murdoch. 3 vols. Cambridge: Cambridge University Press, 1984, 1985, 1991, 2:63–383.

——. *Oeuvres de Descartes.* Ed. Charles Adam and Paul Tannery. 12 vols. Paris: J. Vrin/C. N. R. S., 1964–76.

Dijksterhuis, E. J. *The Mechanization of the World Picture.* Trans. C. Dikshoorn. Oxford: Oxford University Press, 1961.

Doney, Willis. *Eternal Truths and the Cartesian Circle.* New York: Garland, 1987.

Driscoll, Edward A. "The Influence of Gassendi on Locke's Hedonism." *International Philosophic Quarterly* 12 (1972): 87–110.

Dunn, John. *The Political Thought of John Locke: An Historical Account of the Argument of the Two Treatises of Government.* Cambridge: Cambridge University Press, 1969.

Egan, Howard T. *Gassendi's View of Knowledge: A Study of the Epistemological Basis of His Logic.* Lanham, Md.: University Press of America, 1984.

Encylopédie ou Dictionaire Raisonne des Sciences, des Arts et des Métiers, par une société de Gens de Lettres. Neufchastel: Samuel Faulche; facsimile reprint, Stuttgart-Bad Cannstatt: Friedrich Frommann Verlag, 1966.

Epicurus. *Epicurus: The Extant Remains.* Trans. Cyril Bailey. Oxford: Clarendon Press, 1926.

Erasmus, Desiderius. *The Colloquies.* Ed. and trans. C. R. Thompson. Chicago: Chicago University Press, 1965.

Festugière, A. J. *Epicurus and His Gods.* Trans. C. W. Chilton. Oxford: Blackwell, 1955.

Ficino, Marsilio. *Three Books of Life.* Ed. and trans. Carol V. Kaske and John R. Clark. Binghamton, N.Y.: Medieval and Renaissance Texts & Studies, 1989.

France, Peter. *Rhetoric and Truth in France: Descartes to Diderot.* Oxford: Clarendon Press, 1972.

Funkenstein, Amos. *Theology and the Scientific Imagination from the Middle Ages to the Seventeenth Century.* Princeton: Princeton University Press, 1986.

Garin, Eugenio. *Astrology in the Renaissance: The Zodiac of Life.* Trans. Carolyn Jackson and June Allen. Revised in conjunction with the author by Clare Robertson. London: Routledge & Kegan Paul, 1983.

Gassendi, Pierre. *Opera Omnia.* 6 vols. Lyons, 1658; facsimile reprint, Stuttgart-Bad Cannstatt: Friedrich Frommann Verlag, 1964.

——. *Pierre Gassendi: Lettres familières à François Luillier pendant l'hiver 1632–1633.* Ed. Bernard Rochot. Paris: J. Vrin, 1944.

——. *The Selected Works of Pierre Gassendi.* Ed. and trans. Craig B. Brush. New York: Johnson Reprint, 1972.

Gassendus, Pierre. *The Mirrour of True Nobility and Gentility. Being the Life of the Renowned Nicolaus Claudius Fabricius Lord of Peiresck, Senator of the Parliament of Aix.* Trans. W. Rand. London, 1657.

——. *The Vanity of Judiciary Astrology or Divination by the Stars.* Translated by a Person of Quality. London: Humphrey Moseley, 1569.

Gauthier, David P. *The Logic of Leviathan: The Moral and Political Theory of Thomas Hobbes.* Oxford: Clarendon Press, 1969.

Gay, Peter. *The Enlightenment: An Interpretation. The Rise of Modern Paganism.* New York: Knopf, 1966.

Gilbert, Neal W. *Renaissance Concepts of Method.* Cambridge: Cambridge University Press, 1960.

Gilson, Étienne. *The Christian Philosophy of Saint Augustine.* Trans. L. E. M. Lynch. London: V. Gollancz, 1961.

———. *La liberté chez Descartes et la théologie.* Paris: Félix Alcan, 1913.

———. *Reason and Revelation in the Middle Ages.* New York: Scribner, 1938, 1969.

Gough, J. W. *The Social Contract: A Critical Study of its Development.* Oxford: Clarendon Press, 1957.

Gouhier, Henri. *La pensée métaphysique de Descartes.* Paris: J. Vrin, 1962.

Gregory, Tullio. *Scetticismo ed empirismo: Studio su Gassendi.* Bari: Editori Laterza, 1961.

Grene, Marjorie. *Descartes.* Minneapolis: University of Minnesota Press, 1985.

Guyau, J. M. *La Morale d'Épicure et ses rapport avec les doctrines contemporaines.* Paris: Félix Alcan, 1917.

Hacking, Ian. *The Emergence of Probability: A Philosophical Study of Early Ideas about Probability, Induction, and Statistical Inference.* Cambridge: Cambridge University Press, 1975.

Hahn, Roger. *The Anatomy of a Scientific Institution: The Paris Academy of Sciences, 1666–1803.* Berkeley: University of California Press, 1971.

Halbronn, Jacques E. "The Revealing Process of Translation and Criticism in the History of Astrology." In *Astrology, Science, and Society: Historical Essays.* Ed. Patrick Curry. Woodbridge, Suffolk: Boydell Press, 1987.

Hall, Marie Boas. *Robert Boyle on Natural Philosophy: An Essay with Selections from His Writings.* Bloomington: Indiana University Press, 1965.

Hallie, Philip P. "Stoicism." In *The Encyclopedia of Philosophy.* Ed. Paul Edwards. 8 vols. New York: Macmillan and Free Press, 1967, 1972. 8:19–22.

Halliwell-Phillips, J. O., ed. *A Collection of Letters Illustrative of the Progress of Science in England from the Reign of Queen Elizabeth to that of Charles the Second.* London: R. and J. E. Taylor, 1841.

Hampton, Jean. *Hobbes and the Social Contract Tradition.* Cambridge: Cambridge University Press, 1986.

Hazard, Paul. *The European Mind (1680–1715).* Trans. J. Lewis May. New York: Meridian, 1952.

Herbert, Gary B. *Thomas Hobbes: The Unity of Scientific and Moral Wisdom.* Vancouver: University of British Columbia Press, 1989.

Hervey, H. "Hobbes and Descartes in the Light of some Unpublished Letters of the Correspondence between Sir Charles Cavendish and Dr. John Pell." *Osiris* 10 (1952): 69–71.

Hine, William L. "Marin Mersenne: Renaissance Naturalism and Renaissance Magic." In *Occult and Scientific Mentalities in the Renaissance.* Ed. Brian Vickers. Cambridge: Cambridge University Press, 1984.

Hirschman, Albert O. *The Passions and the Interests: Political Arguments for Capitalism before Its Triumph.* Princeton: Princeton University Press, 1977.

Hobbes, Thomas. *The Moral and Political Works of Thomas Hobbes of Malmesbury:*

never before collected together; to which is prefixed, the Author's Life, extracted from that said to be written by Himself, as also from the Supplement to the said Life by Dr. Blackbourne and farther illustrated by the editor, with historical and critical remarks on his writings and opinions. London: MacDonald & Hargeaves, 1750.

———. *Opera philosophica quae Latine scripsit omnia in unum corpus nunc primum collect studio et labore Gulielmi Molesworth.* 4 vols. London: Ioannem Bohm, 1839–1845.

———. *Philosophical Rudiments Concerning Government.* In *The English Works of Thomas Hobbes of Malmesbury.* Ed. William Molesworth. London: J. Bohn, 1839–45; reprint, Aalen, Germany: Scientia, 1962.

———. "A Short Tract on First Principles." In Thomas Hobbes, *The Elements of Law Natural and Politic.* Ed. Ferdinand Tönnies. London: Sempkin Marshall, 1929; reprint, New York: Barnes & Noble, 1969.

———. *Thomae Hobbesii Malmesburiensis Vita.* London: Typis, 1679.

Huffman, William H. *Robert Fludd and the End of the Renaissance.* London: Routledge, 1988.

Jacquot, Jean. "Sir Charles Cavendish and His Learned Friends." *Annals of Science* 8 (1952): 13–27; 175–94.

Jardine, Lisa. *Francis Bacon: Discovery and the Art of Discourse.* Cambridge: Cambridge University Press, 1974.

———. "Humanistic Logic." In *The Cambridge History of Renaissance Philosophy.* Ed. Charles B. Schmitt and Quentin Skinner. Cambridge: Cambridge University Press, 1988.

———. "Lorenzo Valla: Academic Skepticism and the New Humanist Dialectic." In *The Skeptical Tradition.* Ed. Myles Burnyeat. Berkeley: University of California Press, 1983.

Jardine, Nicholas. "Epistemology of the Sciences." In *The Cambridge History of Renaissance Philosophy.* Ed. Charles B. Schmitt and Quentin Skinner. Cambridge: Cambridge University Press, 1988.

Jones, Howard. *The Epicurean Tradition.* London: Routledge, 1989.

———. *Pierre Gassendi, 1592–1655: An Intellectual Biography.* Nieuwkoop: B. De Graaf, 1981.

———. *Pierre Gassendi's Institutio Logica (1658).* Assen: Van Gorcum, 1981.

Joy, Lynn Sumida. "Epicureanism in Renaissance Philosophy." *Journal of the History of Ideas* 53 (1992): 573–83.

———. *Gassendi the Atomist: Advocate of History in an Age of Science.* Cambridge: Cambridge University Press, 1987.

Kahn, Victoria. *Rhetoric, Prudence, and Skepticism in the Renaissance.* Ithaca: Cornell University Press, 1985.

Kargon, Robert H. *Atomism in England from Hariot to Newton.* Oxford: Oxford University Press, 1966.

———. "Walter Charleton, Robert Boyle, and the Acceptance of Epicurean Atomism in England." *Isis* 55 (1964): 184–92.

Kavka, Gregory S. *Hobbesian Moral and Political Theory.* Princeton: Princeton University Press, 1986.

Kelley, Donald R. "Civil Science in the Renaissance." In *The Languages of Political Theory in Early-Modern Europe.* Ed. Anthony Pagden. Cambridge: Cambridge University Press, 1987.

——. " 'Second Nature': The Idea of Custom in European Law, Society, and Culture." In *The Transmission of Culture in Early Modern Europe*. Ed. Anthony Grafton and Ann Blair. Philadelphia: University of Pennsylvania Press, 1990.

Kenny, Anthony. "Descartes on the Will." In *Cartesian Studies*. Ed. R. J. Butler. Oxford: Basil Blackwell, 1972.

Kent, Francis William. *Household and Lineage in Early Modern Florence*. Princeton: Princeton University Press, 1977.

Keohane, Nannerl O. *Philosophy and the State in France: The Renaissance to the Enlightenment*. Princeton: Princeton University Press, 1980.

Kerferd, G. B. "Aristotle." In *The Encyclopedia of Philosophy*. Ed. Paul Edwards. 8 vols. New York: Macmillan and Free Press, 1967, 1972. 1:151–62.

Kettering, Sharon. *Patrons, Brokers, and Clients in Seventeenth-Century France*. New York: Oxford University Press, 1989.

Kieckhefer, Richard. *Magic in the Middle Ages*. Cambridge: Cambridge University Press, 1989.

King, Peter, Lord. *The Life and Letters of John Locke with Extracts from His Journals and Common-Place Books*. 1884; reprint, New York: Burt Franklin, 1972.

Knowles, David. *The Evolution of Medieval Thought*. London: Longman, 1962.

Koyré, Alexandre. *Newtonian Studies*. Cambridge: Harvard University Press, 1965; reprint, Chicago: University of Chicago Press, 1968.

Krailsheimer, A. J. *Studies in Self-Interest from Descartes to La Bruyère*. Oxford: Clarendon Press, 1962.

Kraye, Jill. "Moral Philosophy." In *The Cambridge History of Renaissance Philosophy*. Ed. Charles B. Schmitt and Quentin Skinner: Cambridge University Press, 1988.

Kristeller, Paul Oskar. *Renaissance Thought and Its Sources*. New York: Columbia University Press, 1979.

——. *Renaissance Thought and the Arts: Collected Essays*. Princeton: Princeton University Press, 1990.

Kroll, Richard W. F. *The Material Word: Literate Culture in the Restoration and Early Eighteenth Century*. Baltimore: Johns Hopkins University Press, 1991.

——. "The Question of Locke's Relation to Gassendi." *Journal of the History of Ideas* 45 (1984): 339–60.

Kuhn, Thomas S. *The Copernican Revolution*. New York: Vintage Books, 1957, 1959.

Laertius, Diogenes. *Lives of Eminent Philosophers*. Trans. R. D. Hicks. 2 vols. Cambridge: Harvard University Press, 1925.

Lasswitz, Kurd. *Geschichte der atomistik vom mittalter bis Newton*. Hildesheim: Olm, 1963; Hamburg and Leipzig: L. Voss, 1890.

Leff, Gordon. *Medieval Thought: St. Augustine to Ockham*. Baltimore: Penguin Books, 1968, 1958.

Lennon, Thomas M. *The Battle of the Gods and Giants: The Legacies of Descartes and Gassendi, 1655–1715*. Princeton: Princeton University Press, 1993.

Lenoble, Robert. *Mersenne ou la naissance du mécanisme*. Paris: J. Vrin, 1943.

Levi, Anthony. *French Moralists: The Theory of the Passions, 1585 to 1649*. Oxford: Clarendon Press, 1964.

Lilly, William. *An Introduction to Astrology*. 1647; reprint, Hollywood, Calif.: Newcastle Publishing, 1972.

Locke, John. *An Early Draft of Locke's Essay.* Ed. R. I. Aaron and Jocelyn Gibb. Oxford: Oxford University Press, 1936.
———. *An Essay concerning Human Understanding.* Ed. Peter H. Nidditch. Oxford: Clarendon Press, 1975, 1979.
———. *Two Treatises of Government: A Critical Edition with an Introduction and Apparatus Criticus.* Ed. Peter Laslett. Cambridge: Cambridge University Press, 1960, 1967.
Long, A. A. *Hellenistic Philosophy: Stoics, Epicureans, Sceptics.* 2d ed. Berkeley: University of California Press, 1986.
Long, A. A., and D. N. Sedley. *The Hellenistic Philosophers.* 2 vols. Cambridge: Cambridge University Press, 1987.
Lorch, Maristella de Panizza. *A Defense of Life: Lorenzo Valla's Theory of Pleasure.* Munich: W. Fink Verlag, 1985.
Lucretius, Titus Carus. *On the Nature of the Universe.* Trans. James H. Mantinband. New York: Ungar, 1965.
Lux, David S. *Patronage and Royal Science in Seventeenth-Century France: The Académie de Physique in Caen.* Ithaca: Cornell University Press, 1989.
MacIntosh, J. J. "Robert Boyle on Epicurean Atheism and Atomism." In *Atoms, Pneuma, and Tranquillity: Epicurean and Stoic Themes in European Thought.* Ed. Margaret J. Osler. Cambridge: Cambridge University Press, 1991.
Macpherson, C. B. *The Political Theory of Possessive Individualism: Hobbes to Locke.* Oxford: Oxford University Press, 1962.
Mandon, L. *Étude sur le Syntagma Philosophicum de Gassendi.* New York: Burt Franklin, 1964; originally published, Montpelier, 1858.
Mandrou, Robert. *From Humanism to Science, 1480–1700.* Trans. Brian Pearce. Atlantic Highlands, N.J.: Humanities Press, 1979.
———. *Introduction to Modern France, 1500–1640: An Essay in Historical Psychology.* Trans. R. E. Hallmark. New York: Harper & Row, 1975.
Mason, S. F. "Science and Religion in Seventeenth-Century England." In *The Intellectual Revolution of the Seventeenth Century.* Ed. Charles Webster. London: Routledge & Kegan Paul, 1974.
Mauzi, Robert. *L'idée du bonheur dans la littérature et la pensée française au XVIIIe siècle.* Paris: Armand Colin, 1969.
Mayo, Thomas. *Epicurus in England (1650–1725).* Dallas: The Southland Press, 1934.
McDowell, J. "The Role of *Eudaemonia* in Aristotle's Ethics." In *Essays on Aristotle's Ethics.* Ed. A. O. Rorty. Berkeley: University of California Press, 1980.
McInerny, Ralph. *Ethica Thomistica: The Moral Philosophy of Thomas Aquinas.* Washington, D.C.: Catholic University of America Press, 1982.
Mersenne, Marin. *Correspondance du P. Marin Mersenne, religieux minime.* Ed. C. de Waard, R. Pintard, B. Rochot, A. Beaulieu. 17 vols. to date. Paris: Beauchesne (vol. 1); Presses Universitaires de France (vols. 2–4); Centre Nationale de la Recherche Scientifique (vol. 5-), 1932-.
Mesnard, Jean. "La modernité de Bernier." In *Bernier et les Gassendistes.* Ed. Sylvia Murr. *Corpus: revue de philosophie* 20–21 (1992): 105–13.
Michael, Fred. "La place de Gassendi dans l'histoire de la logique." In *Bernier et les Gassendistes.* Ed. Sylvia Murr. *Corpus: revue de philosophie* 20–21 (1992): 9–36.

Michael, Fred S., and Emily Michael. "The Theory of Ideas in Gassendi and Locke." *Journal of the History of Ideas* 51 (1990): 379–99.

Miel, Jan. *Pascal and Theology*. Baltimore: Johns Hopkins University Press, 1969.

Milton, J. R. "Locke and Gassendi: A Reappraisal." In *Studies in Seventeenth-Century Philosophy*. Ed. M. A. Stewart. Oxford: Oxford University Press, forthcoming.

——. "Locke at Oxford." In *Locke's Philosophy: Content and Context*. Ed. G. A. J. Rogers. Oxford: Clarendon Press, 1994.

——. "Locke's Life and Times." In *The Cambridge Companion to Locke*. Ed. Vere Chappell. Cambridge: Cambridge University Press, 1994.

Mintz, Samuel I. *The Hunting of Leviathan: Seventeenth-Century Reactions to the Materialism and Moral Philosophy of Thomas Hobbes*. Cambridge: Cambridge University Press, 1970.

Mitsis, Phillip. *Epicurus' Ethical Theory: The Pleasures of Invulnerability*. Ithaca: Cornell University Press, 1988.

Molina, Luis de. *Concordia liberi arbitrii cum gratia donis, divini praesciendi, providentia praedestinatione et reprobatione*. Lisbon, 1588; reprint, Paris: P. Lethielleux, 1876.

——. *On Divine Foreknowledge (Part IV of the Concordia)*. Trans. Alfred J. Freddoso. Ithaca: Cornell University Press, 1988.

Montaigne, Michel de. "Essays: In Defence of Raymond Sebond." Trans. Arthur H. Beattie. In *Classics of Western Thought, Vol. 2: Middle Ages, Renaissance, and Reformation*. Ed. Karl F. Thompson. New York: Harcourt Brace Jovanovich, 1980.

Morford, Mark. *Stoics and Neostoics: Rubens and the Circle of Lipsius*. Princeton: Princeton University Press, 1991.

Morin, Jean-Baptiste. *Astrologia Gallica principiis et rationibus propis stabilita, atque in XXVI Libros distributa*. The Hague, 1661.

——. *The Morinus System of Horoscope Interpretation*. Trans. R. S. Baldwin. Washington, D.C.: AFA, 1974.

——. *Remarques Astrologiques*. Paris, 1654.

Mourant, John A. "Pelagius and Pelagianism." In *The Encyclopedia of Philosophy*. Ed. Paul Edwards. 8 vols. New York: Macmillan and Free Press, 1967, 1972. 6:78–79.

Mousnier, Roland. *The Institutions of France under the Absolute Monarchy, 1598–1789*. Trans. Brian Pearce. 2 vols. Chicago: University of Chicago Press, 1979.

Murr, Sylvia. "Bernier et le gassendisme." In *Bernier et les Gassendistes*. Ed. Sylvia Murr. *Corpus: revue de philosophe* 20–21 (1992): 115–35.

——. "Foi religieuse et *libertas philosophandi* chez Gassendi." *Revue des sciences philosophique et théologique* 76 (1992): 85–100.

Nelson, Nicolas H. "Astrology, *Hudibras*, and the Puritans." *Journal of the History of Ideas* 37 (1976): 521–36.

Neuschel, Kristen B. *Word of Honor: Interpreting Noble Culture in Sixteenth-Century France*. Ithaca: Cornell University Press, 1989.

Nichols, James H. *Epicurean Political Philosophy: The De Rerum Natura of Lucretius*. Ithaca: Cornell University Press, 1976.

Norton, David Fate. "The Myth of 'British Empiricism.' " *History of European Ideas* 1 (1981): 331–44.

O'Connor, David K. "The Invulnerable Pleasures of Epicurean Friendship." *Greek, Roman, and Byzantine Studies* 30 (1989): 165–86.

Osler, Margaret J. "Baptizing Epicurean Atomism: Pierre Gassendi on the Immortality of the Soul." In *Religion, Science, and Worldview: Essays in Honor of Richard S. Westfall.* Ed. Margaret J. Osler and Paul Farber. Cambridge: Cambridge University Press, 1985.

——. "Descartes and Charleton on Nature and God." *Journal of the History of Ideas* 40 (1979): 445–56.

——. *Divine Will and the Mechanical Philosophy: Gassendi and Descartes on Contingency and Necessity in the Created World.* Cambridge: Cambridge University Press, 1994.

——. "Eternal Truths and the Laws of Nature: The Theological Foundations of Descartes' Philosophy of Nature." *Journal of the History of Ideas* 46 (1985): 349–62.

——. "Fortune, Fate, and Divination: Gassendi's Voluntarist Theology and the Baptism of Epicureanism." In *Atoms, Pneuma, and Tranquillity: Epicurean and Stoic Themes in European Thought.* Ed. Margaret J. Osler. Cambridge: Cambridge University Press, 1991.

——. "The Intellectual Sources of Robert Boyle's Philosophy of Nature: Gassendi's Voluntarism and Boyle's Physico-Theological Project." In *Philosophy, Science, and Religion, 1640–1700.* Ed. Richard Ashcraft, Richard Kroll, and Perez Zagorin. Cambridge: Cambridge University Press, 1991.

——. "Providence, Divine Will, and the Theological Background to Gassendi's View of Scientific Knowledge." *Journal of the History of Ideas* 44 (1983): 549–60.

Ozment, Steven E. *The Age of Reform, 1250–1550: An Intellectual and Religious History of Late Medieval and Reformation Europe.* New Haven: Yale University Press, 1980.

Paganini, Gianni. "Épicurisme et philosophie au XVIIème siècle. Convention, utilité et droit selon Gassendi." *Studi Filosofici* 12–13 (1989–1990): 4–45.

——. "Hobbes, Gassendi, e la psicologia del meccanicismo." In *Hobbes oggi.* Milan: Angeli, 1990.

Parker, Geoffrey, and Lesley M. Smith, eds. *The General Crisis of the Seventeenth Century.* London: Routledge & Kegan Paul, 1978.

Pascal, Blaise. *Pascal's Pensées.* Trans. H. F. Stewart. London: Collector's Book Club, 1950.

Pegis, Anton C. "Molina and Human Liberty." In *Jesuit Thinkers of the Renaissance.* Ed. Gerard Smith. Milwaukee: Marquette University Press, 1939.

Peiresc, Nicolas-Claude Fabri de. *Lettres de Peiresc.* Ed. Philippe Tamizey de Larroque. In *Documents inédits sur l'histoire de France.* 7 vols. Paris: Imprimerie Nationale, 1888.

Pelikan, Jaroslav. *Reformation of Church and Dogma (1300–1700).* In *The Christian Tradition: A History of the Development of Doctrine.* Vol. 4. Chicago: University of Chicago Press, 1984.

Peters, R. S. "Thomas Hobbes." In *The Encyclopedia of Philosophy.* Ed. Paul Edwards. 8 vols. New York: Macmillan and Free Press, 1967, 1972. 4:30–46.

Petrarca, Francisco. "On His Own Ignorance." In *The Renaissance Philosophy of*

Man. Ed. Ernst Cassirer, Paul O. Kristeller, and John Randall, Jr. Chicago: University of Chicago Press, 1948.

Pico della Mirandola, Giovanni. *Disputationes adversus astrologiam divinatricem.* Ed. E. Garin. 2 vols. Florence: Vallecchi, 1946, 1952.

———. *Oration on the Dignity of Man.* Trans. Elizabeth L. Forbes. In *The Renaissance Philosophy of Man.* Ed. Ernst Cassirer, Paul O. Kristeller, and John Randall, Jr. Chicago: University of Chicago Press, 1948.

Pintard, René. "Descartes et Gassendi." In *Travaux du IXe Congrès de Philosophie—Congrès Descartes.* Paris: Études Cartesiennes, 1937.

———. *Le libertinage érudit dans la première moitié du XVIIe siècle.* 2 vols. Paris: Boivin, 1943.

———. *La Mothe le Vayer—Gassendi—Guy Patin: Études de bibliographie et de critique suivies de textes inédits de Guy Patin.* Paris: Boivin, 1943.

Plutarch. *Plutarch's Moralia.* Trans. B. Einarson and P. H. De Lacy. Cambridge: Harvard University Press, 1967, 1984.

Polin, Raymond. "Locke's Conception of Freedom." In *John Locke: Problems and Perspectives.* Ed. John W. Yolton. Cambridge: Cambridge University Press, 1969.

———. *La politique morale de John Locke.* Paris: Presses Universitaires de France, 1960.

Popkin, Richard H. *The History of Scepticism from Erasmus to Descartes.* Revised edition. New York: Harper & Row, 1964.

———. "Skepticism." In *The Encyclopedia of Philosophy.* Ed. Paul Edwards. 8 vols. New York: Macmillan and Free Press, 1967, 1972. 7:449–61.

Poppi, Antonio. "Fate, Fortune, Providence, and Human Freedom." In *The Cambridge History of Renaissance Philosophy.* Ed. Charles B. Schmitt and Quentin Skinner. Cambridge: Cambridge University Press, 1988.

Queralt, Antonio. *Libertad Humana en Luis de Molina.* Granada: Facultad de Teologia, 1977.

Rabb, Theodore K. *The Struggle for Stability in Early Modern Europe.* Oxford: Oxford University Press, 1975.

Ranum, Orest. *Artisans of Glory: Writers and Historical Thought in Seventeenth-Century France.* Chapel Hill: University of North Carolina Press, 1980.

Redondi, Pietro. *Galileo Heretic.* Trans. Raymond Rosenthal. Princeton: Princeton University Press, 1987.

Rice, Eugene F. *The Renaissance Idea of Wisdom.* Cambridge: Harvard University Press, 1958.

Riley, Patrick. "How Coherent Is the Social Contract Tradition?" *Journal of the History of Ideas* 34 (1973): 551–64.

Rist, John M. *Epicurus: An Introduction.* Cambridge: Cambridge University Press, 1972.

Rochot, Bernard. "Gassendi et la 'logique' de Decartes." *Revue philosophique de la France et de l'étranger* 80 (1955): 300–308.

———. "Gassendi: Le philosophe." In *Pierre Gassendi: Sa vie et son oeuvre.* Paris: A. Michel, 1955.

———. "Gassendi, vie et caractère." In *Pierre Gassendi: Sa vie et son oeuvre.* Paris, A. Michel, 1955.

——. *Les travaux de Gassendi sur Épicure et sur l'atomisme, 1619–1658.* Paris: J. Vrin, 1944.

——. "Les vérités éternelles dans la querelle entre Descartes et Gassendi." *Revue philosophique de la France et l'étranger* 141 (1951): 288–98.

Rogow, Arnold A. *Thomas Hobbes: Radical in the Service of Reaction.* New York: Norton, 1986.

Rosenthal, David M. "Descartes on the Will." In *Essays on Descartes' Meditations.* Berkeley: University of California Press, 1986.

Rossi, Paoli. "Hermeticism, Rationality, and the Scientific Revolution." In *Reason, Experiment, and Mysticism in the Scientific Revolution.* Ed. M. L. Righini Bonelli and William R. Shea. New York: Science History Publications, 1975.

Rothkrug, Lionel. *Opposition to Louis XIV: The Political and Social Origins of the French Enlightenment.* Princeton: Princeton University Press, 1965.

Ryan, Alan. "Hobbes and Individualism." In *Perspectives on Thomas Hobbes.* Ed. G. A. J. Rogers and Alan Ryan. Oxford: Clarendon Press, 1988.

Sarasohn, Lisa T. "Epicureanism and the Creation of a Privatist Ethic in Early Seventeenth-Century France." In *Atoms, Pneuma, and Tranquillity: Epicurean and Stoic Themes in European Thought.* Ed. Margaret J. Osler. Cambridge: Cambridge University Press, 1991.

——. "The Ethical and Political Philosophy of Pierre Gassendi." *Journal of the History of Philosophy* 20 (1982): 239–60.

——. "French Reaction to the Condemnation of Galileo." *Catholic Historical Review* 74 (1988): 34–54.

——. "The Influence of Epicurean Philosophy on Seventeenth-Century Ethical and Political Thought: The Moral Philosophy of Pierre Gassendi." Ph. D. dissertation, University of California at Los Angeles, 1979.

——. "Motion and Morality: Pierre Gassendi, Thomas Hobbes, and the Mechanical World-View." *Journal of the History of Ideas* 46 (1985): 363–80.

——. "Nicolas-Claude Fabri de Peiresc and the Patronage of the New Science in the Seventeenth Century." *Isis* 84 (1993): 70–90.

Saunders, Jason Lewis. *Justus Lipsius: The Philosophy of Renaissance Stoicism.* New York: Liberal Arts Press, 1955.

Schiffman, Zachary Sayre. *On the Threshold of Modernity: Relativism in the French Renaissance.* Baltimore: Johns Hopkins University Press, 1991.

Schmitt, Charles B. *Gianfrancesco Pico della Mirandola (1469–1533) and His Critique of Aristotle.* The Hague: Martinus Nijhoff, 1967.

——. "The Rise of the Philosophical Textbook." In *The Cambridge History of Renaissance Philosophy.* Ed. Charles B. Schmitt and Quentin Skinner. Cambridge: Cambridge University Press, 1988.

Schneewind, J. B. "Locke's Moral Philosophy." In *The Cambridge Companion to Locke.* Ed. Vere Chappell. Cambridge: Cambridge University Press, 1994.

——, ed. *Moral Philosophy from Montaigne to Kant: An Anthology.* 2 vols. Cambridge: Cambridge University Press, 1990.

Schouls, Peter A. *Reasoned Freedom: John Locke and the Enlightenment.* Ithaca: Cornell University Press, 1992.

Schwarz, Hermann. *Die Unwalzung der Wahrnehmungshypothesen durch die Mechanische Methode.* Leipzig: Duncker & Humblot, 1885.

Shapin, Steven, and Simon Schaffer. *Leviathan and the Air-Pump: Hobbes, Boyle, and the Experimental Life.* Princeton: Princeton University Press, 1985.

Shapiro, Barbara J. "Early Modern Intellectual Life: Humanism, Religion, and Science in Seventeenth-Century England." *History of Science* 29 (1991): 45–71.

———. *John Wilkins, 1614–1672: An Intellectual Biography.* Berkeley: University of California Press, 1969.

———. "Latitudinarianism and Science in Seventeenth-Century England." In *The Intellectual Revolution of the Seventeenth Century.* Past and Present Series. Ed. Charles Webster. London: Routledge & Kegan Paul, 1974.

———. *Probability and Certainty in Seventeenth-Century England: A Study of the Relationships between Natural Science, Religion, History, Law, and Literature.* Princeton: Princeton University Press, 1983.

Sharp, Lindsay. "Walter Charleton's Early Life, 1620–1659, and the Relationship to Natural Philosophy in Seventeenth-Century England." *Annals of Science* 30 (1973): 311–40.

Shumaker, Wayne. *The Occult Philosophy in the Renaissance.* Berkeley: University of California Press, 1972.

Skinner, Quentin. *The Foundations of Modern Political Thought.* Vol. 2: *The Age of Reformation.* Cambridge: Cambridge University Press, 1978.

———. "Thomas Hobbes and His Disciples in France and England." *Comparative Studies in Society and History* 8 (1965–66): 153–65.

Sorbière, Samuel. *A Voyage to England concerning many Things relating to the State of Learning, Religion, and other curiosities of that Kingdom.* London: J. Woodward, 1709.

Sorell, Tom. *Hobbes.* London: Routledge & Kegan Paul, 1986.

———. "The Science in Hobbes's Politics." In *Perspectives on Thomas Hobbes.* Ed. G. A. J. Rogers and Alan Ryan. Oxford: Clarendon Press, 1988.

Sortais, Gaston. *La philosophie moderne depuis Bacon jusqu'à Leibniz.* 2 vols. Paris: Paul Lethielleux, 1920–22.

Spink, J. S. *French Free-Thought from Gassendi to Voltaire.* London: Athlone, 1960.

Spragens, Thomas A. *The Politics of Motion: The World of Thomas Hobbes.* London: Croom Helm, 1973.

Stanley, Thomas. *The History of Philosophy: Containing the Lives, Opinions, Actions, and Discourses of the Philosophers of Every Sect.* 3 vols. 2d ed. London: Thomas Bassett, 1655–62, 1687, 1701.

Striker, Gisela. "*Ataraxia*: Happiness as Tranquillity." *Monist* 73 (1990): 97–110.

———. "Commentary on Mitsis." In *Proceedings of the Boston Area Colloquium in Ancient Philosophy.* Ed. J. J. Cleary. Vol. 4. Lanham, Md.: University Press of America, 1988.

Strozier, Robert M. *Epicurus and Hellenistic Philosophy.* Lanham, Md.: University Press of America, 1985.

Struever, Nancy S. *Theory as Practice: Ethical Inquiry in the Renaissance.* Chicago: University of Chicago Press, 1992.

Surtz, Edward L. *The Praise of Pleasure: Philosophy, Education, and Communism in More's Utopia.* Cambridge: Harvard University Press, 1957.

———. *The Praise of Wisdom: A Commentary on the Religious and Moral Problems and Backgrounds of St. Thomas More's Utopia.* Chicago: Loyola University Press, 1957, 1981.

Taylor, A. E. *Epicurus.* London: Constable and Constable: 1911.

Taylor, Richard. "Determinism." In *The Encyclopedia of Philosophy.* Ed. Paul Edwards. 8 vols. New York: Macmillan and Free Press, 1967, 1972. 2:359–73.

Tester, S. J. *A History of Western Astrology.* Woodbridge, Suffolk: Boydell, 1987.

Thomas, Keith. *Religion and the Decline of Magic.* New York: Charles Scribner's Sons, 1971.

Thorndike, Lynn. *A History of Magic and Experimental Science.* 8 vols. New York: Columbia University Press, 1923–58.

Trexler, Richard C. *Public Life In Renaissance Florence.* 1980. Reprint, Ithaca: Cornell University Press, 1991.

Trinkaus, Charles. *In Our Image and Likeness: Humanity and Divinity in Italian Humanist Thought.* 2 vols. Chicago: University of Chicago Press, 1970.

Tronson. *La Vie de Maistre Jean Baptiste Morin.* Paris, 1660.

Tuck, Richard. "Hobbes and Descartes." In *Perspectives on Thomas Hobbes.* Ed. G. A. J. Rogers and Alan Ryan. Oxford: Clarendon Press, 1988.

———. "The 'Modern' Theory of Natural Law." In *The Languages of Political Theory in Early-Modern Europe.* Ed. Anthony Pagden. Cambridge: Cambridge University Press, 1987.

Tully, James. *An Approach to Political Philosophy: Locke in Contexts.* Cambridge: Cambridge University Press, 1993.

Valla, Lorenzo. "Dialogue on Free Will." Trans. Charles E. Trinkaus. In *The Renaissance Philosophy of Man.* Ed. Ernst Cassirer, Paul O. Kristeller, and John Randall, Jr. Chicago: Chicago University Press, 1948.

Vander Waerdt, P. A. "The Justice of the Epicurean Wise Man." *Classical Quarterly* n.s. 37 no. 2 (1987): 402–22.

Vasoli, Cesare. "The Renaissance Concept of Philosophy." In *The Cambridge History of Renaissance Philosophy.* Ed. Charles B. Schmitt and Quentin Skinner. Cambridge: Cambridge University Press, 1988.

Vaughan, Frederick. *The Tradition of Political Hedonism from Hobbes to J. S. Mill.* New York: Fordham University Press, 1982.

Verdon, Michel. "On the Laws of Physical and Human Nature: Hobbes' Physical and Social Cosmologies." *Journal of the History of Ideas* 43 (1982): 653–63.

Vickers, Brian. *In Defence of Rhetoric.* Oxford: Clarendon Press, 1988.

———. "Rhetoric and Poetics." In *The Cambridge History of Renaissance Philosophy.* Ed. Charles B. Schmitt and Quentin Skinner. Cambridge: Cambridge University Press, 1988.

———, ed. *Occult and Scientific Mentalities in the Renaissance.* Cambridge: Cambridge University Press, 1984.

Vyverberg, Henry. *Human Nature, Cultural Diversity, and the French Enlightenment.* New York: Oxford University Press, 1989.

Wade, Ira O. *The Intellectual Origins of the French Enlightenment.* Princeton: Princeton University Press, 1971.

Walker, D. P. *Spiritual and Demonic Magic.* London: Warburg Institute and University of London; reprint, Notre Dame: University of Notre Dame Press, 1975.

Walker, Ralph. "Gassendi and Skepticism." In *The Skeptical Tradition.* Ed. Myles Burnyeat. Berkeley: University of California Press, 1983.

Wallace, William A. "The Certitude of Science in Late Medieval and Renaissance Thought." *History of Philosophy Quarterly* 3 (1986): 281–91.

———. "Traditional Natural Philosophy." In *The Cambridge History of Renaissance Philosophy.* Ed. Charles B. Schmitt and Quentin Skinner. Cambridge: Cambridge University Press, 1988.

Watkins, J. W. N. *Hobbes's System of Ideas: A Study in the Political Significance of Philosophical Theories.* London: Hutchinson, 1965.

Westfall, Richard S. "The Foundations of Newton's Philosophy of Nature." *British Journal for the History of Science* 1 (1962): 171–82.

———. "Science and Patronage: Galileo and the Telescope." *Isis* 76 (1985): 11–30.

———. *Science and Religion in Seventeenth-Century England.* New Haven: Yale University Press, 1958.

Westman, Robert S. "The Astronomer's Role in the Sixteenth Century: A Preliminary Study." *History of Science* 18 (1980): 105–47.

———. "Nature, Art, and Psyche: Jung, Pauli, and the Kepler-Fludd Debate." In *Occult and Scientific Mentalities in the Renaissance.* Ed. Brian Vickers. Cambridge: Cambridge University Press, 1984.

———. "The Reception of Galileo's *Dialogue,* A Partial World Census of Extant Copies." In *Novità celesti e crisi del sapere.* Ed. P. Galluzzi. Florence: Giunti Barbera, 1984.

Wilcox, Donald J. *In Search of God and Self: Renaissance and Reformation Thought.* Boston: Houghton and Mifflin, 1975.

Williams, Bernard. *Descartes: The Project of Pure Enquiry.* Harmondsworth: Penguin, 1978.

Wilson, Margaret Dualer. *Descartes.* London: Routledge & Kegan Paul, 1978.

Yates, Frances A. *The Rosicrucian Enlightenment.* London: Routledge & Kegan Paul, 1972; reprint, Boulder, Colo.: Shambhala, 1978.

Index